Delusion is Good

Great spirits will always confront the violent opposition of mediocre minds.

—Albert Einstein

Delusion is Good

A Visionary Guide to Extraordinary Outcomes

Robert Joseph Ahola and Paul John Peccianti

Writers Club Press
San Jose New York Lincoln Shanghai

Delusion is Good
A Visionary Guide to Extraordinary Outcomes

Writers Club Press
an imprint of iUniverse.com, Inc.

For information address:
iUniverse.com, Inc.
5220 S 16th, Ste. 200
Lincoln, NE 68512
www.iuniverse.com

ISBN: 0-595-18630-0

Printed in the United States of America

To Mr. Wizard

Contents

Author's Note

As Robert Ahola and I have talked and interacted over the years, I soon realized that our conversations came from the hearts and minds of kindred spirits. Able to share ideas, feelings, hopes and dreams, we both came to the conclusion that it was time to share our message with the world. Armed with a faith that held together our thoughts and beliefs, we embarked on this journey called *Delusion is Good,* determined to see the dream become a reality.

That's what delusion, true delusion, is all about.

Personally, I have always been deluded. I'm proud to say so. Although such declarations have raised a few eyebrows, even among those close to me, it is an innate vision of ultimate truth that I have always held dear. Consciously, over the last years of my life, I have carefully chosen my inner circle of friends. These are people who share my range of vision and who have embarked upon paths that allow them to see through the prism of potential rather than be stifled by the chokeholds of what is commonly perceived as reality. Life is an incredible experience. Yet so many people trudge through their daily routines and miss the splendor of what God has laid at our feet. Trapped in the formation of their minds as they gear daily activity towards "just getting by" rather than "getting on." My personal journey is to awaken the world to the phenomenon of constant miracles available to us all. My inner core is love, and everything must come from that point of reference in my mind and in my heart.

A wise man once told me, "If you want something you've never had, you must do something you've never done."

Open your hearts and minds to your dreams!

—*Paul John Peccianti*

Author's Note Too...

When my longtime friend Paul Peccianti first approached me about co-authoring this book with him, it took me about fifteen seconds to grasp the meaning of the title *Delusion is Good*. It took a little longer than that for me to untangle the fabric of the mission as it pertained to me. I felt I had, for a very long time, embraced the righteous fire of my own oversoul's call to be the scribe of great ideas—those of others and, one would hope, a few of my own as well. I had always believed myself to have been the defiant child, the one who held onto his fantasies, and continued to build castles to my ideals despite the doubts of others, and the pressures of many friends and loved ones for me to conform to the easier talents available to me. Nevertheless, I remained a soul in conflict, one who was always trying to reconcile my writer's gifts with those of advertising, marketing and promotion that had made me so much more money in such a short period of time.

What I discovered was that, through the processes we've developed together and articulated in this book, I have been able to lay to rest the doubts about my life's choices and to reconcile the path I had chosen with the ones others felt would bring me more prosperity and less suspicion.

Finally, I realized that I had been doing the right thing all along, and that there wasn't a choice to make. It was merely an opportunity to wink at my angels and keep on going. This process has helped lighten the weight on my wings and has freed me from the demons of dissonance that I felt had often plagued me in the past.

"If a man will begin with certainties," Sir Francis Bacon wrote, "he will end with doubts. But if he will be content to begin with doubts, he will end with certainties."

I, who have often doubted my path, have—through this remarkable pathway to Delusion—ended with greater certainties than I had ever thought possible.

It is my firm belief that the reader too will find these awakenings and, through the simple opening of those lost passages in one's ideals, discover new awakenings in the soul. It is our intention that *Delusion is Good* be a simple, honest, direct, and useful unlocking of your potential for unlimited success and a clearer perspective, not only of who you really are but also of whom you have the potential to be.

—*Robert Joseph Ahola*

Introduction

This begins as a personal "thank you" from us for taking the time to think. What we have found, almost without fail, is that our entire premise for creating *Delusion is Good* has been met in the title. And most of you now reading this have already helped confirm it.

Not everyone agrees with that premise, and that's what makes this endeavor so worth the while, because we found out rather quickly that telling people that "delusion is good" prompts reactions that are both emotional and extreme.

In fact, whenever we introduced anyone to the concept that *Delusion is Good,* they responded in ways that qualified them to fit into one of three categories. The first group, which we will define as *Group 1,* rejected it out of hand with an emphatic, "No! That can't be! That's wrong. Delusion is not good. Delusion is the worst thing people can experience. It is a form of illness." This spate of near-violent opposition usually came from traditional behavioral therapists, other motivational speakers, semantic purists, and hard core conformists.* For most members of this group, the term *delusion* is used as a tool to define a pathology, something that is innately out of whack with human nature—a gear in the human psyche that has slipped and needs to be locked back into place. They were our toughest audience, and fortunately, a very small percentage of the total number we canvassed.

Nevertheless, their high voltage response to *"delusion"* convinced us that we were onto something.

Our *Group 2* respondents to the term *delusion* were at the very least credulous; they kept an open mind. They found the title intriguing and

---

* In other words, anyone who was stupid enough to disagree with us.

were willing to listen when we explained to them that, by our definition, "delusion" was the gift of ultra-dimensional insight, the ability to pierce the veil of circumstance and see all possible worlds. And they responded very well when we pointed out that almost all great visionaries, because of the course they took to pursue their dreams, were thought in their time to have been deluded. Conventional wisdom (which is usually far more conventional than wise) branded them extreme. In fact, we came up with a whole new term to describe such people: "Delusionist," which you will soon find is our summary compliment for all those we hold dear. This new term is used to describe the visionaries who were believed to be way outside the lines in the ways they pursued their obsessions with their appropriate truth. In fact, we have a saying that we feel applies to so much: "A delusionist in the beginning is a visionary in the end." In other words, those who are willing to risk everything for their adherence to the truth will be honored in time. And time is the only arbiter of truth.

Our *Group 3* got it right away. When we told them our intention with *Delusion is Good,* some even pumped their fist with an emphatic "Yes!" that was as reflexive as it was convincing. To our surprise, this third group was nearly as large as Group 2 and cross-cut all age profiles, careers, races and levels of social status. They were also equally divided as to gender. These highly enthusiastic women and men, however, did seem to have one quality in common: They all still had that spark of wonderment about this life of ours. They hadn't dulled that edge of passion that makes each day worth living.

It is to these groups—all of them!—that we offer both our gratitude and our resolve. What is in this book will make a difference in your life, provided you take it to heart, apply it and understand its core belief—*that life is a matter of finding love and setting fear aside.* The total of all our awareness resides in this discovery, as does the sum of all our success.

The question is: How can we accomplish this?

The answer is: Only through the path of true delusion—by rediscovering the ability to think again for ourselves. It begins with rediscovering the hidden chambers in our selves that only true visionaries have the courage to seek. And with it comes the realization that there is a price to pay. You must be willing to work at it, and to realize that all true people of vision were considered "deluded" in their time. And as you will often see, the greater the perceived delusion, the more significant the accomplishment. These are the individuals, the dedicated delusionists, who were willing to risk everything—their credibility, their social standing, their safety, even their lives—to achieve what they knew was right.

For this, we bring you role models by the score—some very famous ones, some lesser known—whose lives and actions will give you support and encouragement. And we offer a step-by-step plan to help you rediscover that lost map to the hidden regions of your soul's desires. At times, it may seem to resemble steps you've taken before and courses you may have touched upon. In rare instances they are. After all, we would be both foolish and arrogant to ignore the teachings of others who have gone before us.

Most of the time, you will find that what you discover along this delusionist's path is a daring new waltz with chaos, one that you will win—one that will bring you peace in ways that will resonate inside you.

All we ask is that you study it, take it to heart, and put it to work.

To do so, however, will challenge you to open your mind to a new universe, and to see this life with new eyes.**

That is the visionary viewpoint.

That is the role of delusion.

** And somewhere along the way, remember to keep your sense of humor.

Chapter 1

Delusion: Wings for the Soul

You are, by birthright, meant to fly.

This is the consummate delusion and the ultimate truth. Of course, there is a generous portion of metaphor packed into our meaning here. But think about it for moment. In your heart of hearts, don't you really believe you possess that ability?

How many of us, hundreds of times during the course of our lives, have dreamt of flying? How often, in those deepest downdrafts of our REM sleep when dreamscapes flash before us in their most vibrant washes of color, have we found ourselves soaring over perilous terrain and indeterminate city skylines, or even the fantasy world of our perfect contrivance? We feel timid at first, uncertain, until we realize that we are in control of the outcome. Suddenly, we are diving, climbing, executing Immelmanns and soaring with the realization that this might in fact be a natural condition of who we are. Always, seemingly without fail, these dreams are the ones that bring us awake. And we bolt upright in our beds, slightly disappointed to find that we are grounded in "reality" after all.

Dream analysts and psychotherapists offer a laundry list of interpretations for these subconscious soarings. A "flight from responsibility," a strong desire on the part of the dreamer to free her or his untapped creative urges, a feeling of needing to flee one's current environment—all these descriptions are

1

palpable. Some are ill advised. Most come out of a box of conformities that leave nothing to the imagination and everything to a limiting sense of order.

Heaven help those of us who dare to insist that our dreams have substance, that we really were meant to accomplish all those wondrous flights of fancy. No doubt, we'll be told that we need to grow up, or something even worse—that we're deluded.

All the while, we are shown greatness in others while we ourselves are taught that this greatness was not intended for us. Early on, most of us have already been brought to abandon what we were meant to be. In place of a clear contact with our destiny, we've been cross-currented in a force field of lies that we must accept, embrace and take to heart. We must do so, we are told, because that's the direction in which the universe flows, and by all means, we must "go with the flow." Instead of embracing our boldest moments, we're bridled to hold back. We're told we must abandon the truth of our dreams and accept instead the mythology of limitation.

The Mythology of Limitation.

"Facts and the truth really have little to do with one another."[1]

—*William Faulkner*

The mythology of limitation is as insidious as it is galling. On the surface, we accept without challenge what we have been told is "reality," when what we need is the Delusion.

We have been taught that a delusion is, by definition, "a belief, though false, that has been surrendered to and accepted by the whole mind as the truth, and so may be expected to influence action."[2] In another definition, delusion is referred to as "a...persistent belief, unconquerable by reasons, in something that has no existence in fact."[3] In other words, delusion is believed to be a failure to deal with what we are told really exists. In the vernacular of psychotherapists, delusions are the dangerous worlds in which many dysfunctional personalities live, those for whom reality is a lost notion. And of course, no insult can be more demeaning for any of us than to hear that we have "delusions of grandeur."

This is often what young children are told when, against the assaults of adult reasoning, they hold fast to their own personal dream dance. That prompts the slow certain war of attrition that begins to be waged against their innate ability to fantasize, a war that they will invariably lose because those "unreal" perceptions are abandoned and they are taught how to fit in the "reality-based world," the so-called world of reason. So they grow up, they put away childish things, and they come to stand in the light of adult peer group acceptance. In the process, in the midst of their broken toys and the piles of half-built fantasy castles, lie the unhatched eggs of their childhood dreams.

We're here to say that child was right—that those dreams were worth holding fast, whatever the cost. And experience has taught us that, upon reading this, you're already feeling a sense of loss for something you might have left behind, some island toward which that child wanted to sail longer ago than your conscious mind even dares to remember.

Much of it begins with how we are taught.

We are told that we can achieve great things, but we're being presented only with the tools of survival. We have revealed to us all the horizons of greatness. At the same time, we are advised that we dare not take the journey, that the risk is too great, that we must spend our lives instead learning how to avoid error. In other words, we have to take the safe middle path.

We are here to insist that those *horizons* might very well have been your destiny, and that *delusion* was your dream of fulfillment that remains the uncharted land in your life. Until you are willing to set your course, until you're willing to make that exploration once again, your world will remain incomplete.

This book is committed to being your navigator on that voyage, to helping you find that way to that continent of potential.

Before we do, however, we extend the invitation to you to become a *delusionist*, to *zap* some old patterns of behavior, and have some fun while you're doing it. That entails the willingness to make a few changes. One is in your use of vocabulary, how it is applied, and why certain words and phrases are often adopted to lock us in place. Another involves your willingness to redefine some commonly held perceptions, including a reexamination of who you really are and what your true mission is in life. The last one comes in the form of a personal housecleaning, including a kind of emotional exorcism, a decisive gutting of your own data closet—the one that has information stacked inside it that is probably conflicting with what you really need to see.

In fact, we feel so strongly about it that we're going to take you on a step-by-step process to show you how to do just that, and not only to see it but also to become it. Understand as well that this is a process you will not have to undertake alone. You will have guides, helpmates, and stable points of reference all along the way. All you have to learn to do is release your ego's need to control every issue, and surrender that control to the higher sources that are in each of us. In order to do that, you'll have to rediscover your natural ability to trust. That is the first challenge of Delusion. And it entails understanding your relationship to the two guiding emotions in our lives: *Love and Fear.*

These are the Matrixes of our lives. All things spring from them. All things return to them. In fact, we think we understand them and how they function in our lives. In truth, we do not.

Nothing was ever accomplished through fear and nothing ever lost through love. This may sound like an oversimplification. We contend that it is not, because the simple fact is that few people know how to love as love was meant to be expressed—without expectation, condition, or a sense of terror; without limitation, sense of loss, or a laundry list of desires; and with total attunement to divine intent. We catch glimpses of the Love Matrix—unconditional love—but see it as too perfect, too remote, and too ethereal to be "real."

By the same token, almost all of us drive our lives by an antiquated set of rules based in Fear. We are taught to succeed, to achieve, to acquire, to amass a body of work, to build a portfolio, to follow certain patterns of success that we can never reach because we've been conditioned never to take the risk in the first place. We are taught to avoid pain, to elude bold pursuits that might lead to folly, to evade error, and whatever we do to take the safe pathways of life. In other words, we are socially baptized in the aching throat of the Fear Matrix, and trained to obey its teachings in every action we take.

After a while we perform these safe actions by rote; we take them reflexively without understanding why. At the same time, we balk at them and end up confused and defeated when we find that, even by carefully adhering to the standards set for us, something has gone wrong along the way. Somehow, we have sabotaged ourselves without realizing why.

The reason is as simple as it is terrifying to discover. Somewhere in the course of our lives—usually very early in our childhood—most of us have fallen out of our contract with our personal destiny and have never gotten it back. It was our soul's design for our lives that was erased because it was "educated" out of us. And it is only by rediscovering our inner purpose and our soul's true path that we can ever find peace. We do this through our *higher self.* But our contact with it gets blurred.

Our higher self is our soul's ambassador to this world. It enters with us from the womb. It sings to us when we acknowledge all that is right and good in life. Yet it is sensitive to moral confusion and must cloak itself at times, waiting like a wizard to reveal itself to us.

There are paths that reveal the way back to the wizard. Delusion is such a path. And once you have mastered that very simple but very major course in self-examination, you'll be ready to continue on your way to let this book help you fulfill your true meaning in life and to eliminate the doubts that may have been holding you back thus far.

Ultimately that is the purpose of this book: to clearly define the faith— and beyond the faith, the conviction—that the real power in life is within *you,* and that you have been entrusted by a Higher Source to fulfill a very special mission while you walk this earth. That is the "Delusion" you should never lose. You have the power inside you, the magnificent super-consciousness, to take your life precisely where it was intended to go, to play at the larger game; to be more fulfilled, more successful, more prosperous, and able to make greater contributions to your world than you ever thought possible.

We call it The Eureka! Factor. *Eureka!* is the Greek word, meaning "I have found it!" Originally it referred to the spontaneous exclamation made by the Greek mathematician Archimedes when he realized he had discovered how to determine the true weight of gold. Since that time it has become synonymous with discovery itself, for all of us, in finding the true gold in our lives and the meaning of life itself.*

So, armed with Delusion and fueled by boundless enthusiasm, we sail new skies toward the continent of Eureka! knowing that is the highest form of exclamation there is. But your journey will only be as successful as your preparation to undertake it, your willingness to be the delusionist, and your courage to crack the eggs of those hidden dreams inside you, hatch them, and give them the wings to fly home.

---

* **Warning:** *Delusion is Good* is a book with a strong spiritual center, so atheists aren't going to like it very much. So, if you're an atheist and you're reading this, we have a suggestion for you. Either close this book and save yourself a great deal of time and effort, or give it to someone who might appreciate it. Then again, if you're continuing to read this, maybe you're not as atheistic as you thought you were.

Chapter 2

Mind Candy, Heroes, and the Flak Zapper

By now, we feel compelled to establish one common accord. Man, woman—the species *Homo sapiens*—is a spiritual entity, a creature with a soul. That soul comes into this life with a mission and a clear contract with our Creator, Divine Force, Universal Mind, or whatever name we choose to give our God. It is our belief, that if we maintain contact with our original mission, our success is guaranteed. The challenge arises when that contact is either blurred or distorted, invariably at a very early age.

But because we human beings have souls and are constantly in search of contact with our higher selves, we can accept no substitutes. The soul's quest for answers cannot be denied. The Truth is its destiny. That's why, in its quest for cosmic integrity, it revolts when it gets hit with false realities. And that is when, especially in the child, delusion can be the individual's greatest ally.

It is our innate desire as spiritual creatures to accept what is told us as the truth. But depictions of the truth take many forms and are often only as valid as the source from which they come. Often, we find it is merely a string of facts that are disguised to resemble the truth, what we come to find are "half-truths." These do not resonate with us and never will, and yet we are told we must accept them, that this is "the way the real world is."

We learn, in time, to return to that Great Universal Truth; our *GUT feel* that tells us something else is at issue—that we need to suspend judgment and dig more deeply, probe more warily, investigate. As we shall soon learn, that GUT feel is the delusionist's greatest ally. It is something every child is born with, only to have it "rationalized" out of them at a very early age.

Once lost, the gift of delusion, like the cradle of trust in which it is born, is difficult to get back. And yet helping you rediscover your trust through the path of delusion is exactly what we intend to do in this book. But we can't do that until we illustrate just how insidious the game has become—the one we are asked to play every day whose name, for lack of a better word, is *reality*.

Take heart! The delusion that cradles your true destiny cannot be destroyed. It is the dragon that sleeps in magnificent suspension, dreaming the dream that has always danced in your soul. The issue that confronts you now is knowing where to find it, and once you've found it, knowing how to wake it up. Once it has been aroused, it can fill you with the fire that will brighten the rest of your life.

But first we search the world of illusion—the one we've been told is real.

Delusion vs. Reality.

"I hate reality. But where else can you get a good steak?"

—*Woody Allen*

Reality bites. We all claim to be its advocates. All our informational points of reference—broadcast, print, the Internet, telecommunications—presume to be based in it. Our social structure tells us that it is the only thing that matters, that we must deal with it. We are, throughout the course of our lives, told to "get real" to "face reality," and to cultivate "real people" who are being "realistic."

In truth, nobody believes it for a moment. That's because, by the time we've reached adulthood, we've already been hit with so many sets of rules and regulations about what reality is that we no longer trust it as being anything it appears to be.

On the surface we struggle to accept it. We go along with the changes in the game we come to call life. We play by whatever new sets of rules we are given. We even seem to understand why they keep changing and why they ostensibly serve the greater good. But what about the storm that churns within us?

In the universe of the deeper self there dwells the child who knows where the truth is kept—the inner door that opens to the land of our lost ideals. It never perishes. It cannot be destroyed. But it is camouflaged by our egos in order to keep it safe. We promise ourselves that we'll remember our pact with our higher self, that we'll come again when the time is right, somehow dig up our contract with our destiny, dust it off, and bring it back it into the light. Finally, we come to a point when we've hidden our treasure too well, when we lose all reference to where we are and what we were trying to protect.

In the beginning, in the infant's universe, all worlds are one—our fantasies and realities intermingle. There are no limitations, no barriers to achievement. Just as the small child finds it easy to learn several languages at once and develop the skills to speak them with great facility, that child also sees his proximate universe as boundless. To help expand our childrens' cache of potentials in the beginning, we introduce them to all sorts of fantasy figures who become their helpmates along the way.

Santa Claus brings them toys at Christmas. The Easter Bunny hides eggs and candy for them to look for in the spring, and the Tooth Fairy brings them money for teeth they leave under their pillow. These mythical creatures are often accompanied by real figures, historical heroes who they are told performed feats of uncommon valor, all of them pointing the pathways to their potential. (These are the heroes that we can be, if we just apply ourselves!)

Then in a series of concussions, the child is informed that all his or her fantasy friends were by and large made up to make them feel better about life and that they now have to say goodbye to them. With a methodical efficiency that is almost cultural in base the child is also made to know—at about the same age—that his or her real life heroes were also not quite "all that." They too were merely stories to show us proud examples of how we ought to be. We learn about new sets of heroes—inventors, military commanders, sports figures, political visionaries. Historical accountings about them abound. But by now (at least if we're thinking at all) we hear that nagging voice inside us that questions their credibility and whether or not they are what they seem. There are other things we have to abandon: Those come in the form of our dreams.

Rather abruptly, the child is informed that we all have limitations. And somehow they are decided for us, and the boundaries are clearly defined. Before we know it, we are being shaped in every way to be who we are not, and yet are given little or no support in finding who we are. The small child, filled with honesty and curiosity, is taught to suppress his quest for brilliance and lower the level of his game, all with the conspired acknowledgment that we are being protected from the pain of disillusionment.

There is something deadening about blind acceptance. And yet we are asked to do so every day of our lives. Especially as children, we are told that those natural perceptions we hold of our immediate universe, our very instincts toward our own outlandish potential, are misguided. We learn somewhere to bite off our inclinations to dream. We're told they are delusions, so we stop speaking of them. Unwittingly, we do so at our own peril.

Rest assured. That which is not talked about begins to pass from existence the moment the energy of voice is taken from it. Desire without the song cannot be heard by the cosmic ear. Eventually our dreams become sublimated, buried so deeply inside us that all that remains are echoes of our contract with our selves.

Meanwhile, as we grow, we find ourselves returning to those lost worlds, to those "fantasies" that were once so clear to us, because somehow they catch a glimmer of the Light that was our hope. Books, film, television—a boundless assortment of entertainment locks onto what remains of our imagination and claims it for its own. Especially in this new era of the electronic nanny, we as children quickly become trained in the mastery of diversion.

Recent studies indicate that in today's working couple homes, children—even as early as 18 months of age—are plopped in front of a television set and plunged into a world that is preordained to reprogram their thinking. By now the statistics are such common knowledge that we accept them without regret—that the average American child spends more than 14 hours a week watching television just for starters. Tack on another 11 hours a week for such activities as video games, the Internet, rock concerts, complete immersions in sense-shattering music, and going to the movies, and you have a youth that is baptized in the void of manufactured environments. We rail against it, but by now we're all a part of it as well.

By now, we have awakened as adults in the dawn of the 21st century. And suddenly we're told that we should congratulate ourselves, because now we can create our own realities. We now dwell on the fringes of a virtual pleasure planet where, with a keystroke or the push of a button, we can alter our state of consciousness.

Just for the price of admission or by tapping into someone's pay-as-you-go entertainment website, we can find new ways to hone the edges of our awareness. We can hop on a ride and plunge into the depths of a virtual Atlantis or strap on some headset and goggles and duke it out with the hologram bad boys from *Mortal Combat*. We can buy into a multimedia music video complete with erotic playmates formulated to perfectly fit our tastes. Or, if we're inclined to group dynamics, we can collectively climb into the control deck of an intergalactic Stealth cruiser and knock out a Death Star perfectly poised to vaporize a peaceful planet.

What's more, we're told these things are available right now—all for actual pocket change or a plastic pass-key to nirvana. We use the small "n" to describe what has become an artificial gigabite paradise because every scrap, frame, and note of it is an appeal to a mind driven by the ego's need to gratify itself. That's because through the murky filter of both mind and ego, we somehow recollect a faded notion that touched upon the dreams we held so deep inside our soul.

Media mogul Aaron Spelling, progenitor of the "prime-time soap," once coined a phrase to describe this stampede to escapism and the media that feeds it: *mind candy*. Today the term "mind candy" is an integral part of street smack and the jargon of the computer elite, and resides in our level of Consciousness Three as the fun but useless fluff of life. And though all these things may be candy for the mind, they clog all spiritual arteries to the heart. They're anesthesia to the senses and starvation to the soul.

Almost all mind candy is Fear Matrix activity in that it is action-driven, morally manipulative, largely violent, presents the illusion of danger and is designed to titillate a viewing public already desensitized to all but the most extreme of sensations.

Awash in this sea of false impressions, the ego flounders, uncertain of its role, trying to command a ship of self that it senses is out of its control. It does the best it can, but it lacks a spiritual compass. So when hit with reality—the real thing this time—the ego goes into hyper-drive, into a rhythm of attack and defend, of conspiracy and complaint, of wrestling with paranoia and of justifying itself.

Again the Fear Matrix seizes us fully, much of the time without our even being aware of its presence. And if you should doubt for a single moment that you're susceptible to this kind of behavior, do yourself a favor some time and carry a voice-activated recorder with you just for a day. Replay your conversations at the end of that day and write down how many times you engaged in complaint, gossip, negative comments, motives of attack and defend, self-justification, and even the casual deprecation of others. Then compare them to the moments when you spoke with love, passion, compassion, and inspiration and other Love Matrix comments.* We are willing to bet you that your ratio of negative comments versus positive ones will shock you. And if you managed even a 50/50 split, you may count yourself truly as a highly evolved human being.

We make this observation with the firm belief that, just as there are no neutral thoughts, there are no neutral words or actions. Everything in the realm of human experience leans either toward resolution or conflict.

We also realize that we've made frequent mention of the terms Love and Fear with references to the Matrixes that they represent.

We intend to explain them fully in Chapter 4, "Love and Fear," and how these Matrixes control every aspect of our lives. But first, we have to lead you on a step-by-step learning process that will bring you up to our Love Matrix/Fear Matrix section of this book. For now, your current understanding of these two powerful forces will suffice. What matters now is that we understand that it is Love and the passion that derives from it that takes us to the farthest reaches of our potential—to our delusions. And it is indifference that is the delusionist's mortal enemy, because it is poison to passion and all the dreams we hold dear.

Yet isn't indifference the harvest we reap whenever we seek diversion?

Holocaust survivor and human rights activist Elle Wiesel once observed that it is not hate but indifference that is the opposite of love. He made his comment to drive home the point that the Nazis, in their campaign of pogrom to annihilate the Jews and other political enemies, were not hateful. On the contrary: their methods were, in their efficiency, terrifyingly indifferent. They treated their prisoners as raw material, as they did the world they sought to conquer. Author C.S. Lewis observed in *The Abolition of Man* that if we as human beings continue to regard ourselves as raw material, we will become raw material. It is indifference that isolates us all from one another, that ultimately turns us all into grist for the cosmic mill. And at this point, doesn't the term, "techno-zombie," jump to mind?

Even as we write this, it has been announced that there are now computers under development that can out-think the smartest human being. It is also predicted that, by the year 2030, these machines will be able to perform every human mental and physical function better than we. They'll be able to do them more quickly, more invariably, and with virtually no margin of error. They will also be able to initiate their own courses of action, duplicate human behavior, and do so without the neurosis of human ego.

Assuming predictions for these super-machines do come to pass, we have to ask ourselves the question: What will justify us to this new mega-tech society, one that is dominated by our flawless alter-egos? If in the meantime we will have embraced intellectual isolation and plunged ourselves into a kind of pleasure-driven personal downgrade, what is going to keep us from being replaced? If we're already becoming reliant upon this new task force of super-tech media to create our realities for us, of what consequence do we become if they can absorb us entirely? Other than merely imperfect extensions of the environments they create for us, what roles do we fulfill?

At this point, our intentions may be good enough. We dash to entertainment megamalls in hopes of borrowing a few moments of inspiration. We strap on virtual reality paraphernalia in order to brush against the extremity of our potentials. It's a means of borrowing a kind of glory that has somehow been denied us. Instead we fall into a trap of multi-image stimulation and all the stuff that's made to seem real without ever touching us at the heart of our actual selves. We blunt our initiative and dull our will until we finally become unable to accomplish a single thing outside the perpetuation of pleasure for its own sake.

Certainly, diversion serves its purposes. Everyone needs to escape from the pressures of the world once in a while. But they don't need to spend their entire lives in pursuit of it. Such things are not delusion. Instead, they dwell in the heart of The Lie. This is a lie that goes back to the beginnings of history. It is the political ploy of "Bread and the Circus" employed by the Roman Emperors to keep the mob at bay. It is *religion as fear* practiced in the Europe of the Middle Ages.

Yet, in the heart of the Lie, the truth is born, if you know what to look for inside. That's what delusionists do, and that is what we find.

And what we find is the voice of the child trying to find the way back home—back to its pact with the oversoul and the contract with its dreams. We take wild swings at altering our consciousness because we're longing for fulfillment. If we recognize it for what it is, we can start the move to correct it. So let's acknowledge mind candy as a wonderful warning sign. And the greater the addiction, the stronger the need to change

We're looking for answers. We long for heroes. So we all play let's pretend. And yet we expect reality to woo us like a lover. We try to win the waltz with chaos and get caught up in the storm. We try to flow with the stream of events and find ourselves drowning instead.

That's why it's so disillusioning when we are bombarded daily with news, impressions, and reportage that we are told are "fact." We accept them as fact only to be informed later that, in truth, they were "spin," misinterpretations of what actually happened and often outright lies. We're fed misinformation disguised as fact proffered by a job-scared press-corps desperate to scoop the news rather than allow it to unfold. They have to feed the monster, and any fiction will do especially if it creates a scrabble that can be sorted out later.

We are lied to by our national leaders. Our presidents cheat, steal, and commit sexual indiscretions. Our major corporations hype financial analysts to run up the price of their stocks, manipulate the news about their earnings, and dump their senior level employees. Our financial moguls swindle the public. Our sports figures batter their wives and overdose on performance-enhancing drugs. And our entertainment celebrities often appear amoral, clueless and naïve.

Aren't they all terrible? And wait a minute! *We* are *they.* And *we* have become that which we would both admire and hold in contempt.

Father Albert A. Taliaferro, a very wise spiritual leader and personal counselor once observed that, "In a democracy, government is a direct extension of public consciousness… We get exactly the kind of leadership we deserve. No more No less."[4] He also noted by the same token that he was amazed that anyone of quality would ever want to run for President of the United States, or for any other major public office. "We elect a man to the highest office of the land, and then tens of millions of us spend the next four years firing psychic darts at him week-in, week-out."[5]

Truth is a fire that sometimes burns. As far as we the people are concerned, that places the responsibility for what happens to us squarely on our own shoulders, where it belongs. We have the power to make changes. We possess the skill and capacity to alter the course of our collective destiny. We also own the responsibility for all our thoughts, words, and deeds—the sum total of what we think, how we speak, and how we behave. And we emphasize once again; it is our focus that consumes us.

So, what is the answer? Compassion, commitment, involvement—all Love Matrix qualities—are what are needed to bring us back into domain over our public lives, just as we must recultivate our relationship with true delusion to regain control of our personal lives. That requires some visionary thinking. And in this day and time opportunities for it not only abound, they are rewarded at light speed.

Today, in the age of the megamogul, billionaire entrepreneurs appear on media-drenched panels and share their perspectives of a limitless future where their projections for technological advancement and international Internet horizons push the limits of our comprehension. Nowadays, it seems as if new billionaires are being created every week just for having a good idea. New dot.com purveyors of everything from dog food to digital dress designs are heralded as marketing prophets and funded out of some high-tech guru's pocket change. Millionaires are made overnight just for thinking up a domain name that some brokerage firm wants to buy. And novice investors who think EBIDTA is a food preservative have gotten to watch their stock portfolio triple in the course of a year—at least for a while.

Brilliance is now rewarded with the flick of a wrist. So the nagging question remains. Why are so many of us still petrified of reaching for our potential? Have we lost the will to achieve? And why do we fling ourselves into a welter of negativity, obsessions with security and addictions to escape? It's not that we lack the courage to do so, it's that we've forgotten how. We've been trained to be mediocre yet still allowed to dream.

Delusion offers another path, the one that shows us heroes, the one that tells to search again in those lost corners of ourselves. That's where our heroes will be found—not in some distant star but in what we decide to become in this very moment in time.

In Search of Heroes.

"Die every day. Be born again every day. Deny everything you have every day. The important thing is not to be free but to be willing to die for that freedom."

—Nikos Kazantzakis,
The Saviors of God

Passionate words often sound extreme to the diffident mind. But think about it for a moment. The occasions in our lives when we felt most alive were those in which our passions were at their peak. A passionate romantic involvement, a passionate cause in which we believed, a sport at which we excelled and a big game in which we shined, playing anything at a higher level, even a night of supremely memorable entertainment—these are the times when we, upon reflection, would remember having felt most charged with purpose, when we brushed against the edge of our own excellence. Our potentials realized, or at least glimpsed, we felt truly filled with the cup of life. Our responses to a special moment might even be so extreme as to say it was "to die for," or that something was a "killer" experience— meaning that it was the supreme expression of what it should be.

To be on the edge of life, at its highs and lows, brings us in touch with the reasons we are here. Our celebrations of those who are willing to risk their lives for what they believe in fills our history books and our legends. Artists, poets, creators, political progenitors among us who draw from us the most admiration—the Galileos, the Van Goghs, the Herman Melvilles, the Frank Lloyd Wrights, the Martin Luther Kings, the Winston Churchills, the Edisons, the Michaelangelos and Gandhis—they were the ones who lived their lives at the edge of their potential to the extent that they were virtually "willing to die" for their dedication to cause. Some even did. Extreme? Perhaps. Yet there dwells within us the unspoken admiration for the categorical courage of a Julius Caesar who burned his bridges at the Rubicon in order to leave no way but forward toward his destiny as the leader of Rome. We stand in awe of an adolescent girl like Kerri Strug who sticks a perfect vault despite a sprained ankle to gain Olympic Gold for her gymnastics team. We nod in silent respect for a Sir Edmund Hillary who, upon peril of his life, joins his Sherpa guide in becoming the first human beings to ever reach the summit of Mt. Everest.

It takes courage to have this kind of determination, courage filled with the willingness to spare no part of oneself to achieve the desired goal. This is the kind of commitment that we admire, covet, and long to emulate. It ennobles us to experience such moments, even if we do so vicariously.

Nevertheless, we pause. Along with this admiration comes the nagging suspicion that these are prices we are not willing to pay—that we lack the physical, mental, or emotional skills to achieve such things. But would we, if we knew our dreams could be realized, take a different approach to the conduct of our lives? Would we go for it? Would we be willing to sacrifice everything to embrace again that deeply held desire in the soul?

There are two words that trigger emotions here. The first one is *sacrifice*. But what are we really giving up in this reckless, deluded pursuit of ourselves? Comfort, security, the fun of life, the support of our loved ones, what we view of prosperity—these are the anchors to which we attach our momentary pleasure. These are the points of reference that we somehow fear we'll lose. But how comfortable can any life be with that constant gnawing inside, the one that tells we're missing the boat that rows to our destiny?

The other word upon which we would focus is *achievement.* Achievement in any area is the realization of a goal. It is the top of the mountain. And yet what mountain do we climb? We're given a laundry list of things that we're told would be good to "achieve. Many appeal to our vanity. But what of the higher self? What of the "angels of our better nature" who hold our spiritual contract with this life?

Most of us aren't willing to make the necessary sacrifices to achieve our dreams, because we no longer trust our own judgment. We no longer know whether it's *the spirit* that moves us or just the hollow drumming of egos. Even as the ego drives us, we never really trust it, because deep inside us we suspect it's not really up to the job.

So most of us sit, immobile, frozen in a flak field of our own conflicted awareness. We know we're not where we ought to be. Yet we're filled with partially eradicated images of our own heroics that we're no longer sure apply.

It is our insistence as confirmed delusionists that the hero lives in each of us, waiting to be rediscovered. But he or she cannot come back out of hiding until we blow away the clutter around them. We call it *flak.* And its many connotations apply. *A field of dangerous missiles fired from a hostile source, an atmosphere of emotional conflict, a series of negative influences, a sudden blow struck against us, the hum and drum of confusion, the explosives that fly up before us to block our successful mission*—all these descriptions and more define the flak that mauls our lives. And in the delusionist's dictionary, we add a few more definitions as well. *Wastes of time, useless distractions, the petty actions of others,* are all the minions from the Kingdom of Flak that need to be tagged and banished.

For all these and more, we have a secret weapon to help you zap the flak. This is not a weapon of aggression. In fact, its sole function is to bring healing and transformation to any situation. This is the only weapon we'll ever offer. But it always works and seldom needs recharging. So use it with both love and discretion—and feel yourself start to get free.

Proudly Presenting the Flak Zapper™.

Imagine a radiant laser light that you could call to your service at any moment and use to heal and transform any situation, to make it better. If you could be in possession of this light, would you be able to use it with intelligence, compassion and grace? We will wager (and give you odds) that in your present state of mind, you would not. That's the bad news.

The good news is that you are already in possession of this laser light. And if you continue to make delusion your course of study, you will learn how to master it in ways you never would have thought possible until now.

To be sure, we note the irony of introducing you to something that might be referred to as a weapon. But we assure you that in every way it is the sword of the peaceful warrior.

We would prefer that you think of the *Flak Zapper* as an *energy equalizer* in that—in the right hands—it engulfs (or zaps) negative energy and transforms it into positive energy. But in order for it to be 100% effective requires some effort on your part. What you have to do is first understand when you are being negatively affected. You have to be on the lookout for those moments when you are being dragged into areas of negativity, and zap them—stop them cold. But more than just stopping them cold, you are required to equalize them.

This is more easily said than done, because in the first place most of us are so inundated with Fear Matrix influences that we don't even recognize it half the time we're exposed to it.

In the second place, when we do get hit with negativity, our first instinct is to retaliate, and that is precisely what flak zapping should never do.

Let us be specific. Zapping flak should never involve "telling it like it is," giving someone a piece of your mind, or laying it on the line. Candor is like pepper and only seasons well in the hands of an expert. If you're

---

* The Flak Zapper™ is a trademark of Delusion Technologies, Inc. for a lot of reasons.

going to take a bad moment and make it better, then you have to replace it with something positive. And unless you're skilled in the ways of delusion, you might fail in the attempt.

Like any other advancement in the technology of the spirit, zapping flak is an acquired skill that takes both timing and practice. And only a complete awareness of all the principles of unconditional love and constant application of them can make it work for you.

Once you have studied Chapter 4, "Love and Fear," you'll better know what faces you and how to polish your skills. For the time being, however, let's start out with something simple.

Earlier in this chapter, we suggested that you learn to gauge the degree of your involvement in Fear Matrix activity by taking a voice-activated tape recorder around with you for a day. At the end of that time, we suggested you play it back, writing down to take some measure of how much time you spend engaged in negative environments, discord, or counterproductive activities, including all your seemingly innocuous "mind candy" moments.

At this point, we acknowledge the fact that trying to measure an entire day might be a bit too much on the first pass. So we recommend that you take just one or two hours of that day, find reruns of the flak and practice zapping it. In other words, isolate the negative, conflictive or self-indulgent moments, note an approximate length for them, and then decide what you might have done to counteract them by a simple positive act. It might be a form of ruthless compassion or a simple act of kindness. Whatever form it comes in, it will always get to the goodness in an issue and let the rest fall away.

Just as we soon will illustrate that there are no neutral thoughts, we ask you to accept the truth that there are no neutral acts.

We also ask you to note that you are practicing your flak zapping in private, after the fact, and at no personal expense to you. It is a practice session. And because it is one, it will enable you to thoroughly weigh your course of action. What it will also bring to light in a hurry is just how caught up we are—we all are—in the thrall of Fear Matrix behavior, and how often we embrace it out of a simple need to conform. What it will also reveal is the truth that we all come to find. First we must learn to love unconditionally. We have to learn how to give of ourselves and do so without expectation of reward. Once we do, the answers will come with a flow we might not have expected.

The Flak: You're locked in a marketing planning meeting, and everyone is at odds. Deadlines have been missed. The client is furious and everyone is blaming everyone else. Creative is blaming research. Research is blaming production. You're the account supervisor. So top management is blaming you. The cycle of attack and defend has gone to verbal extremes and there doesn't seem to be a way to resolve it. The question is, what did you do? What was your response? Did you shoulder the responsibility and fall on your sword? Did you call an order to the meeting and threaten others if you didn't get the results that you thought you ought to have? Or maybe you just let it run its course. After all, your boss was there, and she was barking too. She was in high dudgeon and the rest of the world was in dread.

Zap it: There are a number of things that you might have done, but we have a good suggestion. Give the prattle a time limit—say five minutes for everyone to get all the negativity out of their system—and then zap it. If there's a graphics board nearby, you might have even written it down. Then at the end of the time, shut down the complaints and write three words on the board: *Positive Ideas Only.* That would be the delusionist's path, because by doing so you've made the meeting yours. You've prompted everyone to raise the level of their consciousness. And you've brought the issue into the flow of solution, its natural home. Part of learning to zap the flak is knowing when you can win. And you only win when everybody wins. That is part of the delusionists creed: that the zero-sum game is an illusion, that the only way we grow is by bringing our world into balance.

The Flak: You lunch with a friend who monopolizes the entire meal with complaints about her marital problems. Her husband mistreats her terribly, she informs you—so much so that she's getting a divorce. You know them both and know for a fact that he is both kind and devoted to her. She asks your advice. What do you tell her? Do you pour out your opinions? Or do you absent yourself from this controversial issue? Do you take sides, and then risk alienating one or both of them should they get back together? Or do you get away from it as soon as possible, let them know that this is "their problem," and that they need to work it out. None of these choices seem workable. So zap them and look for another.

Zap it: In emotionally charged issues, such as this, the options to a third party might seem limited, and that's not such a bad thing. In the vernacular of delusion, limited choices can often be a benefit to all. Since most of your options for participation seem dangerous, look for other options. Try a simple one first. Try being a friend. Simply listen without judgment. Ask her if she has explored all options, then promise to be there for her. Judgment and partisanship are qualities born in fear. You're simply there to give your love and to be a calming influence. And don't let your ego send you into dark places in other people's lives.

The Flak: After listening to the tape that chronicled your day for about an hour-and-a-half, you realized that in that recorded time, you

1) listened begrudgingly to your longtime friend complain about how unhappy he is at work, but thought up a quick excuse and got off the phone.

2) You admonished your son for not picking up his room.

3) You ignored your dog, insulted your cat, and screamed at your computer because your stocks look like they were just hit by a bomb.

4) You blew half-an-hour watching a rerun of an old John Wayne movie you've seen five times before, because "The Duke" is a personal hero of yours.

Zap it: Even though these occasions have passed, you've never really lost them. You can learn from each of them and rectify many.

1) Okay, so you've heard your friend's complaints before. But have you helped him resolve them? Get back in touch with him and tell the loving truth—that he needs to find some alternatives and that you'd be happy to help him put them together. Of course you might have to give up that

half-hour of television you just wasted your time on. So why not? Part of zapping flak is realizing that no good effort is ever wasted, and no kind act ever goes unrewarded. Call him back.

2) Recognize that the fact your son didn't pick up his room is probably a cry for help. So help him. Make cleaning his room a game. Put a reward at the end of it. Show him a system. But share the time. A conflict is but a prayer for harmony.

3) Pet your dog and hug your cat. They're some of the best friends you'll ever have, and affection is a gift that rewards the giver. Then bless your stocks. Recognize that if you are investing for the long term, the day-to-day fluctuations of your equities are irrelevant. Go have a cocktail and rejoice in your prosperity.

4) As far as watching The Duke on TV is concerned, most of us do it because we're either trying to alter our consciousness or search for heroes. If you need to alter your consciousness, try meditating for the same half-hour, or just sitting in silence. If you're looking for heroes, then find a real one, someone after whom you might want to pattern your life. Might we also suggest you begin your search by looking in the mirror? If you don't like what you see, then start making some positive changes. That's what zapping flak is all about.

A Final Caution: Treat the *Flak Zapper* with great discretion until you learn how to use it well. Rest assured you will come to use it soon enough. In the next few chapters, it will become your laser companion, brought out on those occasions when you know it will have effect. Remember, it knows neither good nor evil and will only be as effective as your sense of delusion permits. That means you use it only to heal, only to give love, only to make better and to transform every situation. Like anything, it's a matter of practice. But when you practice good things, you are learning to become the hero you've always wanted to be.

Summary. A Final Word About The Certain Need for Heroes

At the risk of contradicting ourselves, we proclaim that it is our very ability to fantasize that offers us salvation. In facing the storms of the universe, we are, therefore we dream. That's why mind candy is so irresistible. That's why we constantly search for heroes, because we want so much to believe. Not all our heroes are visionaries. But all our visionaries are heroes, if for no other reason than the fact that they see the universe with eyes unclouded by the flak of common perception.

It is here that we must understand that delusion has molded history by flying in the face of the conventional wisdom of its time, by swimming upstream against the chaos of the universe and creating new currents of thought. And it is delusionists above all others who have changed the course of our lives, our history, and even the shape of the universe as we know it. The truth can never be second-guessed. It has to be brought into light. And that must be done by someone with both the courage and wit to do it.

The delusionist will always look beyond the veil of reality and see all possible worlds. That sense of "delusion" teems in all of us. It is what the child sees that the learned adult has been conditioned to veil from his perceptions. But those higher perceptions are not dead in us; they are merely dormant. They need merely be awakened.

They were awakened in Leonardo da Vinci, a man who by any measure would be the epitome of the visionary mind. Leonardo was the consummate delusionist because he saw beyond his physical world to every conceivable potential of art, physics, physiology, botany, and astronomy. Because of that, he was able to conceive of such radical concepts as human flight, submarines, advanced anatomy, rocket launchers and what amounted to the first helicopter. By the late fifteenth century, when da Vinci flourished, the "realities" of the Renaissance intellectual elite had broadened considerably. Still, except for the few learned scholars who understood his genius, he was widely regarded as eccentric, bizarre, blasphemous, and largely a misfit.

Even now, we can hear the cries of protest from those who would embrace mediocrity as a lifestyle that, "da Vinci was a prodigy, a genius of enormous proportions, one in a thousand years."

Then we offer you another delusionist, equal in his impact, yet unexceptional in either his appearance or his demeanor: Mohandas K. Gandhi, an Indian lawyer of modest means, slight of build, with no exceptional visible skills. And yet he was a man possessed of incredible focus, an infallible GUT feel that almost never failed him about the correctness of his life, and a devotion to cause. How else could he have become the spiritual revolutionary, the Mahatma Gandhi, the "Great Soul" who never wavered from his delusion that the nation of India, deemed "impossible to govern" by the British Governor general, could be made whole, independent, and at peace? By perfecting the art of civil disobedience, he accomplished the impossible and succeeded in extracting "The Jewel in the Crown" from the British Empire without a shot being fired. His was a quality that could only be accurately described as *ruthless compassion,* the relentless pursuit of universal goodness. Gandhi harmed no one and yet conquered entire armies. He was the rose that cracked the stone.

"Ah, but Gandhi was an astute visionary with an exceptional sense of devotion to cause," they cry out. "And he was from a political family, schooled in the skills of government and of motivating others."

Then we submit for your approval yet another choice. Her name is Helen Keller. Born both deaf and blind, written off as hopeless even by her loved ones, she merely managed to become a prize-winning author and one of the foremost educators of her time who virtually revolutionized our teaching techniques for the sense impaired.

Often quoted, Helen Keller once made this timeless observation: "Security is mostly a superstition. It does not exist in nature... Life is either a daring adventure or nothing."[6]

And doesn't that strike us all at the heart (If it doesn't, at least it should!) that a woman, who, by all ordination of conventional wisdom could have become a vegetable, chose instead to change the ways in which we regard our physically disadvantaged?

To be sure, Helen Keller had a teacher like Ann Sullivan to tap the genius trapped inside her. But it is our belief that a genius sits locked inside us all, waiting to be set free by the higher self.

The difference between genius and mediocrity is often a matter of focus. Great souls among us—the visionaries, the delusionists, the heroes—are blessed with inquisitive minds. They never tread the same ground twice. They possess a will to know everything about themselves and the universe around them. They never accept the life they're given. And they always begin with questions.

So it is questions we will next put before you, ones we hope will put you on the path to true delusion. At the very least they will make you think about where you stand in your life and where it is you truly want to go.

Chapter 3

Twenty of the Most Important Questions You Will Ever Ask[*]

"What is the answer?
In that case, what is the question?"

—Gertrude Stein
(Spoken from her deathbed to Alice B. Toklas)

It's easy to feel overwhelmed, particularly at the important choices we face in our lives. We want to dig deeply to find the destiny that drives us, but sometimes that little voice that calms the soul inside has grown so faint we are daunted even at the prospect of trying to call it out.

The dread of uncertainty brings even gods to tremble. That is the curse of free will—and its greatest blessing as well. No matter how much we long for certain outcomes, it is that very element of not knowing that spices our lives.

We long for the law of probability; but, if it is to favor us at all, it must reinforce it with a resolution of our own Determination, conviction, and

---

[*] We know you've been hit with jillions of questionnaires in your life. But this one goes toward the core of who you truly are—at the level of your soul's contract. Respect it. And take the time to make the honest choices some of these will require of you.

dedication to purpose all become our allies. But sometimes they come late to our cause. And if they come, it is usually because somewhere along the way we were encouraged by our use of them. It is a favor to those of us who were. Those of us who were not must look to another source to find our grit. And that requires a different kind of tactic altogether. It is called surrender.

We admonish you to do so, because you will win—because, in the individual's search to rediscover his or her true purpose on this earth, failure is not an option. By surrendering, you release expectation of outcome while holding fast to your intention to achieve what is right. It is the delusionist's greatest skill. It is your inheritance, by birth.

Another way of saying surrender is to say "let go and let God." That implies trust—not necessarily trust of the hard-edged world that has taught you its pain, but the trust that the infant carries with it when it comes into this plane of consciousness. Trust is the ability to hear your angels when they sing.

You must also trust this: Fear is your personal message that you are getting nearer to a truth. It may not be a truth you want to hear, but it is most certainly one you need to know. So when you are challenged to answer the questions you are about to put to yourself, be willing to play through the pain of discovery, and realize that by doing so, you will find great joy on the other side.

We have already emphasized, but let us emphasize again: Fear is the Lie of the left-hand path. Fear is the flip side of love. And yet fear, like everything in our divine universe, serves a purpose—in this case, a beneficial one. "Love and Fear" is our very next chapter. So, you'll learn about the Fear Matrix soon enough. For the time being, we invite you to look upon fear as an ally in your process of personal discovery. Just as a disease without symptoms is far deadlier than one in which the symptoms clearly reveal themselves, those little ticks of pain you feel as you verge on certain moments of discovery just might prove to be your best guides to some accurate answers. Questions that do not create some measure of discomfort are often not a challenge to the answerer and therefore offer little opportunity for growth.

The other issue lies in the nature of the questions themselves. They are meant to trigger responses on two levels. Your conscious response level is important, to be sure. You are expected to weigh your replies, to think them out. You can also be expected to rationalize away some of the right answers. It's a part of the process. But then, so is relying on your instinct. So, we encourage you to listen to your GUT. What was the first instinctive, visceral response that churned through you when you asked the question? Take note of that and be willing to readdress it as you continue on your search for the truth.

Remember, above all else, that these questions are being posed to help you tell the truth about who you really are and where you want to go in your life. From the outset, we acknowledge that no twenty questions, however astutely designed, will carry all the answers. What these can and should do is act as conduits. Properly asked, they'll bring forth new cascades of questions from within you, all of which can be addressed by means of an honest communication with your higher self—the one that is always with you, the one whose voice you often hear but do not always heed.

Well, now it's time to retune your dial. But in order to do so even more effectively, we ask you to do it with a system that we find effective. Throughout this book we, will ask you to make a series of lists, and to answer certain questions, like the very important ones that will follow on these pages. As is the case with all things in life, your participation in these lists is optional. It simply depends upon whether or not you truly desire to make a difference in your life, or to read a book that may prompt you to examine your life a bit more seriously. In either case, you will experience some exceptional results. In the former instance, however—the one in which you participate more actively—we can assure you of even more dramatic outcomes.

But for you to do this requires that you either use a note-pad or get your *University of Delusion Playbook* and follow the chapter directives that you will find in it. Whatever you do—if you do nothing else!—please answer these next twenty questions as if the rest of your life depended upon it. You never know; it may.*

Question 1: When your heart is truly open, what are you doing? There are certain times in our day, in our week, in our lives, when we are so "in the zone" with what we do that there is no other feeling like it. We resonate oneness with our universe. We feel unified in mind, body and spirit.

This feeling doesn't have to be merely during the accomplishment of some grand project like brain surgery or having painted a masterpiece. It can come when you're walking your dog or building a cabinet or reading a book or helping with a recycling drive in your neighborhood. It can come with being with your loved ones, or being by yourself. It can come through a frantic game of racquetball or a serene morning's meditation. The important issue is to take note of it, evaluate how much time you spend doing it and why. And if this feeling appears to be entirely missing from your life, flip back to those past moments when you felt such spiritual harmony.

(Caution: The tendency here is to confuse the opening of your mind with the opening of your heart. So many people can enjoy an activity, an accomplishment or a success with an open mind. Usually these are appeals to the ego—a board-room victory, a standing ovation for a speech you've just given, a low score on the golf course, a big night at the casinos in Las Vegas. These experiences are pleasant as far as the ego will allow them to be.

True openings in the heart resonate throughout your entire being. They are the notes of a spiritual awakening, and once the inner self rediscovers

---

* We also offer you a suggestion. Answer these twenty questions now. Then, a few days after you have finished reading *Delusion is Good,* answer them again. We think you'll be amazed at how differently you answer some of them, and how others—some of the more important answers—might not vary at all.

that attunement—that atonement, that *at-one-ment*—it cannot fail to recognize it when it happens again.

An Additional Caution: Addictive personal relationships seldom if ever get the job done. Sex is only cause for euphoria if an overwhelming unconditional love precedes it. That is something that is tested in time, not in the quick ins and outs of transitory passion.)

Question 2: What subject makes your heart and mind flutter with excitement? What pushes your happy button? Everyone has a personal passion. The subtext that must be answered is whether or not it is beneficial to everyone around you. And do you, in pursuing it, feel as good once you've done it as you did when you began?

(**Caution:** Remember the *mind candy trap* and how deliciously deceiving it can be. Movies, television, and entertainment media events are okay, but they are attempts to alter our consciousness by retreating from life rather than participating in it. Obsessions with various forms media magic, however, do serve a positive purpose. They are a good indication that an individual is not in touch with his or her true delusion. It is also indicates that your oversoul is knocking on your windows of perception. And if you find yourself fixated upon a film or a score of music, it is important to note the nature of the vehicle itself, and how it affects you emotionally. If it triggers you to higher aspirations, it could be an indication that you are ready for some major changes. It if opens passages in the dark side of your soul, it is mind candy at its worst, Spit it out and find an activity that will help you make a complete about-face in how you focus your energy.)

Question 3: Who is your Hero? And why? It never fails. We define ourselves by what we find to admire in others. That's why this question may be more important than it first appears to be. Even a human being who is utterly out of balance with everything else in their life is able to find a hero, someone who epitomizes those qualities that make an impact on them.

You can approach your answer to this in one of two ways. You can make a short list. Look at your alternatives, and select one individual from that—probably the one who most closely summarizes your values. Or you can write down the first figure who pops into your mind. They have to be people who have actually lived—no cartoon characters please! And they may be either alive today or be some figure from the past.

The authors, for example, have their personal favorites. Paul selected the conqueror Alexander the Great as his hero. Paul believes, Alexander may have been the most successful delusionist of all time. A student of Aristotle, Alexander was remembered as having said, "I count him braver who overcomes his desires than he who overcomes his enemies; for the hardest victory is the victory over self."[7] Alexander followed the call of his destiny, took a small Macedonian fighting force out against insurmountable odds and conquered half the known world all before the age of 32. (Paul, who likes meeting tough challenges and cutting Gordian knots found this particularly appealing.)

Robert chose Thomas Jefferson as the person he most admired. Perhaps the most gifted Renaissance man since da Vinci, Jefferson was not only an accomplished architect who set forth much of the design for the nation's capital, as well as many of the important structures in Virginia and Maryland; he also managed to draft the framework of U.S. government, serve as this nation's President, and patent a score of inventions. And yet it wasn't his list of accomplishments that made him most admirable. It was his sense of vision. He was aptly called the father of modern democracy, and never wasted a moment of his life. Ever the student, he was constantly learning. Acquiring knowledge of everything new in life was his only form of mind candy—food for the soul, with no artificial preservatives.

(**Note:** It's easy to fall into a trap on this one and name some positive role model who will make you look good to others. Don't fall for it. These are your 20 questions, and they are here for your benefit. Your hero is your personal choice, and so are your reasons for choosing her or him. Honest answers are the only viable means to self discovery.)

Question 4: What would you do if you had unlimited funds, excellent health and one year to live? Given the allowances made for family and loved ones, what would you do then? What hidden dreams would you tap? What would you want to accomplish? What contributions would you make to the world you leave behind? Don't be afraid to probe for this one and pull out your long buried dreams; the ones you haven't shared with anyone for a long time. Given that short span of time, compare this list to your list of goals and objectives in Question 3. (By the way, we realize that we are asking additional questions inside each category. But consider them prompts, if you will. Be aware that we do this in order to stimulate your thinking.)

Question 5: If you knew there was one thing at which you couldn't fail, what would you like most to do? We assume everyone is at least in some command of his or her proximate universe. We're looking for possible worlds here—the careers, pursuits, accomplishments that have been just out of your reach, the ones you have postponed. If necessary, make a larger list of five or more, then narrow it down to three. Sleep on your choices, then narrow the list to one. If you truly can't narrow the list to one, then accept the fact that you have more faith in your abilities to achieve than you might have originally thought. That in itself is cause for celebration.

Question 6: Up until now, what do you consider to be your greatest accomplishment in life? We all have something at which we have truly excelled. Whether it is a sport, an academic achievement, a professional accomplishment, a superb long-term love relationship, or bringing up a child, we truly feel we've done it the right way. Keeping that in mind, we emphasize that it is a very good thing to give ourselves a stroke for having achieved that level of excellence. The question that is born out of this is whether or not it fits into our most deeply held dreams; those goals we would—forsaking all else—like to have achieved.

Once you reveal that moment, go back step by step and review how you did it. And make a note of everything you did correctly. How many things did you do incorrectly? How quickly did you amend them and move on toward the corrected solution? Now, ask yourself this question: If you did everything right in this winning endeavor, why can't you apply the same principals to other endeavors you would like to accomplish?

Question 7: What has been your most agonizing failure? This question is truly significant for a number of reasons, because it prompts us all to look at other facets of that failure. First, we have to acknowledge whether that failure was the result of a supreme effort that fell short. If it was, congratulations. You didn't fail. You just haven't succeeded yet. But only you can answer the question that also ties to it: How hard did you really try? Did you try everything? When asked these questions, almost everyone admits they didn't. Then the logical question follows: If you didn't give it your best effort and try everything, how could you expect to have succeeded in the first place?

Did you even try at all? Or was your failure a failure even to try. When asked this question, an amazing number of people will also admit that they did not try. They were too afraid even to make the attempt. If you're one of that very large collection of souls, congratulations. You not only didn't succeed, you didn't even play the game. The good news is that you still can.

Having said that, there are some things you are no longer physically equipped to accomplish, so we now invite you to be realistic. And we use the word "realistic" both advisedly and sparingly.

Question 8: On those occasions when you have failed, did you try again to accomplish the same thing? A surprising number of people give up after just one pass at something. Others, even more sadly, gave up after years of trying a game, a skill, or a profession. Resigned to their own misplaced sense of mediocrity, they simply felt unsuited to the task at hand.

We have all been bombarded with the host of homilies that admonish us to "press on," when confronted by defeat, rejection, or what is commonly perceived as failure.

Yet we can only maintain the delusionist's point of view that no one fails at a bond that is made in the soul. If you are guided by your destiny toward a major goal, you will achieve that goal. We can also assure you that you will recognize it by the inner peace it gives you do to it. Once you have discovered it, success in other areas will often follow. On the other hand, denying it or ignoring it can create a level of dissonance that will remain with you like a constant low-grade fever.

Now, what you are well served to tap into is the pain that causes you to recoil at some of your decisions not to continue. How much of a sense of loss do you feel? If it is accurate, some of the sense of loss should be considerable.

From that shorter list, put a mark by those abandoned dreams, no matter how faint, that still have spark. How much would you still like to achieve that goal or desire? What steps would you have to take to reach it? Are you still willing to take them? What would you have to give up to take them? How would this fulfill you spiritually, mentally, emotionally, and financially?

Question 9: What are the goals or desires in your life that are still within reach? If they are still within reach, how close are you to achieving them? What steps are you taking toward that achievement? If you're not close, what would it take to make it happen? How can you begin to bring that about? Once you do achieve the goals or desires in question, how will they fulfill you? Would you have a full heart, or a full pocketbook? (They're not mutually exclusive, by the way.)

Are you driven by your higher self? Or your ego?

Can you tell the difference?

This question entails a series follow-up questions that may make it seem like a load to answer. But it's all a part of the same matrix. And, like Question 8 before it, it is intended to get you closer to the source of your most deeply held dreams. What we find is that many people, when answering these questions, go to financial gain, fame, and material advantage as criteria for fulfillment. These are manifestations of fulfillment. They are symbols of fulfillment. But, in and of themselves, they never fulfill anyone.

True fulfillment has to come from the heart. It has to come from our deepest soul's desires. Those are our connections to the higher self, and the delusions that just won't die. So, unless your list already only contains one, we recommend that you cut it in half. Compare your list to the answers you gave to Questions 3 and 4. How close does this list come to that one? What can you do to bring the two together?

Question 10: How would you define success? We mean for you to include yourself in this question. To evaluate such an intangible as success, one must inevitably come back to one's own perception of it. That in itself can bring on a broad spectrum of personal perceptions, and that is at least a part of the process.

The important consideration is the criterion you use. We won't attempt to dictate that paradigm, because it has to come from you. That's the challenge of this question. However, we do offer you some instances of measurement.

Almost always in his smaller seminars, success counselor Tony Robbins asks his clients to give their definitions of success, and never fails to be surprised by some of the answers he gets. One multi-millionaire entrepreneur in his group felt himself a failure because he had not achieved the status of a mega-millionaire. Another multi-millionaire, when asked the same question, considered every day above ground to be a success. Both men had achieved the same approximate level of financial reward, professional status, and high regard in their community. Yet almost anyone could answer the rhetorical question: Who felt better about the life he was leading?

In his "Treatise on Self-Reliance," Ralph Waldo Emerson defines success as follows:

> "To leave this world a bit better... whether by a healthy child, a garden patch, or a redeemed social condition. To know that even one life has breathed easier because you have lived, this is to have succeeded!"[8]

That comment, in itself, can be construed as settling for little or nothing. However, we have found that what you perceive as success will not only determine your level of drive but also your level of stress. And though there are certainly positive kinds of stress, constant feelings of falling short or failing are not contributory to them. Just as we all have failures in our lives, we all have successes too. And striving to become even better than you already are is a good indication that you are already a winner.

Question 11: How would you define integrity? On the surface of it, this response should offer fewer variables and make fewer demands on your levels of interpretation.

We find that this question also serves as a bellwether for one's level of intention. People who are operating from a spiritual center, those who are more closely in touch with their core delusion, tend to give a more precise answer. Those who are not, tend to flounder for their truth. That is not to say they lack integrity if they're floundering. But there exists the possibility that they are out of touch with their integrity of purpose in life.

There are, by the way, several definitions for integrity—yet only one. Just as the element of gold possesses an integrity that protects it from corroding even when influenced by an oxidizing atmosphere, a human being's personal integrity protects that individual from the corruptions of a toxic environment.

Question 12: What do you want to accomplish in your life—today, tomorrow, two years from now? At this point, it is more important to be positive than "realistic." Don't spare yourself the hidden dreams and the little abandoned wishes. Dig them out, take a look at them, and acknowledge the degree to which you are close to attaining them. Make a list, and cut the list in half; then cut that list in half.

Examine your short list—every item on it—and write each item on a large sheet of paper, along with the benefits to others that will come out of it. Then put them up on the wall and study them. Repeat them aloud if you will, and decide at that moment if that is how you want the world to see you.

The manner by which you answer should prompt you to examine both your short term and long term goals. It does not necessarily mandate that you bring the focus of your accomplishments on monetary gain, career achievements, or personal glory. Nor does it dictate exclusively that you conjure a host of noble causes. Balance is often the signature of the well-spent life. But only you can determine what that balance is, and ultimately how it will make you feel at the end of your day.

It is also important to note that you need to have a plan, set your course and follow that plan. Very often people will list what they have to do for the day, but they will do nothing about what they have to accomplish in the next year, or five years. That is very much like traveling to a city to which you have never been without either directions or a road map. Will you get there? Eventually, perhaps. The challenge is how much time are you willing to waste looking, when consulting a map will take you there right away and with certainty.

Question 13: As you continue to progress, what obstacles are in your way? How real are these obstacles? (Many, you will find, are manufactured to keep you from achieving your delusions of total fulfillment. In other words, they are a part of the lie that keeps you from achieving your truth—your ultimate dream). Real obstacles never present problems; they merely offer challenges that require solutions. Look upon your obstacles as hurdles in a race. Runners who finish see the hurdles, take their measure, and take each hurdle one at time. Winners see the tape at the finish line beyond the hurdles. They have already topped them on the way to it, even before the starter's pistol fires.

Question 14: If these blockages do exist, what steps can you take to eliminate them? If your obstacles present real challenges, then you can build a vehicle to either plow through them, fly over them, or swift around them. Obstacles are usually fixed, circumstantial, and rigid. That description also applies to people who might be obstructing your path. So, just remember that, as the free-to-fly deluded soul, you are flowing and highly motile. That means, by virtue of your own divine right, the advantage is with you now. You can accomplish all the things you desire at this very moment. But you must decide and take the action.

Right now, upon reading this, you're screaming out.

"Hold it!" You cry. "I don't have the answers. I don't know!"

Congratulations. "Not knowing" is the delusionist's first step toward making real progress. When you read the rest of this book, you'll have a complete design for the machine that will help you go through, over and around them. (Flying is usually the best way, but there are others as well.)

In the meantime, try thinking for yourself first. You'd be amazed at some of the good answers you'll come up with. By the way, have a good time while you're doing this. And if any obstacle you confront seems overwhelming to you, you have an opportunity to see it again. Is it a hard physical present-day barrier to your achievement, or is it something more deep-seeded?

For now, recognize what is seemingly the most sinister barrier to your achievement, and acknowledge the impeccable truth that you are certain to overcome it.

Question 15: *Who is in control of your life?* If you are, if you can look into the mirror and say you're financially, personally, and spiritually in complete control of your destiny, you're either an ascended master, a multi-millionaire entrepreneur, a completely self-actualized human being, or immersed in severe denial.

Truly insightful people are the first to recognize that someone else is always in control of aspects of their lives. They have obligations to finances, mortgages, car payments, family, spouses, ex-spouses, children, cause groups, churches and business associations.

Most of us are tethered in one way or another to all these things and all these people. The question to you then persists: Is it by your design that you do so? If you had to free yourself from these encumbrances, how difficult would it be?

Are your relationships dependent, interdependent, codependent or independent? Take each one and evaluate it honestly. If your mutual relationships are dependent, they will have either a termination date (like putting a child through school). If they are independent, they will involve personally complete people who could operate independently but choose instead to benefit from their participation in the group dynamic. The more independent relationships you have, the closer you are to being in control of your own life (and surrounded by people in control of theirs).

Question 16: If you are not in control of your life, how do you gain control of your life? Well, of course, you don't know. Otherwise you would be in control of your life. But take each set of situations in which you are not in control and outline the steps it will take to get you in control. Take the easy ones first. What you will find after a short time is that, situation by situation, you are going to develop some ingenious ways of doing so.

If you still can't, stick around. We'll be offering some designed suggestions for that later on as well.

Question 17: Assuming you have taken control of your life, what are the first three things you would do? You may make a larger list to begin with. But remember, we are trying to get to core issues here. We also encourage you to be constructive. Did the initiatives you set include gaining control over others? Or did you seek to empower those within your sphere of influence? Part of the delusionist's mission is to go to the larger issues of life—virtually to get larger than life. That is the thrust of what we intend to teach in this book, and the supreme design of life that we can all share with one another.

Question 18: At the end of your life, how will you want to be remembered? Everyone wants to be remembered well. They also, in the winter of their years, want to be able to look back and recall what they stood for and what they accomplished with a certain measure of pride and warm regard. The question that grows out of this might also be phrased another way: *What would I like to be spoken about me at my testimonial dinner?* We would probably all like to be thought of for a lifetime of contribution, to making our world a better place. But are we spending that lifetime in ways that would truly facilitate that condition?

By the same token, few of us can be expected to be a Mother Theresa or a St. Francis of Assissi. Life is not just sacrifice, service, résumés and testimonials. It is always about the cultivation of positive influences. The question that begs the answer is, how have you positively influenced others in your life? How will you evaluate it at the end? Are you headed on the path toward the kind of fulfillment you truly desire? At this point, you have probably tapped into a core issue or two about what you're doing with your life and where you're heading with your intention to make it complete.

If you have, congratulations. You're completely deluded and probably never lost sight of your dreams in the first place. You are a true delusionist. Or you could be lying to yourself, in which case you may be closer to the right answers than you think.

We'll explain. And that explanation quite possibly might come with the next question.

Question 19: Summarize yourself in two words. If you could use two words to define how the world sees who you are, what would you want them to be? This is the shortest list you will make, so it will require the most thought. By now, if you've been asking the right questions, you will have tapped into your true delusion, some of your earliest and dearest dreams.

So, now define yourself. It is a very important decision for you to make. Dig deeply. Give it all the appropriate consideration it deserves. Don't be surprised, by the way, if you find that what lies at the core of who you truly desire to be is a far nobler soul than you might have first perceived. Just as we are all put on this planet to make a positive difference, to contribute and to do service, the closer we come to that standard, the more at peace we will feel with the answer. To be sure, it is not something you can manufacture, conjure, or fake. That desire resides patiently inside the core of who you are. It is longing to express itself. It will not be denied.

Question 20: Summarize yourself in one word. What is the one word that should represent you to the world? At this point, you have reached the delusionist's summary statement. So this word should say everything for which you stand.

Once you have inscribed that word, go on a search for the first set of beliefs you held as a small child. If you've gone through this process correctly, it might well be the same word. Naturally, we must acknowledge that the evolution of one's dreams and perceptions is a part of the process. And of course there persists the maxim that states, "As I am, yet am not, the same person I was as a child, I am (but am not) the same person I was yesterday."

Change is as inevitable as it is relentless, but there also exist some magnificent constants about delusion. Your innate contact with your destined purpose in life never varies. Nor does it pretend to be more than it is. By its very nature, it offers us an entire horizon of choices as to how we carry out our contract with our higher self. The issue is that we do so, and that we are equally determined in our pursuit of it.

Magnificent Intention: A Summary.

Most of what we experience in life has us clamoring for answers when, invariably, we are not even clear about the correctness of the questions that will lead us to them. But remember, we didn't title this chapter "The Twenty Most Important Answers You Will Ever Receive," because it is not the answers but our search for them that causes us to grow.

There are no right or wrong answers to these questions. There is only the process. That process, properly undertaken, leads you through the maze of situation to the truth, and through that truth to the kind of future we can expect.

What many believe to be the definitive book of prophesy, the *I Ching*, teaches above all else that answers to questions about the future are supreme vanity. Even the master-teacher Lao Tzu, who conceived and structured the book, was said to have observed that he who prophesies the future does the work of a fool.

With that in mind, the process dictated by the *I Ching's* oracle leads the seeker through such a disciplined structure of seeking that the search itself alters the consciousness of the seeker. By the time the answer to any question is revealed, it has first become apparent that there is no good or bad outcome, no right or wrong decision. There is only the conduct of the superior or inferior man as he confronts the challenges each situation presents.** So, outcome is dictated both by response and by intention.

It is also significant to note that the literal translation for The *I Ching* is *The Book of Changes*. What remains unstated but evident at the outcome of each reading is that the ultimate change comes not in reward or punishment but in the evolution of the seeker in the midst of the quest.

That's what *questions* do.

We also ask you to acknowledge that your elements of denial in facing many of these questions may have come straight from the Fear Matrix and, conversely, those dreams that you envisioned most passionately, without reservation or remorse, came straight from your contact with the Love Matrix. Those songs from the soul, all of them, are what we must deal with next. Because we can prepare and do exercises until we are blue in the face, but until we make a complete study of the two driving forces of our life and all the decisions that spring from them, we will live in a flak field of conflicting impressions.

Time to turn the page on that.

Chapter 4

Love and Fear

Where no hope is left, is left no fear.

—John Milton
Paradise Regained.

The universe wears two faces and does so for a reason.

These two faces are put in place both to give us perspective and to be our teachers. As a part of the daily ritual of living, we see them, feel them, wear them, and project them into the mirror of our perception. Yet few of us, when pressed to define them, would be able to arrive at the same conclusions about what they are. We must speak of them in the present tense, because they are our constants—as fixed in their nature as we are ever changing in our understanding of them. We define them in narrow, human, emotional contexts that are both fallible and incorrect. Our "realities" of Love and Fear have been learned by rote and are, by the very expression of that learning process, self-limiting.

In the broad universal context, we would find other labels for love. Light, God, positivity, goodness (or God-ness)—all stem from the same positive matrix and all project the same kind of "good" energy. In itself, "God," as a term is an absolute use of the Matrix. And the quote from the First Epistle of John that "God is love" is the absolute perception of the Word as we have been taught it in the Christian faith. We hold to that

45

belief and honor our Creator in such a way. However, we also acknowledge that using the term "God" as such edges us perilously close to groundings in religion. And since religionism generates the kind of partisanship we are looking to avoid in this exposition, we will hold to our use of the term, "Love," as the Matrix for purposes of this study.

Some behaviorist schools of psychology prefer to reduce the love-fear polarities into simplistic psycho-galvanic terms such as "pain and pleasure." But we believe that such perceptions of pain and pleasure can appear to come from both matrixes at the same time, ostensibly for contradictory reasons. Usually, when that occurs, it is because the pleasure is either illicit, self-destructive or comes at the expense of someone else. And that kind of pleasure is an offshoot of the Fear Matrix.

Fear, we feel safe in observing, is the dominant matrix at this material level of consciousness. Love, its very nature and meaning, is what remains the great cosmic enigma, and that is what we intend to give greater clarity in these pages. We also emphasize that these observations—being solely our own and those of about 50,000,000 angels with whom we consort on a regular basis—are entirely subjective and should be viewed as such.

With that in mind, we guide you to the Ahola-Peccianti Love/Fear Matrix and our guidelines for it. With it, we also offer every feasible consideration of how it might help you gain a better insight into the reasons we perceive them the way we do. We also suggest that while you're going down this list, you make notes on the kind of emotional reactions you might have to some of the words as you came across them.

The LOVE/ FEAR Matrix

Love	*Fear*
God	Satan
Light	Darkness
Angel	Devil
Good	Evil
Truth	Lie
Positivity	Negativity
Peace	Conflict (War)
Grace	Disgrace
Atonement	Separation
Enlightenment	Superstition
Abundance	Lack
Harmony	Disharmony
Healing	Hatred
Charity	Greed
Trust	Distrust
Praise	Blame
Kindness	Unkindness
Abundance	Limitation
Acclaim	Envy
Hope	Despair
Elation	Depression
Non-judgment	Judgment
Tranquillity	Rage
Praise	Ridicule
Forgiveness	Resentment/Revenge
Calm	Anxiety
Ease	Disease
Non-violence	Violence
Openness	Bias

Freedom	Constraint
Acceptance	Condition
Intention	Expectation
Inspiration	Manipulation
Helplessness	Attack
Commitment	Avoidance
Submission	Aggression
Disinterested	Partisan
Neutrality	Defense
Serenity	Passion
Passion	Indifference
Detachment	Involvement
Resurrection	Death

Now that you've made a study of this list and jotted down some notes, we must now ask the inevitable, if rhetorical, question: What were your responses when you read these? Unless, you have made an elaborate study of these diametric opposites in the past, you probably experienced some emotional reactions to them on at least two levels. We would note, without fear of contradiction, that the first set of opposites (about two-thirds of the list) found you nodding with complete if not perfunctory agreement. These are perhaps logical aspects of the same matrixes, and one might disagree only in the degree to which some responses to negativity or positivity that fear or love prevail.*

However, when you reached a certain bank of words, we suspect you began to question the emotions these terms conjured as well as the source

---

* Some people who study the list, for example, might feel strongly that rage or anger are more powerful aspects of the fear matrix than fear itself. We agree that they might be more violent and intense aspects of fear. But they are, in themselves, narrower ranges of the fear matrix and, as we will soon show, are merely offshoots of it.

from which they sprang. You found yourself stepping gingerly through some gray areas and might have even come to some conclusions about the matrix that disagreed with their position on the list. If you did, congratulations! That's a very good sign that you are truly measuring the impact that these matrixes may have on your life. And even though it is our sworn mission to clarify these issues for you, we compliment you on your passionate approach to the themes in question. Aspects of passion, as you will note, have been placed into both sides of the Love/Fear equation and fit there for a very good reason. We are, after all, dealing with the facets of rhetoric and find it essential to note that our language, like the endless aspects of love and fear themselves, includes words that carry their own diametric contradictions.

It is important to acknowledge both Love and Fear and honor all aspects of them as the divine gifts they were intended to be. Everything in this life we all share is a gift, but only our discernment can show them for the treasures they are, and true discernment extracts certain disciplines of rethinking the nature of everything we are.

Embracing such platitudes as "All you need is Love," and "God is Love," are at the same time both accurate and incomplete. At the core level of our inner selves, we already acknowledge this. It is just that our conditioning has caused us to redraw the lines according to the ways that we have been taught them, and each of us—tens of millions of us in hundreds of different cultures—have been infused with complex, confusing, and contradictory precepts of what love is. In so many ways, we are "frightened" by our very inability to deal with many aspects of love when we think we recognize it. Often, they are merely facets of fear that we misconstrue to be love.

Whenever our political leaders such as Franklin D. Roosevelt say, "There is nothing to fear but fear itself," or our men of letters such as Frank Herbert (author of the *Dune* Tetrology) insist that "Fear is the mind-killer,"[9] we nod our collective agreement at what we hear or read, while we harbor individual pockets of dread that we are overwhelmed by just such personal demons every day of our lives. We feel impotent to confront them, often even to identify them.

Such behavioral syndromes as *free-floating anxiety*, the kind we get for no apparent reason and from no ostensible external cause, are so prevalent in our sophisticated society that entire pharmaceutical industries have shot up simply to treat the symptoms. Such biochemical marvels as Valium, Librium, Prozac, Halcion, and other anti-depressants, mood enhancers and muscle relaxers are—even at the time of this writing— used by an estimated 70 million adult women and men in the United States alone. That does not take into account such non-toxic herbal alternatives such as St. John's Wort and Kava Kava that are now the rage of the new age.

Yet into what kind of new millennium do we move when so few of us are of one mind as to the significance of the forces that drive us most? We learn what we are taught are the true natures of them without undertaking the delusionist's discipline to rise up from the stew of social dogma into the light of Universal Truth. Instead, we embrace doctrines, laws, and patterns of social behavior that—though they are correct in fact—are dictated by a system of rewards and punishments that stem from the Fear Matrix itself. When placed in juxtaposition to it, Love—the giving, caring, unconditional creation brought on by the cosmic ballet between our angels and our higher selves—appears fragile, tepid, and insubstantial.

That is very much like saying Jesus Christ, standing next to Satan, is a wimp. We would deny it with our dying breath, while it is with all the living breaths in between that we make our burnt offerings to that other guy with the dank thorny wings and the very confident smile.

For a better understanding of our meaning here, we invite you to examine these matrixes in more detail and to keep score on your own responses to them. While you are doing so, be ready to come to some realizations about yourself that you might not at first be willing to accept.

But accept them you must. "Or," as the Jedi master Yoda might say, "grow, you will not!"

It is our undying faith—our delusion if you will—that you will break through all bonds that shackle your infinite mind and see the light of God's love. First, however, you must pass through the gates of Fear and recognize it for the alluring impostor that it is.

We will address the issue of Fear first, because it is the easier of the two universal qualities to define. It throws a clearer shadow, so that we can mark it in all its manifestations and move on to the more perilous terrain of understanding universal Love.

Frighteningly Fun.

Luke Skywalker: "I'm ready to undertake my training, Master Yoda! I 'm not afraid!'

Yoda: "No. But you will be…"

—*Star Wars/ Episode V*
The Empire Strikes Back

Admit it. The Dark Side is fun! It terrifies us, holds us fast, titillates us, frightens and intimidates us—even obsesses us at times—taps into our tawdry fantasies and our most lurid moments of mass mind thinking. It is the great entertainer, the consummate distraction, the bells on the jester's cap that keep those of us in the kingdom of Heaven from being bored with our own perfection. We let its images surround us, pervade our senses, dominate our media, and form the passages through which we find our escapes from the dull realities of day-to-day drudgery. We revel in negativity, danger, and the pyrotechnics of war and destruction! We long for the conflicts, the intrigues, the personal corruptions that bring down the houses of the *glitterati*—both fictional and real—in all we watch and witness. We enjoy it, all of it, *as long as it doesn't affect us directly.*

We are *voyageurs* into those bleak and perilous places in film, entertainment, literature, news, world events and thought, as long as we can keep them at a distance. They form the Hydra—that very singular monster with many heads. It is terrible, frightening, more than occasionally foul, wicked, debasing, even repulsive at times. But at least it isn't devouring us! And for that moment—that string of macroseconds—we are thrilled, our perceptions heightened, our awareness brought to new rushes of energy. And somehow we feel we've managed to bring it all under control while even more minions born from its maw come into our midst.

Mouths agape, we sit and read or watch or become immersed in the Sensurround® experience, while a legion of dazzling villains uncompromisingly evil and unrepentantly compelling prance about in our fantasies, pulling out of us a kind of magnetized repulsion that is degrading, sensual and exhilarating all at once. Darth Vader, Professor Moriarty, Mephistopheles, Richard III, Hannibal Lecter, Caligula, and Dracula—how charmingly seductive they all appear. Even though we are at last permitted to see the hideous depredations they intend for us, we still remain enthralled with the illusions of power they depict.

Then we come down from the artificial high of it, our senses numbed, narcotized by the loud Gestalt of manufactured thrills. We have indulged at a banquet of borrowed emotions—many of them enervating—and now we feel ashamed, spent, and ever so slightly aware of the fact that none of these responses felt natural to us. We promise to do better, to avoid them, to concentrate on the poetry of life. Deep inside ourselves, we know the greater good. We sense the slow rot in the soul. But we still look on. Still we find that all around us the world, that "real" world closer to our own, has conspired to give us more.

The media, the print and electronic press, the rapidly rising Internet—all feed on this even further. They claim to be the messengers of virtue and the arbiters of social justice. In truth, they have become the panderers of sensation.

Does high intent have a part in their plan? Is there virtue in the mix of what they do? Of course! But one loses the taste of it in the commercialization of fear. Killings, maimings, wars, natural disasters, stock market panics, oil spills, nuclear meltdowns, mass murders and domestic violence form the major mural that is framed by the occasional St. Patrick's Day parade or celebrity interview. "If it bleeds, it leads" becomes standard editorial policy not just for the scandalmongering weeklies that supersell at our supermarket checkout counters, but also as the editorial gospel of mainstream newspapers, magazines, and national television networks.

In truth, we are so inundated with the theatre of bizarre and extreme acts that we rush home to our tame little worlds, where we watch nice safe soap operas and serial fantasy sagas where rich, beautiful and powerful people all scheme, plot, manipulate, betray, connive, and seduce one another's wives and boyfriends, and more than occasionally graduate to more sinister sports such as murder, embezzlement and fraud.

Small wonder, the rest of the world leading more mundane existences consider their quarreling, sulking, bickering, excessive discipline of children, neglect of pets, sloppy personal hygiene, and optional road rage to be venial sins—the occasional behavioral lapses of an otherwise normal if somewhat mundane life.

It is here that we emphasize again: We are the sum of our focus; no more and no less. And even though we might not ask for these impressions, they come cascading into our lives with relentless force, pervading our senses, dictating the pace of our daily interactions until we are inextricably caught up in the "negativity of daily living." Whether or not we can explain it away, we can never understand it entirely because— at a very early age—it becomes a part of our cellular consciousness, our senses, our very way of understanding our environments, both actual and contrived. For reasons never quite apparent to us, we feel a hole in the heart that cannot, through any power on earth, be filled.

Psychotherapy may identify it, even reveal it, for the monstrous apparition that it is. But it can never put it to rest. Prescription drugs may provide a brief panacea, but it has limited range and bleak continuous loops of Bell-curve usage.

Many people resort to illegal drugs and alcohol but realize, often too late, that these become nutrients of the soul's dis-ease and have been darkly cultivated to even further feed our fear addictions and spur us on to even deeper levels of depravity.

In our need we turn to religion, any religion, and to what we believe are the arms of an unconditionally loving God. But soon we find the Gods, any gods, to which we turn have been weighed down by the limitations and conditions that human thought have placed upon them. Religions that begin by promising salvation end by being less concerned with love than by gaining advantage over other religions—by being on the winning side. Rather than acknowledge the universality of Love, they demand adherence to the petty details of doctrine—man-made details—whose contrivances they are willing to go to war to defend. So what begin as the citadels of the Love Matrix are inverted to bastions of the Fear Matrix, and entire nations are slaughtered in the bargain. It is a catastrophic chain of retribution that continues even into the new Millennium.

It is this soup of disharmony through which the innocent soul must swim until it wears the armor of fear on every cell, until it becomes a part of it. That is its fate—unless it has somehow kept its hidden covenant with Delusion. Remember the undeniable truth that, even to the moment of our passage from this life, we all remain little children asking not to be hurt. And yet we are hurt by the "thousand natural shocks" that come to be the process of daily living—so much so that we become party to that process ourselves. We attack in order not to be attacked. We defend in order to prevent attack. We gain advantage in order not to be taken advantage of. We do so with an adherence to some code of conduct that we believe to be fair and just. But very often love has no place in it. Love, we feel, is not strong enough; love is a glass dove. Love is some fragile creation from a distant world we can only visit on occasion.

By now, we hope you are engaged in your own personal protest against the mural of unnatural emotions that we have painted for you.

"That's not me!" you cry out. (At least you'll cry out if you've been working to become as personally developed as we believe you have.) If you're feeling that way by now, if you're feeling a sense of outrage, congratulations! You are ready to embrace the delusionist's call to account for your life, and you're refusing to be limited by the network of negativity that the Lie has woven around you.

Then again, if you've come to understand and accept our Pandemic corruption of the spirit and your personal inability to escape it by means of your own individual will, we offer our double congratulations! You are one of the rare few who realizes just how deeply the Fear Matrix has infiltrated every aspect of who we are. So intensely has that penetration become that none of us can free ourselves of it without some extensive changes and some considerable outside help.

In either case, we offer you a test in the form of a chronicle—a daily log, if you will—that we want you to keep for a week (five work days will do). In it, we would like for you to write down or at least mark every Fear Matrix event, encounter, or invasion you experience. This will include more than you have ever realized. So, in order to help you become more aware of them, we offer the following starter's kit of interactions for your consideration:

• Every violent or unpleasant moment you see in film, television, hear on the radio, or read in magazines and daily newspapers. (Hint: This not only includes every violent film such as *The Rock* or *Con Air* but also every episode of reality-based shows such as *Cops* or *911*, every rerun of *Dallas* or the every version or spin-off of the *Jerry Springer* genre of personality freak show, every violent music video, every news that covers some unpleasant news event or national war, every commercial decrying drug abuse… Starting to get the picture?)

- Every violent or unpleasant event you experience in your office. (Hint: Board room quarrels and heated exchanges, office gossip [including the gossip you listen to but think you don't participate in] nasty inter-office memos, industrial espionage, power plays etc.)
- Every phone conversation you have where one or more negative subjects come up—even conversational news of a death or misfortune suffered by another. Include conversations where you listen but don't add to the negativity—this too is silent approval and constitutes participation by consent.
- Every event of animal cruelty or child abuse you see, hear about, or (unwittingly) participate in, including every hunting or fishing show or film about violence to animals or animals who hunt and kill other animals. Include in this mix animals who turn on and try to kill human beings.
- Every piece of promotional material or advertising that brings up unpleasant subjects—even if they are set in place for what is ostensibly a good cause.
- Every in-your-face radio or TV talk show you listen to or watch during which the language is confrontational, hostile, self-serving or involved in ridicule of a third party.
- Every sporting event you see either live or in the media where fights, conflicts, or arguments break out.
- Every violent sport such as ice-hockey or football or boxing—even the *Grand Guignol* of professional wrestling—including blood sports such as bullfighting, cockfights and hunting of any kind.
- Every time you have choked, clutched, tanked, or melted down while playing a sport or participating in a game of chance.
- Every negative artistic criticism, play, musical, opera or ballet in which violence, mayhem or conflict appear as themes.
- Every fire-and-brimstone sermon you hear or spiritual diatribe that condemns another faith, religion or spiritual point of view.

- Every moment of anger, road rage, or hate thoughts you see, feel or experience while driving (This includes everything from wrecks to showing someone in the next car the nice manicure on your middle finger. It also includes any kill thoughts or negative thoughts that may flutter across your consciousness.)
- Every attack thought, punitive thought, or thought of revenge or retribution you have felt toward someone. Note every one, even the casual ones that appear to have no agenda.
- Every time you have fantasized about hurting or even killing someone who made you mad or who had offended a loved one.
- Every time you see cartoon violence either on television or on the Internet, including Internet combat games and films.
- Every time you run across an Internet porn sight, topless dance nightclub or 900 number advertised on television.
- Every time you fantasize about sex with someone, including all those times when the objects of your desire are married or involved with someone else. (This includes fantasy sex, exploitive sex, sex where you manipulate or exploit someone else solely for your pleasure.)
- Every time you boast of your accomplishments or praise yourself to others as having been on the right side of a conflict.
- Every occasion upon which you listened to heavy metal, rap, hip-hop, or rock music that contained bleak, negative, violent or exploitive lyrics.
- Every time you are possessive, controlling, jealous or hostile in your so-called love relationships.
- Every situation in which you started out with a pleasant intention but were dragged into negativity by another party.
- Every instance in which you let someone else drag you down, and every instance in which you dragged someone else down to your level of emotional debris, either by gossip or contentious behavior.

- Every challenge you postponed and every time that you have procrastinated rather than taken on the job at hand.
- Every time you have lied (including little white lies) to serve your own ends.
- Every time you have teased someone, been thoughtless, or unwittingly hurt someone's feelings.
- Every time you have ridiculed someone behind his or her back or made satire or a laughing stock out of someone else.
- Every comedy show you see that either ridicules, satirizes, or brings injury to someone else.
- Every time you've prayed for advantage, revenge or specific benefit to you at the expense of other groups, sects, nations, or opponents of any kind.
- Every time you have had a negative or fearful thought about being harmed, betrayed, or abused.
- Every favor or service asked of you that you either turned down or lied about because it inconvenienced you to do it.
- Every moment you have experienced an unwarranted sense of panic, loss, fear, fright, or depression. (Include panic attacks and suicidal considerations in this).
- Every time you have felt unattractive, unworthy of good things, overweight, dissatisfied with who you are.
- Every occasion during the day when you rerun past failures, past injustices or past negative experiences over which you have no control—events, which persist, in your memory.

Are we taking away all your fun? After all, without a little sex, violence, intrigue, argument, exploitation, and a bench-clearing brawl or two, what is living all about? Right? When you think about it, so many of these little diversions spice the broth of life. Besides, we're only human. We're not perfect, or we wouldn't be here. Right?

We don't intend to take issue with that kind of thinking. We need only remind you that, even when you're indulging in mind candy, you're spending a lion's share of your time personally investing in the Fear Matrix. In fact, we are certain that you'll encounter so many of these experiences that we suggest you again follow the experimental directive we gave you in Chapter 2. Either carry with you a voice-activated mini tape-recorder, or set up a shorthand code that you can use to make and perhaps initial in your notebook, Palm Pilot, or *University of Delusion Playbook*. (For example, a violent two hour and ten minute film might carry the code F/2:10 to denote the topic and the amount of time you spent on it.)

Experience has taught us that you will undergo a graduated awareness of just how much time and energy you spend in the Fear Matrix. At first, only the larger issues and events will catch your notice. Later on in your daily diaries, you will start to take more notice and acknowledge the myriad negative occurrences. The more honest you are and the more willing to push the edge of your psychometric pain-threshold, the more notes you'll find you're taking.

Whatever you find, we caution you not to be too hard on yourself or to edge your score toward the high side of the Love percentage. It is not at all unusual for people beginning this daily chronicle to start out with a Fear Matrix recognition level of 35% and graduate to a 55% or even a 70% level of Fear Matrix experience.

By every system of measurement we have, hard-core negativists (those who would never come near this book) spend at least 85% of their waking hours locked in Fear Matrix activities. The average person spends over 60%. And even some of the more enlightened souls who have undertaken to keep the log acknowledged having spent an average of 15% to 20% of their time in Fear-Matrix occurrences. That is approximately 2.5 hours of their waking day! For the rest of us, it can be as much as 7 to 9 hours a day wallowing in the wash of the Fear Matrix.

And don't think you escape it when you sleep. So much of the weight of negative thought, word and deed gets dumped into the subconscious that even our dreams can become troubled because of them. By design, it is our dream states that frequently redeem us. Our dreams become a kind of waste management for negative thought, so that we can emerge refreshed, even reprieved. We have been able to wander through the arcane mindscapes of our REM state so that we may experience some of the tranquillity that otherwise might be missing from our lives. We have also found, however, that people who spend the majority of their time in Love Matrix activity also have dreams that rise to a higher plane of awareness. So even their subconscious gets a break from Fear Matrix input.

And by the way, if you think spending a week logging and taking notes on what you've become is a lot of work, we invite you to run the math and just figure how many hours a year you spend in Fear Matrix activity. Then multiply that by the number of years that you've been on this planet since the age of three.

Certainly, we acknowledge the inescapable truth that none of us can avoid all the negativity that comes our way. A great deal of it is situational and is nothing more than the by-product of living on a very busy planet. There are, however, some positive steps each of us can take to amend our lives and bring our every thought, word, and deed back toward the Love Matrix. Because it is only by functioning in the Love Matrix that we can not only help heal this world but also bring ourselves more closely in touch with our higher purposes in life.

There are several steps that we have found that can be taken to help accomplish this. Most of them can be found in our examination of the Love Matrix and our directives in how to place the majority of your focus from it. For the time being, however, we ask you to go through one final step in your Fear-Matrix chronicle. Go back to each confrontation or negative experience and note your participation in it: Could you have avoided it? Could you have learned something positive from it? Did it bring you down emotionally? Or did you enjoy it at some level? (Dig deeply for this one.) Did you do the best you could to make something positive out of the situation? If not, would you be willing to try next time? What could you have done to prevent it?

As in everything in life, none of us can hope to have all the answers. What we can do to better understand the nature of the Fear Matrix is to ask the questions that will bring it into focus, so that we may make more positive use of it later on. For that—truly!—all you need is love!

Unconditional Love—The Fire of Purification.

There is no fear in love, but perfect love casteth out fear.

—*1 John 4:18*

We begin this section with a purely subjective observation: Fewer than one percent of us truly knows how to love unconditionally. We may have erratic periods of it, those minutes or hours when we are truly in the flow of what it means, before the tides of circumstance slam us back to earth. Usually they come in a jolt of discord, a cross word, someone we meet along the way whose attitude is a toxin that infects the poetry of that perfect awareness.

As Ralph Waldo Emerson observed, "Our faith comes in moments. Our vice is habitual."[10] We believe it was a comment less cynical than true. And if you kept your Fear Matrix diary conscientiously for one week, we feel confident that you'll be in agreement with it. In view of that, the sad realization we must come to is that a permanent state of grace in which unconditional love exists perpetually is, on this plane of consciousness, unachievable. The good news is that we can get a lot closer to it than we are. But to do so requires some disciplines. In other words, the attainment of unconditional love will take some intense additional effort on your part. You're going to have to work at it.

This, of course, defies all tenets of cosmic logic. By every other premise of measurement, quite the opposite should be true. Love should come as easily and naturally to us as breathing. After all we, as spiritual beings, are born out of the Love Matrix, and are taught the elements of the Fear Matrix out of life's experiences. But it is part of the insidious subtlety of the Fear Matrix that, among its first manipulations of the innocent child, it instantly assails that child's open, loving nature.

We refer you once more to that innocent soul, that tiny child filled with a sense of freedom, joyous expression, and abundant love. If that child is fortunate, he or she spends a period of grace in the company of soft colors, cooing voices, plush toys, and pretty sensations kept in place to smooth out that passage of introduction to the world. If that girl or boy is truly lucky, she or he will have a year or two—perhaps even three—when their senses are nurtured and they are shielded in their positive energy cocoon from the harsh realities of the outside world. (Such environments do exist, especially in this age of enlightened parenthood.)

Unfortunately, all too often in the extremes of our planetary consciousness, the infant is introduced to the perversities of the Fear Matrix within a matter of weeks if not a matter of moments after its birth. In certain underdeveloped societies, deprivations of food and basic sanitation and the incidental chaos of ignorance and personal lack, pervade its senses and violate its sanctity of self. No matter when this takes place (and the later the better), the innocent soul is soon struck with its first sensation of fear. The unexplained discipline, the physical assault, the first exposure to the violence of verbal or physical conflict (to which it may be no more than a witness)—it is at those times when the soul revolts while the tiny body and infant personality ego is forced to deal with that first trace of negativity. It is then, when the blood runs from the cells and that first sick tingling of the skin strikes and the GUT turns against the unnatural invasion it perceives, that the little child must find a way—some way—to defend itself. No longer is it able to hold fast to the helplessness that rendered it one of the most powerful creatures on earth. Now, the child must cope. The child must learn to defend itself against further violations of this kind. The child must cultivate a defense mechanism.

By this time the rules of life have changed. The nurturing and positive interactive love shown the infant is, depending upon the culture, either slowly or abruptly put aside. That child must be "toughened up" in order to deal with the real world. This happens more quickly for the male, but the new rules of survival are quickly being set for both male and female. In the schools, playgrounds, and peer group activities of children, new paradigms are set in place. Almost instantaneously, the child learns that the best defense is a good offense. Every game, sport, board game, video game, fantasy cartoon and classroom exercise are governed by rules of ultimatum: attack or defend; succeed or fail; win or lose. Score, dominate, obliterate, prevail!—these are the new commandments in the bibles of relativity taught the young boy or girl.

Along with this entire *"attack and defend"* lifestyle come sets of rules and regulations, rewards and punishments—conditions, if you will—and honor, integrity, fair play and ethics are learned along with the strategies of winning. But after a time, those noble qualities undergo an insidious kind of shrinkage in the wake of winning at all costs. By now, the patterns of success or failure are set directly in juxtaposition to one's ability to successfully attack and defend. Attacking issues, taking on assignments, task force operations, corporate war room strategies, and "taking no prisoners" during a sports contest or a business pitch become the rallying cries of the acknowledged winners in life. After they have succeeded exceptionally at a project, on a test score, or new client presentation, someone proudly declares they have "kicked butt."

By the same token, "defending territory at all cost," "defensive strategies," and "defending one's honor," are buzzwords for both caution and wisdom. Eventually, even the most virtuous among us think in terms of attack and defend just to get through our day. This carries over into every aspect of personal activity, from casual cocktail conversations to love relationships. And without doubt the most significant cause of rifts, separation, and divorce between seemingly loving couples occur because of the good old-fashioned *power struggle.* Two dominant type-A personalities are irrevocably drawn to one another by the dynamism of their success, attack, and prevalence over their immediate circle of involvement. This sweetens the sauce of sexual dynamics between them in the beginning. In the end, it becomes the potion that poisons their rapport, because neither party will give up the need to dominate the other.

How can they, after all? These are the dynamics they have been taught will work for them in every aspect of their lives. These codes of conduct form the infrastructure not only of survival but also of prevalence in everything they see. It is "Darwinian economics," the politics of love and the law of the jungle. This kind of attack-and-defend positioning is visible in everything we behold, witness, emulate and become. It is attractive, compelling, and vigorous; and every bit of it is based in the Fear Matrix.

At this point, we are the first to recognize that we're supposed to be talking about Love in this section, and we're still railing on about Fear. Yet it is the very pervasiveness of this matrix in all its manifestations that has to be both understood and dismantled before we can even begin to take Love to the full expression of its potential.

This attack and defend, sword and shield mechanism, after all, is the best parade of positive alternatives the child sees in a world that might otherwise be unbearable with all its shocks and frights and legions of neon negativity.

Along the way, the child also beholds the subtle poetry of life. The kindness from a loving parent, the compassion from a teacher, the loyalty of a friend, the beauty of high thought, the moments of unconditional love from those they first hold dear—these instances of redemption appear like flashes of sunlight in a darkening room. Even then, these still-caught moments, fragile in their content, must be protected, must be defended, must be taken to those hidden lands where the other treasures of unconditional love are kept safe: the fantasy friends, the sweet creations of their delusions who keep their counsel; the animal companions such as dogs or cats who never ask for more than sharing the moment as it is; the angels who guide them to "sounds and sweet airs that give delight and hurt not." These become the phrases of poetry that can never be lost to us.

God bless the child! For he or she knows, despite the bombardments of hostile new impressions, that these caretakers of our high intent must be kept safe at all costs. And it is that wise innocent to whom we return time and again for spiritual clarity. For what the child remembers that the wounded adult has lost sight of is that these crystalline moments can never be destroyed. They are, in their fragility, eternal; their integrity endures.

We are the first to recognize that once the child comes to a certain age, and especially once the boy or girl has reached young adulthood, the treasures of its unconditional world become sublimated. Like the iron butterfly they become buried, encased in the grit of real experience, and yet remain indestructible. Whenever the soul cries out to them, they explode from their chrysalis and reappear, even if for momentary glimpses of the Truth. It is those that the innocent child works with us to cultivate, to relearn, and to embrace through unconditional love. The quest to get back to unconditional love, though it may be unconscious at times, is both resolute and incessant. It is the voyage back home. And we refer again to the little child because, as we shall illustrate shortly, it is that innocent who will guide us back to that haven and help to reacquaint us with our true purpose for being on this planet.

First, however, for our study of the power of absolute love and its absolute Power, we direct your attention to its paragon, and the significance that it brings.

The Master Class.

Whatever your faith, whatever your belief system, whatever your religious affiliation, we offer this impeccable observation: All great master teachers were delusionists. Whatever great souls began our primary spiritual schools of thought—Jesus the Christ, the Sidhartha Gautama Buddha, Lao Tzu (teacher of the TAO and the initiator of Zen), Confucius—all based their teachings on similar doctrines. Without exception, each of them taught their followers to seek answers outside the confluence negative energies born of the Fear Matrix. They based virtually all of their spiritual tenets in the Love Matrix. In so doing, most of them were initially believed to have been deluded:

As the Prince Sidhartha, Gautama Buddha, born to the royal purple, renounced a life of abundance beyond measure to pursue true enlightenment. At the time, everyone thought him deranged for his pursuit of unconditional love and self-denial as pathways to Nirvana. His belief in living positively in the present moment, of devoting the entirety of one's life to *dharma*—good works and compassionate speech, and to kindness to all creatures were considered radical concepts for his time.

Confucius, a minister of justice in his home province, was considered to have been a misguided and contentious civil servant for his insistence upon equal justice for the poor and downtrodden of his state. "There is no profit in collecting injustices," he declared and set about to establish a philosophy of balanced conduct that is still a metaphysical manual for compassionate conduct.

Jesus Christ was, for all his adult life, denounced by those in power as being both deluded and a rabble rouser. Herod belittled him as a clown, a mockery of the Messiah, and a parody of his own declared intention. Pontius Pilate believed him to be a well-intended but deluded fool. And yet Jesus, the man, transcended all skepticism, abuse, and ridicule to bring us into the light of universal Truth.

Jesus Christ's final gift to us was his summary statement that death is the nadir of all lies and that life eternal awaits all of us who understand Love and the Great Universal Truth that flows from it. In so doing, he always preached from the positive point of view and constantly taught us that miracles were not merely optional, but our divine right as a matter of our daily lives. His guidelines were simple—that we love one another as we love Him, that we honor God above all else, and that we do unto others as we would have them do unto us—simple, all-encompassing, and non-judgmental in their infinite capacity both for understanding and for love.

It is here that we note again that Jesus' teachings carry striking parallels to those of the Gautama Buddha, Lao-Tzu, and Confucius, and other great master-teachers. Barring slight cultural variances, there is little in the crux of them that is either divergent or contradictory.

In every set of circumstances with which these great teachers were faced, they invariably did one of four positive things: *1) They made positive every situation they faced and brought it to its fullest potential.* In other words, they looked to their own power and ours to transform the gnarl of negative condition into an opportunity and, ultimately, into a transforming experience. *2) Often that transforming experience, the spiritual solution, entailed a miracle or two.* Miracles were a matter of our entitlement, something they accepted as matter-of-factly as their right to breathe, as a simple matter of living. ("If thou canst believe, all things are possible to him that believeth." [Mark 9:23]). *3) All master-teachers uplifted, empowered, and inspired others, and showed them the light of their own ability to achieve both love and fulfillment. 4) They understood and practiced the laws of manifestation—that every act in life was "bread cast upon the water" that would come back to the giver a thousand-fold.* This included not only good deeds, but evil ones as well. The modern interpretation for this would be to say, "What goes around, comes around." Such thoughts have become so much a part of the common vernacular that they actually experience no opposition when brought into conversation. It is Universal Law acknowledged even at the basest levels of human contact.

Such things form the compendium of masterful vision. The entire process of the lives of such impeccable human beings was to make better each challenge presented to them. Whether by the working of miracles or the power of positive instruction, they transformed every aspect of the Fear Matrix and brought it under the influence of the Love Matrix. They carried what had been perceived as delusion into its highest form of expression: *The Visionary Experience.* And it is to that truth and through the reengagement of the wise little child that we offer our secrets of winning the world through Love. Like any good plan, the process is simple in concept while altogether challenging in execution.

Winning the World through Love.

Initial Advisory: What we offer here is not some tepid formula filled with platitudes. It will take courage, insight, and persistence to carry out. It will also go against the grain of some learned social skills that have served so many of us for such a long time.

All we can say is: consider this to be a form of spiritual skiing. In the beginning, like skiing, it seems as though you are going against your sense of balance. Soon, however, you learn how the true intention of your movements will become a part of the natural flow of the Mountain. You soon come to be at one with the constant drifts of the slope and the shifts in the winds that help you to gauge the stems and turns you need to make. That is when true recognition comes to you, that love—like the truth to which it gives birth—comes without effort, thought or bias. It simply is, in its own way, perfect.

With that in mind we offer our recognition of the fact that there are dozens of different kinds of love—romantic love, maternal love, familial love, love of humankind, compassionate love of the universe, love of animals, love of friends, love of Nature, love of God, love of all good things, love of justice, love of beauty, of truth. All loves are but one Love, and they only endure if they are *unconditional.*

Condition as a term of confinement is an aspect of the Fear Matrix and, by its very definition, *limits* (another Fear Matrix term) the application of love. Love with conditions, limitations, stipulations, or expectations is fragile at best and short-lived at worst. And it cannot endure for long until it becomes something else entirely. Jealousy, possessiveness, control, manipulation, suspicion, spite, desire, discipline and expectation—all are faces on the monster that passes itself for various kinds of love.

Unconditional love is impenetrable, indestructible and eternal. It is our natural, God-given state of being when we came into this world as the infant child but has been sublimated by the *attack-and-defend survival mechanism* taught us by our real world experiences. The "real world," as we know by now, bases its commerce almost entirely out of the Fear Matrix. Unfortunately, although our attack and defend survival mechanism may help us survive, it blocks us from flourishing and actually blunts the superior sensory awareness (the GUT feel) we brought with us into this world. So immersed do we become in the human churn of Fear Matrix conduct, so bombarded are we with Fear Matrix impressions, that *we confuse it with its intended purpose to act as our warning system.* After a while, it becomes the only music we hear, so we cannot react properly when it arrives in waves to warn us.

Only by embracing unconditional love, and by applying the principals of the Love Matrix can we ever hope to attune ourselves to the symphonic chords of our destined purpose.

Like all aspects of the Love Matrix, the principles of unconditional love are both simple and explicit. But in order for them to work, they have to be applied diligently and with exceptional determination. Certainly there are hundreds of ways to put unconditional love into play and to make it work. We have found the best way is to acknowledge that it is a quality that, though innate to the human condition, has to be relearned in order for us to be able to activate it at all times. There are a number of processes that can work to activate unconditional love, in almost any situation. And we encourage everyone to apply their own system as long as it truly meets the Love Matrix criterion. Ours is a six-step process, each carrying its own set of applications:

Step One: Recognize that every thought, word, and deed carries an energy of its own. Also recognize that they almost all carry equal weight in terms of their impact on you and every one else around you. Positive or negative thoughts may not net the same immediate responses as words or deeds. Yet in every sense they are the parents of words and deeds. They precede them; they birth them; they design them. So, the word and deed are mere fulfillment of the thoughts and take place on this earth dimension as manifestations of what has already been put in place by the thought. Thoughts are multidimensional. They never cease. They carry on in limitless procession and, because of that, they can be both powerful and volatile in geometric progressions that the conscious mind cannot fathom. Positive thoughts alone can carry us to our highest notions. Proliferations of negative thoughts will gradually but inevitably destroy all we hold dear.

It is most important for us to recognize, in our approach to our attack and defend lifestyle, that attack thoughts are greater toxins than we can possibly imagine. Unless we are some kind of criminal sociopath, we seldom if ever conduct physical attacks on anyone. Our verbal attacks, though more frequent, are fortunately not acted out nearly as often as they are plotted. Our attack thoughts, however, number in legion. They are planned, choreographed, and carried forward in our darkest fantasies. But invariably they forge swords that turn inward. By defiling every cell in our body with cascades of mental toxins, they form a cone of negativity around us that blocks all positive energy. We are burned in the ice of our own calculations. And the only way we can melt it is through the fire of unconditional love.

In order to achieve that, however, we must introduce the concept of forgiveness. Earlier we touched upon the concept of forgiveness and stressed its importance as an aspect of unconditional love. Now we emphasize its use as a matter of personal survival. Unconditional forgiveness is both source and substance of all the success we can hope to have in our interactions with every being on this planet. The very acts of hating, resentment, vengeance, and retribution bond us by laws of energy to whomever we bring into the focus of those powerful fear-based energies.

Only by means of forgiveness can we be free of the bonds. That includes forgiving everyone who might have been responsible for perpetrating them, including yourself. It also entails releasing them not only from your table of rage but also from your field of recollection. Leave nothing that will connect you to them in a negative way.

To dwell on past injury is to place all your energy against both the source and the resentment that accompanies it. Resentment, as a part of the Fear Matrix, must be released with forgiveness. Forgive, let go, and move out of the past and into the present. A caveat is necessary, here, however, because, as is taught in *A Course in Miracles*, forgiveness can only be effective if it is *unconditional.* Like unconditional love, unconditional forgiveness precludes all attack, all anger, all rage, all grudges, and all obsessions. It is our bulwark against evil.

For now, recognize that any other options to unconditional forgiveness carry with them the seeds of self-defeat. For example, people who hold onto the old chestnut, "I can forgive, but I can't forget," have just announced their bond with non-forgiveness. They have placed the maximum condition on their ability to forgive. So, they remain focused on their own resentment, if not fixated by it.

We are all ruled by whatever we bring into focus, by whatever occupies the majority of our energy. If your focus is on rage over limitations placed upon you in the past, if you can't forget them, you will be stuck in that point in time as if you were frozen there.

If Love is truly the fire that melts all Fear, then unconditional forgiveness is the flint that ignites that fire. And it is through the next steps in the Love Matrix that we can find unconditional forgiveness as a matter of our soul's desire and our divine right.

Step Two: Accept the fact that every act in life is either a cry for help or an answered prayer. This step is a paradox in that the second part of it is easy to accept. The first part is exceedingly difficult. Finding one of your prayers answered, in whatever form it comes, is a matter of recognition and gratitude. A stroke of luck, a dream fulfilled, the kind words of someone your respect—all complete the spectrum of your desires. One needs to merely acknowledge them, give thanks, and recognize them for the little miracles that they are.

Recognizing the cry for help can be a challenge at times, and one must work to cultivate the gift of it. Especially when one confronts what appears to be a hostile situation, it is a challenge to even engage it, much less bring it to its highest possible outcome. First recognize that it is within your power to bring the answered prayer to that cry. You can help heal the most difficult situation by recognizing your own power to be the peacemaker, the arbiter, and the bringer of reason. People in conflict, whether great or small, seek deliverance. Whether you are the outsider who happens to be brought into a situation of conflict or the object of what seems to be an attack, acknowledge your power to make it better and the willingness of everyone involved to join you in that quest.

Step Three: See whomever you are interacting with as a little child— one who is two or three years of age, able to speak (and to reason more than we dare acknowledge). That child exists in all of us, so use your child's eyes to behold them. Remember the maxim that we are all little children asking not to be hurt. Take that child into your care and acknowledge that this child is on the same journey as you. By seeing what that child is trying to accomplish, recognize that it is either crying for help or answering a prayer of yours.

Just remember, only you can acknowledge the little child and bring it the gifts of both unconditional forgiveness and limitless healing. The child—no matter how unseemly its outward appearance—is looking to you to be healed and to be comforted. How can any of us harm the child who asks not to be hurt? We are that child, just as we are the source to whom the child looks for deliverance.

(**Note:** We're the first to acknowledge that there are times when it is very difficult to apply these principles. It's hard to see some steroid-stoked 300-pound "attitude" who wants to punch your lights out in a grocery store line for no apparent reason as a little child crying out for help. But that is often the acid test. In such cases, it is best to enlist helpers. By extending your good will to everyone around you and creating the energy that grows out of that loving attitude, you will soon see that the fool who confronts you is often immersed in the joy of it and begins to recognize the degree of his foolishness. It's also an excellent time to use your *flak zapper* in all its many forms, an aspect we will cover in Step Five.)

Step Four: Apply the principles learned from our Master Class Manifesto. First, recognize your God-given ability to make something positive out of any situation and bring it to its fullest potential. No matter how negative the situation appears to be at first, ask yourself this series of questions: How can I make it better? How can I help this child feel safe? How can I empower everyone involved in this to take positive action? Second, never overlook the potential for miracles to take place, or for our ability to effect them. The biggest mistake in our approach to miracles is to believe they are grand events that take place outside us. There are miracles by the thousands that surround us every day. Third, recognize that you have within you the power to uplift and inspire others, and to empower them to achieve great things. You can do this only through unconditional love and the desire to lead one another to the best of all possible worlds. By exploring those unlimited possibilities and by showing faith in your shared dreams, you will find no enemies and a legion of fellow travelers. Fourth, recognize that everything you do is subject to the laws of manifestation. Your good or evil works will come back to you a thousand-fold, and even the least enlightened among us possess some awareness of this. What goes around always comes around; always! It is the immutable law of the universe that has been proven so often it can no longer be denied at any level. The fact that it so often continues to go ignored provides you with the notable opportunity to reinstruct others in the ways of its truth.

(**Note:** If you've noticed that some of this seems to reiterate the steps that preceded it, congratulations! You've been paying attention. We also find, in this as in all things in life, it is good to place a miniature plan inside the larger one, in case we lose sight of our objectives somewhere along the way. Consider it a kind of cosmic spare part.)

Step Five: Use your Flak Zapper. And do it often! Now that you have a more complete understanding of the flak of human confusion that surrounds us every day, you begin to see how many opportunities you have in your power to transform it, and to make it better. And what gives the Flak Zapper its unique personality is that it enables you to look upon it as a tool of both practical and creative transformation. That means seeing every moment as an opportunity to do something good, to give love and to put the best of your higher self into it, so that you can make the most out of it. Zapping flak can be something as simple as a smile or as intricate as solving a complex set of challenges. It means taking that extra moment in time to perceive with your extra senses the goodness in every situation, extract it, distill it and reveal it to everyone concerned. Guided by total love and unconditional forgiveness, flak zapping also means the ability to use those gifts that help you discern a corrupt situation that you can not help by any personal means. When these instances present themselves in our lives, when you see that you cannot help them and they in fact may harm you and those you care for, zap them: acknowledge them, bless them, and then get out as soon as possible!

Step Six: Gratitude is the grace of angels. Just as unconditional love brings us to new levels of higher awareness, perpetual gratitude draws to us both the energy and the resources we need to carry them out. There is an old Persian saying that goes to the heart of this: "For that for which I am grateful, I cannot be denied."

Gratitude doesn't just mean being grateful for your prosperity, your good life, the riches you have, your loved ones. Those are all important, of course. It means beholding the entire world around you as a blessing. The air you breathe, the sky above you, the accidental creatures in our life who come with joy to delight and entertain us.

Perpetual gratitude not only grows the flowers of its own fulfillment but also forms the perfect prayer; one of both acknowledgment and commitment. It is remembering to thank God, God's universe, and this life for all that we have been given. So if you're going to pray, begin every prayer with a statement of gratitude for your abundance. When one addresses one's day in such a way, it tears away the armor of the Fear Matrix and lays it open to abundant positivity.

Such language is the acknowledgment of that which already exists. Since we know all prayers are answered in time, the secret remains in knowing how to ask them. Begin with gratitude and the rest will become a matter of natural consequence.

Making this Work: A Summary.

It becomes immediately apparent to us after having written this that Love and Fear are such prime movers in our lives that no chapter, however thorough, could complete a study of them. They merit a book of its own. For the delusionist's specific purposes, however, let's review their significance here:

First, we made the observation that the universe wears two faces, but broke some patterns of expectation by noting that they both serve a purpose. In the divine plan, nothing goes to waste. And Fear and the aspects of the Fear Matrix can be effective tools if they are brought to serve us in the smaller context for which they were intended.

Second, we brought forth the (purely subjective but nonetheless peerless) Ahola-Peccianti Love/Fear Matrix to examine all aspects of both and how they are perceived—sometimes incorrectly.

Third, we made a detailed examination of fear and at least some aspects of the Fear Matrix, offered the categorical observation that most of us spend over half our time in the Fear Matrix and assigned you to keep a Fear-Matrix chronicle (or diary) for one week to note every Fear Matrix event that crowded your consciousness. In order to help you do that, we provided you with a "starter's list" of just a few of the Fear Matrix encounters you could experience every day, and asked you to note the length of time you spent on each. (And by the way, we encourage you to keep an ongoing log of your Fear Matrix activities. By becoming even more acutely aware of your participation in it, you can continue to clean it up, clear it out, and bring in the aspects of the Love Matrix that will clear up not only your mental process and your emotional disposition but also the very body of energy that surrounds you.)

Fourth, we made a study of the "attack-and-defend" lifestyle, including an exposition of how the young are inculcated into having this lifestyle become the negotiating force in their lives. We also offered the means to help us all out of that viciously efficient cycle by rediscovering our "natural" ability to give and share unconditional love. This, we emphasized, could be accomplished by putting *The Master Class Teachings* into play—the quality that all great spiritual teachers have in common of positively meeting every challenge, empowering every person, and showing everyone the path to unconditional love and unlimited fulfillment.

Fifth, we made the immediate observation that it is unconditional love, not the "attack and defend" consciousness, *that is our natural state of being.* We also recognized that there are many possible pathways to achieving unconditional love and offered our Six-Step Process, which we felt could help you introduce unconditional love not only into your life but also into every situation that life presents to you.

If you have followed at least some of the disciplines we've recommended in this chapter, we firmly believe that you'll be able to clean out your spiritual closet and rid your life of so much of the fear-debris that has crowded out your potential for total abundance. Simply by reducing your entanglements in the Fear Matrix by one half (50%), you will discover that the space created by the voided negativity can now be filled with trust, compassion, caring, cooperation, inspiration, and all the other aspects of the Love Matrix to which your spirit is naturally aligned. That will mark the beginning of a cascade of more positive experiences, allow you to live and conduct more of your daily activities by finding support from the Love Matrix, and help return you to the lifetime of contribution that you have always wanted to lead. You will also understand that once Fear no longer governs you, when its hum is no longer the only song you hear, fear and all aspects of its matrix can be brought into your service as the superbly efficient warning system it is.

Make no mistake about it: People who operate primarily from the Love Matrix will have better health, will digest food more easily, will breathe in more negative ions (which generate positive energy), and will even tend to look younger. That is the kind of energy shift that this changeover can help create.

Rest assured, there are no neutral thoughts in this world. We are all at choice every moment of our lives to gravitate toward the light or into the darkness.

We encourage you to choose lovingly, to fear not, and to read on!

Chapter 5

Of Painting Fences, Cleaning Closets, and Getting Crystal Clear

"If seven maids with seven mops
Swept it for half a year,
Do you suppose," the Walrus said
"That they could get it clear?"
"I doubt it," said the Carpenter,
And shed a bitter tear.

—Lewis Carroll
Through the Looking Glass.

Any course in personal awareness occasionally requires some fence painting. Let us explain by drawing an analogy.

In the popular film, *The Karate Kid,* the kid (played by the actor Ralph Macchio) pleads to the martial arts master (played by Pat Morita) to take him on as a student. Reluctantly the master agrees, then commences his training by handing the kid a paint brush and bucket with orders to paint the fence around his house. Disbelieving but obedient, the kid does as he is told and paints the master's fence. Exhausted at the end of the day, he returns to the master to announce that the fence is painted—when he is told that there is still a great deal left to paint, and that he has to start again tomorrow. This begins an entire schedule of seemingly meaningless chores that the kid must do—painting, scrubbing, brushing, reaching, climbing, reaching again—every day, until at last he feels he can take no more. At this point, he runs to the master and shouts his frustration. "Good," he is told, and then is informed he is now ready for his training.

As we soon come to find out (and not entirely to our surprise), all of the motions the kid made while he was doing these boring, distracting, time-wasting chores have come to form the very foundation of his skills as a fighter.

So, in our own instructional metaphor, we're asking you to paint some fences for a while. That means we're going to revisit our own kid for a page or two—that child in all of us—and relive a journey most of us have taken.

In a way, you might call this a process of untraining, or unpainting the fence.

A Child Again.

Verily I say unto, Except you be converted and come as little children, you shall not enter into the kingdom of Heaven.

—*Matthew 18:3*

What a splendidly divine gift the newborn child is when it enters our world. Flush with new life and unconditional love, filled with hope and unlimited potential, it comes into this plane of consciousness with all its sentient spiritual wisdom intact.

In the beginning, the little child does not know how to lie. It does not know the meaning of fear. Its only negotiation with its proximate world is the honest perception of its unbridled imagination.

Then, like a series of concussions that take place in a terrifyingly short period of time, the little tyke gets slapped with restrainers, gets put in cages (called playpens), gets battered by admonitions of denial at every natural move he or she makes, and then gets punched in the psyche with the stigma of Original Sin. That's just for starters. Soon, it is disciplined at every turn—good necessary acts, we are told, that will help make it a more productive member of society. Soon enough comes the pollution of new perceptions. The infant is learning to speak, and yet almost immediately the conversations it learns are negations of its desires.

Almost invariably, "no" is one of the first words this young human being ever hears, and hears often. The child is bombarded with constraints and caveats that come from well-meaning teachers whose lessons often strike dissonant chords in the soul. Wanting to please, now fearful of reprisals if he or she does not, the child complies, learns to adapt, and begins to sublimate its spiritual instincts in order to survive in the "real world."

Soon enough come peer pressure and rules of conformity to strange new, often illogical, laws that one adheres to for fear of being excluded from the group consciousness. It is the innocent child's first introduction to the collective, to mass-mind thinking. What follows is the inevitable corruption of his or her inner voices. The child begins to lose direct contact with the higher self that accompanied it into this world. Its Great Universal Truth is lost in the maze of conflicting sensations and the counter-opinions of others. Its aspirations are immersed in the clangor and drums of false impressions. And yet it is by refocusing on its true spiritual center—the higher self—that the soul can be saved.

The Vase Hypothesis.

We invite you to liken this child to a vase of pure crystal. In the beginning it reflects and enhances whatever it contacts. It is open to all new ideas and nurtures them. It is made full with the pure water of life. And when new elements are added, it fulfills its function as their clear and willing host. The question is, what is planted there? Flowers of infinite potential, to be sure, but with them also come the seeds of doubt and weeds of conflicting concepts.

Life's experiences add new materials, new flowers for the vessel. Many of them are good; many are reinforcements to great new potentials. But by now the receptacle is becoming corrupted. It is crammed with the clutter of new details and the extraneous stuff of survival.

Even worse, the water has not been changed. It becomes clouded over with pathogens. Virtually, the crystal that comprises the vase is beginning to have its integrity questioned because it now reflects the pollution that festers inside. Literally, because the contents of our awareness are corrupted, we as full grown human entities—filled in equal parts with information and misinformation—cannot help but see ourselves, "through a glass darkly."

This poses the question: If you saw the eyesore that this vase has become sitting on a table stuffed full of junk, gunk and dying flowers in the middle of the most prominent place in your home, what would you feel obligated to do?

Empty it, of course. Change the water. Throw out the seeds and the weeds. Scrub it clean. Prune back the fresh flowers and fill it again with clear purified water and new blossoms.

You would do that with the vase on the table, because you are certain of what you could accomplish by having done so. You know that the outcome of your actions will be a flourishing new arrangement, a bower of fresh expressions; a thing of beauty.

Then why, we are compelled to ask, are you so reluctant to pursue the same process with your own life?

You are that vase.

The pollution with which you must cope has become a large part of what fills you. And yet until now, you lacked the certainty to continue, partly because you don't know exactly where to begin.

The key word to which we attach our focus is *certainty*. Knowing the outcome of anything helps to ignite our lives. Not knowing, doubting, and failing to act because of your doubt is the ice that freezes us into place. Certainty is what we long for, but we require a sense of direction.

Direction is thaw. But that can only be properly determined by knowing where to begin. That means knowing where you have been as well as where you're going.

Now we know, because at this point in our delusionist's training we have at least been made aware of the forces that govern us. In a way, we have identified the sources of the pollution and started emptying out. Now is the time for a bit of scrubbing. The rest is a matter of putting in play some of the things that we have learned.

To do that, we begin with a simple exercise that we feel will help you learn a little more about yourself and about the things you deem important in life. It's something we've all done. In fact, there are now professional firms to help you do this sort of thing. However, we recommend that this is something you do yourself. Consider it a kind of emotional scrubbing out. It's a process, we have found, which will bring you large measures of awareness about where you are in your life.

When in Doubt, Clear it Out.

We discovered something quite interesting recently. Good things start to happen to people who clean out their closets. Originally, it happened seemingly by chance, when a good friend who had not been able to get the job she had wanted decided to divest herself of every needless trinket in her life, and gave herself a good house-cleaning. In other words, she started *"feng shuiing"* her life. As a result, she either sold or gave away to charity everything she did not absolutely need. Within two days of completing this personal catharsis of her material goods, she was offered the dream job she had always wanted in advertising design, for precisely the salary she had desired—including bonuses and perks.

Accident? Coincidence? Of course, not.

By now, everyone who applies the least bit of spiritual logic knows there are no accidents. The wheels of the universe turn on *Synchronicity.* As almost everyone knows by now, synchronicity is the term coined by Carl Gustav Jung to define a divinely ordained action that appears as a coincidence. In other words, it's the ultimate cosmic surprise.

Mindful of all this, we nevertheless decided to put our friend's synchronistic career move (which she directly attributed to her personal housecleaning) to a series of field tests and random surveys. Without exception, everyone we had contacted who had done a similar closet-cleaning, housecleaning, or recent purging of their material possessions had experienced a similar spate of good fortune.

So, we decided to apply the process to ourselves.

Robert, who had an enormous closet full of retro fashions—enough to start a men's boutique—thoroughly cleaned it out and gave away a score of sport coats, old shirts, and bags of gym clothes to homeless shelters and AIDS relief centers. Within two weeks, he experienced renewed film producer interest in a screenplay he had long since written off, and got his property optioned.

Paul, who was sympathetic to the process but too busy traveling at the time, had his closet cleaned out for him by a pair of burglars. Ironically (or perhaps synchronistically), these thieves seemed to show little interest in any part of the house other than Paul's closet and its contents—especially his dress pants. Disregarding the fetishes the thieves seem to have shown for his suit pants and dress slacks, Paul acknowledged the good in the rather bizarre occurrence, blessed his long-term relationship with a very skilled tailor, replaced his missing trousers, released any attachment to the event, and changed his residence. Shortly afterward, he not only found the ideal dwelling but also the perfect antique furnishings to go with it.

The point we make is this: Our field survey, however crudely constructed, netted results that were virtually 100% in the affirmative. Score one for *Feng Shui*, and for making physical spaces in your life. Of course there's a modicum of symbolism attached to this, but there are some dynamics of physical energy that come into play as well. In order for anything new to enter your life, you must first rid yourself of that which you desire to replace.

The basic laws of the universe are immutable.

Among the most important is the law of displacement (Archimedes Law!)—the one that says no two objects can occupy the same space at the same time.

Understanding this law can have a great bearing on the trends our lives take. It is also the beginning of our process of "cleaning out the vase."

Originally, we referred to our mutual friend telling us she had applied the art of *feng shui* to her closet, and the good result that came from it. Originated in China more than 4,000 years ago, Feng Shui (pronounced *fung shway*) has become the rage among the *beau monde* of the western hemisphere for the last few years, primarily because it apparently works.

The literal translation for Feng Shui is "earth and water." It emphasizes *harmony in living* through understanding the ebbs and flows of life, and by creating appropriate currents of prosperity and good fortune in one's own immediate environment.

In itself, Feng Shui is an algorithm of positions and procedures that make-up an intricate study all its own. Still, it offers a premise that strikes a harmonic note with everyone: *Simplicity widens the gateway to prosperity.*

A major part of this philosophy of simplicity is the process of pruning down our own environment by cleaning out everything that is no longer of actual use. That means physically cleaning things up and getting rid of the junk, the deadwood, and the collection of useless possessions that often clutter our lives. To the pack rat and the sentimentalist, this kind of discipline can be anathema. Yet, when you think about it, it only makes sense.

Physical elements have lives of their own. They occupy places in our consciousness whether we're mentally aware of them or not. Some schools of higher awareness refer to them as "attention bits." These attention bits, these memories, these tethers to our past, take up space in our psyche.

They weigh us down. They strike dissonant chords in our mental processes that might actually fatigue us. Just like the stack of unpaid bills or the pile of unreturned phone calls, they vie for our attention; they itch in the back of our mind. And just as the law of societal survival dictates that we pay our bills, and the rules of business protocol and social decorum dictate that we return our phone calls (unless you live in L.A.), we must also clear up our past clutter. We must clean out our closets and drive away the specters of recollection.

Whether you choose to interpret this as metaphor or as physical necessity, we view it as an essential process for two very good reasons: First, it helps you rehearse for the essential process of the decisions you must make about your ultimate purpose in life. Second, this provides a terrific opportunity to practice your skills with your Flak Zapper. So you not only learn how to zap the extraneous stuff in your life, you also enjoy the opportunity to transform it into something special and to put it to use somewhere else.

It's an operation of which you have to take charge, just as you might take charge of your life. You have to have a plan, a course of action, and a destination.

You get to decide where things are to go, and what must be removed. Since a good many of the items you address will have value to someone else somewhere, you should also have a game plan about where the discards should go and how they might benefit someone else—cause groups and communities in need.

Every object you pick up during the process of your cleaning will bring you to a point of decision. You will decide what is important, what is essential, what must be gotten rid of, what is marginal. It is then that you will come to your first awareness that, if you are truly going to have room to grow and progress, a little ruthless discernment is in order.

It's a practice you will have to put into effect more than once. But as you do, a new awareness will come to bear. You'll start to realize that so much of what you are holding onto are out of habits born in fear. We all fear loss. And yet we hold onto things that long ago lost their meaning.

Love them. Bless them. Zap them. Give them away. You will begin to realize as you do so that you are losing nothing. Rather, you are redistributing it to others—to those in need. That which no longer fits you, that which you no longer value, will become a prized possession to someone else. That's what zapping is all about. These are now gifts of love. These will set you fee and clear your energy to boot.

Suddenly, you'll find that you're making more and more conscious choices—where to give what you are losing from your glut of possessions. Old items will take on a particular new value. Somewhere along the way, you will even find that you've uncovered some cherished treasure, something you had lost (and perhaps even forgotten).

You will rediscover parts of yourself. And at the end of the process, you will have touched others—those to whom your belongings are being bestowed. What a simple joy it is to give. What a frenzy of fulfillment it creates, knowing your discards might form the fabric of someone else's new moments of self-esteem. Finally, you will be surprised by the fact that you have discarded very little yet given very much. You have answered the call of universal law. Most important, you will have made room for yourself to grow personally.

As the universe abhors a void, you will have just helped fill the empty places in someone else's life, and you will have made some new spaces in your own. Those spaces will be filled with all the good things you have long ago sought to bring in. From it, some new truths will even arise; some decisions for new beginnings will be born—some new resolutions and even a new sense of direction. It will help prepare you for the true cleaning out—of your personal list of hopes, dreams, desires, concerns, fears, and closely held secrets.

It is both prelude and dress rehearsal for the journey ahead. Be bold. Be brave. Have faith. Set your wings in motion. And never doubt your ability to fly.

Chapter 6

Go With Your GUT

Heroism feels and never reasons and therefore is always right.
Ralph Waldo Emerson
"On Heroism"
Essays and Journals.

We begin this chapter with the realization that we've been sold a bill of goods where our more esoteric senses are concerned.

Once again, we've been told that when it comes to our instinctive natures we *Homo sapiens* have somehow managed to backslide on the evolutionary scale, that somewhere during the course of growing a highly developed cerebral cortex and an opposing thumb and forefinger, we forgot to fine tune our more subtle levels of awareness.

That is the commonly held belief. And it's backed by all kinds of scientific evidence—field studies, sensory response tests, and other psychometric measurements.

It is our obligation as true delusionists to challenge such clinical bromides.

The truth is that we human beings are the most acutely calibrated instruments of broad-spectrum awareness on this tiny young planet. And our instincts are not dead or even dormant. We've still got them. We use them every day. And with a little refresher course, we can get them back into top form, because the other good news is that our instincts are only a part of the supersensory gifts we have.

We grant you that, compared to what they once were hundreds of thousands of years ago, our instincts are vestigial, and our creature companions have developed levels of sensory acuity in far greater profusion than we. But we have the Great Universal Truth. We have intuition. And only we, as far as we know, have been blessed with them.

This merits some explanation.

Intuition, by virtue of both custom and usage, is a purely "human" characteristic. It is the overdrive of higher awareness that empowered the Adam of Genesis 1:26 to "hold dominion" over the beasts of the field and the birds of the air and the creatures that swim in the sea (except perhaps dolphins). Even now, it affords us a readable GUT reaction to what may often seem to be a complex set of circumstances. It is in its way a combination of instinct with knowledge that forms the intuitive response, and can be drawn as a kind of equation:

Instinct + knowledge = Intuition.

So, when we truly learn to apply the natural, spiritual gifts we've been given, we can make correct decisions with astounding accuracy, provided we are able to observe correctly in the first place.

Basic instincts, those of so many of our planetary cohabitants in the animal kingdom, are imbedded at such deep levels of cellular consciousness that they can find spawning beds and breeding grounds that are hundreds or even thousands of miles away without ever having been to these locations themselves. These genetic calling codes are the texture of their survival as a species. As such, they are perpetual, unerring, and almost always unequivocally obeyed. That's how they survive. That's how they flourish. And on certain rare occasions, that is how they destroy themselves. But instincts for our animal friends are almost always followed without question, debate or variance. In other words, they are involuntary. An animal's inclinations to fight or flight are both spontaneous and unreflected. Their relationships with the Fear Matrix and Love Matrix are immediate, direct and uncomplicated by the shadings of abstract thought.

And let's hear it for our creature teachers. They are here to guide us—to instruct us, comfort us, and demonstrate to us the wisdom of following the flows of Nature. They are stripped of the conscious clutter of ego. So their relationships with their proximate worlds are free of hidden agenda. They love unconditionally. They're quick to forgive. They spend little time awash in the maze of judgment and condemnation. Their responses to pain and pleasure are direct, honest, and generally predictable. And they possess a universal wisdom that extends often beyond our ability to measure. Of course there are nuances—thousands of them, relative to various species. But in the main, our "creature connection" is readable, reliable, and beneficial. They are our support system on this planet.

By our very complexity, we are more blessed than they—and more cursed. Even where our instincts are concerned, we have been given a choice. We have free will. We have simply unlearned the cosmically intelligent application of it. We have done so primarily because the cacophony of fear has drowned out the spiritual symphonies that have been available to us. Our minds and egos try to help, but they are—in the destiny of our soul's design—instruments that were meant to serve and not command.

However, if we've been following our delusionist's game plan, we have begun to retrain our instincts by scrubbing away the mental debris that the Fear Matrix has created for us. But mental debris is only part of the issue. It is, for lack of a more appropriate word, psychic debris as well. Fear creates an energy of its own. It recognizes itself in its myriad forms and draws those bodies of energy to itself as familiar patrons if not welcome guests. In such cases, fear bombardment becomes a matter of fact. When it does, the confusion of fear-based activities irrevocably smothers intuition and renders GUT feel virtually impotent.

Love embraces its own as well, and in equal or greater measure draws to itself its multifarious aspects. But when one draws a predominance of love to oneself, it forms a different body of energy. It is pure positive vibration attuned to such a clarified awareness that it recognizes chaotic activity and fear-based decisions for what they are.

For clarification, let's return to our Vase Hypothesis for a moment. If we are the vase, and the polluted water now filled with the fungus of negativity has been poured out and scrubbed clean, we should begin to perceive with greater clarity the nature of what is put into us next. If we are filled with the pure water and fresh flowers from the Love Matrix, we can caress them for the positive energy they bring. If corruptions from the Fear Matrix—weeds, dying grass, brackish water covered with algae—are offered to us, we can perceive them for what they are and prevent their further influence. But if the vase is already polluted, there is no ability either to discern or reject further pollution. The pollution recognizes itself and disregards the threat of finality that it brings.

So our GUT feel, along with the intuitions that serve it, works the same way. Unless the receptacle has been cleansed, each event, each challenge to our intuition, becomes an exercise in misjudgment.

We fail in our decisions about life because we fail to observe correctly. We succeed in our decisions about life because we succeed in the correctness of our observations. In other words, the outcome is preordained by the weight of spiritual intelligence we place against it.

To illustrate, we offer this seemingly simple test:

You are driving down the street about ten miles from your home or office when your warning light flashes on your fuel gauge to tell you that you are low on fuel. You are immediately at choice. You may 1) stop at the next available service station for gas, 2) determine that you have enough fuel to make it to your destination without stopping, 3) assume that your fuel alert is inaccurate and that you have plenty of gas left, 4) be worried about the low fuel but even more concerned about being late for a business appointment (so you press on).

Upon review of this menu of choices, you have only one decision that offers you anything close to absolute certainty: that is option *1) stop at the next available service station for gas.* Yet option 2 may also be correct. So may option 3. Option 4 is also viable, even though with option 4 you have thrown fear directly into the mix. And fear, as we surely know by now, can bring a negative energy impact all its own.

And since we are able to observe this chain of choices from a reasonably detached perspective, we again ask you which option has the least potential for either certainty or success?

Even the slightest reflection would prompt you to observe that option 4 would offer more danger of failure of running out of gas, if for no other reason than the fact that in option 4 *fear* has entered the equation.

That is the kind of negative impact fear can have in everything in our lives. Fear presents a life form all its own. Our animal companions can see it on us and on other creatures. Every creature from a dog to a lion, from a polar bear to a shark, knows the scent of fear when it comes from another creature and responds to it with both violence and a kind of social marking. Dogs bark and become vicious at the appearance of it, because it constitutes both negativity and danger to them. Sharks and other predatory fish are actually drawn to it. It has the same aura of victimization as blood. It sends out its own kind of static, drawing only the darkest energy to it.

We recognize it in the fear equation of the person who is worried about running out of gas. Yet we fail to anticipate it in the other two equations as well. In option 2) and option 3) of our "getting gas" multiple-choice, fear also possesses excellent potential for gaining leverage the longer the option is taken. The person who decides he or she can make the destination, may eventually begin to *doubt* it (an aspect of fear), or become *irritated* when they suddenly get caught in an unforeseen traffic jam. Suddenly, they realize they've been a bit *arrogant* in their decision, and sooner or later they become genuinely *worried* that they've misjudged their options. If one assumes the fuel gauge is incorrect, he or she already *mistrusts* the reading they're given. Then again, that creates *doubts* that perhaps the gauge is showing more than they actually have. So, the driver trusts nothing; therefore both *uncertainty* and *misgivings* become a permanent part of their travel relationship with both their gas gauge and their car. So once again, fear, sooner or later, makes its play for dominance.

In truth, how many of us have been offered the peace of mind of exercising option 1 and gone on to option 2, 3, or 4? How many of us have run out of gas? How often, when we ran out of gas, did we know better but chose instead to disregard the readings we'd been given?

The choice then becomes a simple, logical process. Check your readings. Get gas when your fuel gauge tells you it's time to get gas. And do it as soon as possible.

In our GUT, we know the right thing to do. In the more complex decisions we make in our lives, almost without exception, we know the positive consequence of correct action. So, why do we not pursue it every time? We are given the signs in numerous ways. The gauges, whether real or figurative, are lit in invitation, to prompt us to make appropriate decisions. But, at some level, we choose to ignore them. Why? We don't ignore them all the time. If we did, our life on this plane of existence would end much sooner than it already does. So the question persists: Why do we obey our intuition on certain occasions and entirely ignore it on others?

Let's reexamine our intuition equation, in reverse.

Intuition = instinct + knowledge

By this time, we acknowledge that instinct is our creature connection, that visceral rip of awareness that comes when our basic physical well-being is at stake. But what about insight? Insight is that deep personal navigator that always enables us to find true North. It is a product of our highest sense and deserves its own equation.

Insight = information + perception x awareness

This equation becomes a bit more complicated because we are all in receipt of information. The information at hand, for example, is that our fuel gauge warning light has come on. Our perceptions, however, become a bit dearer. They require us to react to the tangible information we receive—the facts—in combination with the unwritten texts of what we perceive and feel. This reference is our spiritual mentor—our Great Universal Truth. It is unerring, beneficial, and angelic. It is effective in direct proportion to our contact with the Love Matrix. As such, it is reflective of powerful levels of positive energy whether or not that infusion of positivity is conscious or unconscious.

The combination of *information* plus *perception* helps form our level of *awareness* and is multiplied by it, because it is our awareness, our spiritual awareness, that makes us more or less than what we are. But in order to be aware, we must recognize both Love and Fear when they are presented to us and use them both appropriately. So our GUT feel comes to be the glorious summer of all knowledge, awareness, instincts, and intuition. It is *divine insight*. And yet it is often unreflected. It comes upon us suddenly, often in such waves of power that we find it irresistible. When it comes to us in such ways, we offer this word to the wise: Heed it! Do not let the hum of fear-based rationalizations neutralize that brilliant moment. Recognize that instant of glorious opportunity or relentless danger for what it is and realize that your great cosmic computer has already made its evaluations and is reporting to you, "loud and clear."

At this point, we have to recognize that, when it comes to responding to our GUT feel, none of us is perfect. Sometimes we are able answer this call consciously; on other occasions, we simply respond as if we were puppets on strings, as beneficiaries without total awareness. (This, however, requires trust predicated by a certain consistent spiritual attunement.) Still, at other times, we react in contradiction to the signs we are given, and pay the price for it. So, the issue once again comes to attunement. How do we get ourselves in spiritual and emotional shape to recognize the gift when it is offered?

To that purpose, we offer a number of examples that should help show how these variances come to us and how they are met.

GUT Feel: Some That Worked (And Some That Didn't)

Example 1: A man is considering a one thousand share stock purchase of a high profile Internet technology provider—Oracle. As a long-term hold, Oracle (currently selling on the NASDAQ at $26 a share) is on several market analysts' recommend list as a long term accumulate, but is not recommended as a buy for the short or intermediate term. After doing his proper due-diligence on Oracle, the investor goes to sleep and dreams vivid dreams of Oracle's surprising success as an immediate investment. He even awakens at about 4:00 a.m. that morning from an almost vocal alarm of the name, Oracle, thumping out of his dream state and flowing into his conscious thoughts. Bounding out of bed, he goes on to get dressed and, somewhere in the process of his daily routine, dismisses the dream as merely the result of his conscious research. Choosing to take the cautious path and wait rather than invest, he checks the market stock quotes later that morning and discovers to his horror that Oracle has had an astounding positive earnings turnaround for the second quarter of 1999 and has jumped 9 points in one day! And he hadn't bought the stock.

Example 2: A middle-aged M.D. and internist with large stores of discretionary income has been introduced to a biotech company's promising new technology (a cure for various types of cancer) that he finds intriguing. After examining the cursory data, the doctor makes a decision to invest a large sum of money in the newly formed pharmaceutical company. Despite the fact that his lawyer and his wife, as well as partners in his practice, assure him that neither the business plan nor the curriculum vitae of the company CEO checks out to their satisfaction, the doctor feels "in his gut" that the product is a winner and agrees to go ahead with a direct purchase of more than $500,000 in shares of "preferred stock" in the soon-to-be public corporation. Ten months later, the product fails a series of FDA tests, the CEO disappears, and the corporation files for bankruptcy. The doctor loses his entire investment.

Example 3: A writer-producer in the Hollywood film community, and a longtime bachelor as well, has given up looking for a balanced relationship with anyone of the opposite sex and has settled into a life of personal tranquillity, meditation, and relative isolation that is only occasionally interrupted by disturbing dreams of the same "ideal" woman. She is slim, gifted with flawless dark Mediterranean features and an overriding sense of joy that sheds a visible light that he can feel and almost taste. Certainly, she is unlike anyone he has ever met. Wisely, he notes the dreams as more than mere aberrations, but then just as wisely releases his attachment to them and gets on with his life. Several weeks later, our producer accepts an invitation to a private art gallery exhibition. On the day of the party, he decides to cancel and curl up instead with a good book. But about two hours before the event is set to begin, he is brought upright out of his chair by a set of voices that tell him, "You have to go to the gallery. Get dressed... and dress to the nines!"

Entirely taken aback by the little voices nagging him but clearly aware that this message is synchronicity in its most eloquent expression, our protagonist gets dressed, attends the gallery showing, and meets the same strikingly attractive woman from his dreams. The two are instantly attracted to one another. (For him it's love at first sight). The week after their "chance" meeting, they begin dating and as of this writing have been inseparable for seven years.

Example 4: April 1999. A young woman, unhappy in her current job, has been *focusing* on a career change for quite some time. Even though she currently holds a well-paying position as a paralegal, she has sent out résumés for a job in advertising, one for which she has no previous experience. Having been rejected a dozens of times, she still envisions the job she will have, even to the kind of office she will occupy. Weeks later, in her darkest moment, she gets a flash of insight that tells her she should run to the Internet and check positions available on *Monster.com.* She does so and finds the perfect opportunity for an advertising assistant account executive "with a background in the legal profession." She applies for the job and is accepted. And when she is shown to her office, she finds it to be the same one she envisioned—right down to the desk chair.

Example 5 (Historical and possibly apocryphal): The country: Scotland. The year: 1312. The place: near Stirling Castle. Robert the Bruce, the new King (Robert I) of the Scots, is about to lead his undermanned force of about 3,000 men against the armies of the English King Edward II, including a cavalry of 1,200 "heavy horse," that outnumbers his own forces by about four to one. Two nights before the battle, Robert the Bruce dreams that the English heavy cavalry are riding to surround him but are sinking into the ground as if they were suddenly and surprisingly caught in a body of water.

After the dream, "The Bruce" repositions his army off the high ground (where it would traditionally enjoy an advantage) and into the nearby lowland marshes of Bannock Burn. Surprised by the seeming tactical blunder, King Edward II decides for a quick thrust to victory and sends his heavy cavalry charging down into Bannock Burn—where horse and rider sink down into the sands and mud of the bog and are rendered helpless. It is a primary factor in turning the tide of battle and winning the day for Scottish independence.

Example 6: Stuck in the Heartland of America during a small-town winter tour, rock and roll icons Richie Valens, Buddy Holly and "The Big Bopper" don't want to get stranded in a small Iowa farm town in the middle of a snowy winter night. So, they hire a private aircraft to fly them to their next tour stop in Sioux Falls, South Dakota. Even though there are storm warnings ahead—and even though Valens has dreamt of his own death by air crash on numerous occasions!—the trio presses on. The plane crashes en route. And the tragic event is remembered in song and verse as "The Day the Music Died."

Example 7: A young man at a blackjack table in a Las Vegas casino is on a roll with his wagers. He has had a few drinks and is now *in the flow* of winning. He has just been dealt a 10 and an 8 and the dealer is showing a face card. By any logical betting method, the young man should stand on the 18 he has been given, but tonight he is fearless. Somehow, he just *knows* he will get a 3 and hit 21. He calls for a hit, and even tells the dealer to, "give me my 3." The dealer tosses out the card. It is a three of clubs.

From all the examples we have just cited, a number of conclusions can be drawn. First is the understanding that there are no accidents. Our universe is in such constant conversation with us that every moment has meaning. The important issue for us to remember is that, once we are able to release Fear and embrace Love as the guiding factor in our lives, our readings of these moments will become more clear, more positive, and more beneficial to us. We grant you, as well, that some lucky individuals innately have more ability to read the flow of energies in their lives. Possibly they're not particularly nice people. They just seem to be luckier about all things in life. But why is it that they are?

In each of the eight examples we offered, there was a pivotal moment in each decision that was made that marked the fate of each person in that decision. Some of them are glaringly apparent; others are more subtle in their expression.

In *Example 1,* the investor should have followed the cosmic alarm that went off in his dream. There was such an urgent call to be heeded. Remember, there are no accidents. And our dreams, like our waking moments, can be read for the helpmates that they are. In this case, the investor allowed himself to rationalize away his decision by thinking more about the expertise of market analysts instead of the innate wisdom of his own well-researched "intuition." His own GUT feel had led him to study Oracle and gather the information about it. His cosmic telephone did the rest. He just failed to answer it. He answered his mind instead of following his heart, when he knew in his heart that Oracle was a good buy. The fear of loss caused the man to mistrust his GUT. And because he did, he lost nearly $10,000 in one day's missed opportunity.

Example 2's medical professional thought his "gut" feel was the overriding consideration in his decision to invest. In following what he thought to be his exceptional instincts, he ignored the practical facts presented to him by his lawyer, his wife, and his associates. In so doing he had disregarded the prime directive of intuition, and that is, "always measure the tangible aspects of any situation first." A laundry list of evidence was in place to condemn both the project and his investment. In this case, the doctor refused to observe them correctly. So, his gut feel was probably little more than good old-fashioned *greed,* combined perhaps with more than a dash of *arrogance*—both aspects of the Fear Matrix.

Our writer-producer friend in *Example 3* did just the opposite. He marked every piece of information he received as valuable, and he listened to his inner voices when their messages came through. Meditation and a clear mental approach to his life probably aided in the correctness of his decision, but he was also less at risk in his choices. Fear was not much of a factor in his decision. He had also been able to focus on his desire for peace and put himself in a positive light. He had removed *expectation* from his focus on the perfect soul mate, and just let it happen.

Example 4 is a classic case of focus, intention, and positive imaging. The young woman in this scenario never lost sight of exactly what she wanted and placed all her reserve energy directly toward getting it. She kept her faith, and in the end the universe rewarded her with a flash of insight that led her precisely to the right place for her goal imaging to be rewarded. What's more, it was rewarded with a sense of detail that matched the intensity of her intention.

Robert I of Scotland, in *Example 5,* lived in a time where dreams were held in high regard as the omens they often proved to be. He also applied to that very specific cosmic alarm a bit of the *Eureka! Factor* and welcomed the subconscious alert for the sound tactical advice he perceived it to be. Virtually, the course of history was altered—for the time being at least—by a national leader's willingness to heed his Great Universal Truth.

Example 6 is a tragic combination of hubris (in the true sense of the word), success self-sabotage, and (in Richie Valens' case) a failure to heed an entire volume of GUT-feel warnings presaging that ill-fated flight. In truth, volumes could be written about this tragic occasion and the decisions that led up to it. They form a classic if not predictable chain of events that dog celebrity calamities such as this and raise additional questions about our human propensity for self-sabotage.

Example 7 was a case of what could only be referred to as *flow momentum*. The young gambler was so much in the zone of what he was doing that losing was not even a consideration; he just saw himself winning. He envisioned it. The fact that he was slightly tipsy also managed, temporarily at least, to remove the elements of fear from his panoply of emotion. He was quite literally fear-less. And for the very short time being he was a "Master of the Universe."

We observe immediately in this study of unconscious momentum technology that we recommend neither drinking nor gambling as a secret either to refining one's intuition or to fine tuning one's contact with one's Great Universal Truth. What we do suggest, however, is an examination of the underlying strength of this man at the moment of his invulnerability: It was the sheer, boundless *joy* of the child at play. He was having a good time. He was standing in a pure cone of light from the Love Matrix. Fear had no hold on him. The pivotal question here is whether his good fortune was an aberration or a permanent state of grace. We suspect the former, and that in itself is a confirmation that we all get occasional random waves of Love Matrix energy that find their way into our lives whether we think we deserve them or not. The issue comes in their recognition as well as their cultivation.

In examining our eight examples collectively, we suggest that each proper use of the GUT feel factor and each equally improper use of the GUT feel quotient had certain qualities in common.

Those in touch with their Great Universal Truth were able to achieve one or a combination of factors that led to their fulfillment:

1) Most of them correctly learned the facts and came to some conscious, intelligent decisions in their application of them.

2) Once they had properly evaluated their current situation, they were able to focus on their objectives and envision them as successfully occurring. In other words, they were able to set their intention to succeed.

3) In several cases, the people who embraced a proper relationship with their objectives also released their expectations.

4) In every case, they relied on positive forces outside themselves—Lady Luck, angels, the cosmic connection, the Love Matrix information—to carry to them the GUT feel they needed to make a correct decision. In other words, they trusted their spiritual natures.

The people who failed to listen to their GUT feel or who totally misread their intuition also obeyed a fixed set of pre-conditions:

1) *They failed to correctly observe the facts presented to them.*

2) They ignored their GUT feel or else misread it as something else.

3) They allowed their pivotal decisions to be dictated primarily from the Fear Matrix.

4) Their behavior was, without exception, errant to the point of being self-destructive.

The question that must be asked then, is this: How could they get so far out of touch with the opportunities for correct decisions so readily available to them?

The question you should now want to ask yourself this: With which of two these distinct groups did you most readily identify? No one wants to admit his or her intuition is out of balance when in truth, for most of us, it is.

It is, by the way, entirely possible to identify with both groups. We have all entertained the dark side of what makes us fail at what we attempt. By the same token, all of us have experienced those moments when we too were in the flow of higher awareness, when our decisions were just perfect—as if they were pre-ordained to have been so!

Your Three Best and Three Worst Decisions

It is simplistic to observe that everything we accomplish in our lives, for better or worse, comes as a result of the choices we make. And yet a troubling set of questions arises from this: How consciously do we make some of them? How aware are we, really? Did we do all our homework on every sensory level?

There have been those moments for all of us that are monumental, life altering—just as these eight examples we have documented proved to be for other people. Sometimes these moments get by us unnoticed, like whispers in a noisy room, yet they transform our lives irrevocably. At other times, they trumpet their importance, announcing themselves with brazen self-awareness and an almost tumescent presence of ego.

The challenge to us comes in our abilities to recognize them—not only those moments themselves but also the underlying connections that brought us to them. And that is what we ask you to do here.

It is both our challenge and our delusionist's prompt to help you recall in detail those times when you came to some surprisingly good decisions, and some amazingly inaccurate ones.

First, list three separate occasions in which you made some GUT feel decisions that were exceptionally good, bright, or fortunate.

(**A hint:** List all the circumstances surrounding each occasion and what might have prompted you to make the decisions you did. How did you feel about them going into the event? What induced you to go for it? Had you been concentrating on the issue that favored you for a long time? Or was it something that just came up? What was your energy like at the time? Was it positive or negative? Were you in the flow of your perceptions of what could be achieved? Or were your desires encased in fear? Did you have integrity of intention when you came to this decision? Was this truly a part of your life's plan? Did this fit in with goals and objectives you have set for yourself? Did you even set any goals?)

Dig deeply, and come up with as many details as you can remember. Then look to the three incidents for any traces of similarity, and come up with your own GUT feel design.

Second, list three separate instances where you made some unfortunate decisions about something. It could be the wrong choice of career, a poor choice of a place to live, or a disastrous choice of a mate, wife, husband or significant other. It could be a bad bet in a game of chance, or a poorly chosen investment.

Once again, what were the circumstances surrounding your decision? What observations did you make that led to your decision? What facts were presented to you that led to your observations? What truths did you ignore in the process? Did you experience any cognitive dissonance when you did so? Were you tuned in at any level of higher awareness during the process of your intuitive choices?

Was the choice you made a part of any grand design, game plan, or mission statement you had set for yourself? Or was it a matter of random selection?

Once again, we're asking you questions within the questions to help energize both your recollections and your evaluations of them.

We also admit to another agenda that comes from a simple point of discovery: People who set goals and objectives, those who design their lives and who have a clear vision of what it is they want to accomplish, are much more apt to recognize those spontaneous events, those GUT feel opportunities, when they do occur in their lives. It is all a matter of attunement to that consciousness, and the immutable *Law of Concentration:* That to which you focus the majority of your effort will bring you a destiny in direct proportion to that effort, *provided* you are working from a basis of love and not fear.

Setting goals and focusing upon them are not only a prayer but also a declaration of trust in the universal good that awaits you. If you set them with positive intention, you are trusting (an aspect of the Love Matrix) and will devote intelligent energy to their accomplishment.

Fear is never an intelligent use of energy. When you fear, you are operating exclusively from your head and not your heart. What's more, fear is an insidious binding agent. Since the vast majority of people are uncertain of their love but immersed in their Fear Matrix, they will spend more time in it and perhaps experience it even more intensely. If you experience an intensity of fear, dread, or negativity, you will draw to you that which you fear the most. That is the *Magnetic Law of Fear*, and we encourage you to release it as soon as you have read this.

Having planted that fear weed, as it were, we immediately offer a formula to uproot it. And you can do so by loving unconditionally all that you hold dear. See it as complete. Understand that it is your divine right and your destiny. And do not let doubt enter the equation of your dreams.

Easier said than done, because we *all* have doubts. But doubts (an aspect of the Fear Matrix) can be like flocks of tiny birds that fly through our lives without either power or occasion. They just occur. If we are practicing the principles of the Love Matrix, we can note their comings and goings without letting them either disturb us or bear weight upon the conduct of our lives.

If we focus upon our desires and envision them with love, our GUT feel will come to us like an eagle returned to its aerie. But it comes to us best when we have a tranquil and untroubled mind. It also finds its way back to us on the clear and silent path.

The challenge with most of us is that the noise and clamor of daily living is so overwhelming that it forms a cycle of entrapment from which we find it difficult to free ourselves. The opportunity for us lies in the fact that we can realign our focus and find our way back into the silent wisdom of self-discovery. It is here that we ask you to understand that our *GUT feel* is a kind of *Divine Multi-sensory Compass (DMC)*. Properly in tune, it is our guide back home to our intended purpose. The challenge now comes with learning how to recalibrate it. And that will take some discipline and a willingness to work.

Resetting Our Divine Multi-sensory Compass. (DMC)

Now that we understand how focus and the disciplines of goal-setting can help us more readily attune to our GUT feel and make proper use of our intuition—now that we recognize that operating in the Love Matrix brings our GUT feel back to us—let us set a simple series of steps that we have found can help anyone regain better contact with their Great Universal Truth.

• Write down an initial set of goals and ambitions. Include everything you desire, dream of, and are investing your total energies into achieving. And be sure that the goals you set for your life have integrity. If they do, you cannot fail. If they do not, if they are zero-sum or mean-spirited, then no amount of goal setting will work for you. And your GUT feel will tell you so. (Note: If you're having trouble doing this, in Chapter 8, "Get Larger Than Life," we will have a specific sample goal-setting plan for you to use as a model, as well as a set of disciplines that will help you bring them about. But for now, embrace the random joy of picking your unlimited potentials. And don't spare the details.

• Review your Love Matrix potentials as well as your Fear Matrix chronicle. Determine to what degree you have been able to use one to replace the balance of the other.

• Begin a five-day process of attunement into a different level of awareness as follows. (**Note:** This test is optional but significant for those who would really like to attune to their GUT feel. Pick a period when you have some extra time, and be willing to experiment with yourself to the degree that you are not regimented to a particular pattern of behavior or perceptual expectation. Once you maintain the disciplines, the freedom of movement and response is yours to enjoy.)

1) On day one spend four hours of intermittent deep breathing. There are several ways to breathe deeply. One is to breathe in for a four count, hold your breath for a sixteen count, and exhale for an eight count (or multiples thereof). Another is to breathe in quickly for a six count and breathe out slowly, gradually for a twelve count. A third is aerobic exercise. Swimming, jogging, and active cycling are excellent means of accomplishing this. So are active sports such as tennis, basketball, squash skiing, in-line skating and racquetball. This will serve you in a number of ways we will discuss in detail in Chapter 8, "Get Larger Than Life." But for the purposes of this exercise, spend at least ten minutes of each hour in the four-hour period deep breathing as we suggested. As you do, breathe-out your negative emotions, thoughts and feelings. Release them. Let them go as if they were birds flying from captivity. Then breathe in positive thoughts and ideas; let them flow into you as if you were drinking in sunlight and the scent of sweet flowers. At the end of the four-hour period, note how it made you feel. Did you feel more positive about your life and world? Or did you feel more anxious. Did you feel energized or sleepy? Note each response. It's better if you jot them down on a piece of paper or journal.

After this first day, start each of your next four days' exercises with at least five minutes of deep breathing. It will help clear your head as well as your lungs and blood vessels. (It's something like scrubbing out your vase at the energy level.)

2) *The second day* may seem a bit radical, and only undertake them, if you're absolutely sure of your environment. *Pick a time of morning or evening when you can spend four hours blindfolded.* (It would be wiser to stay close to home while you're doing this.) And you might want to block off access to any staircases. You may play soft music. Other than that, we recommend that you run no television, radio, or other electronic media). Use your sense of hearing and your sense of touch to note the world around you. Become aware of how objects feel, how sounds affect your movements, how odors and smells become a

more significant part of your life. In the last hour, you may hold phone conversations, but do so with the intention of hearing for the first time. Listen to the silence during the pauses. And make a mental note of the subtle shifts in energy you are able to pick up. At the end of your four-hour period, note how your perceptions have changed—how you have taken certain levels of your awareness for granted. Make a written note of them, if you choose to do so.

3) *For the third day, spend four hours in complete silence.* Use ear plugs if necessary. Don't play music. Don't answer the phone. Get away from the noisy daily interactions with your family, and feed your pets early. Begin to use your sense of sight, your sense of touch, and your sense of smell to interact with your proximate world. While you are in this silence, begin the active process of cleansing all your negative thoughts. If they are directed at other people or external forces, forgive them, bless them and release them. If they are turned inward, again forgive and release them, but also remember to forgive yourself for the lack you feel. In the last hour, close your eyes and meditate. And as you do allow only positive images in—images of beauty and fulfillment. Don't force them. Rather, permit them to flow naturally to you. Trust and understand the natural flow of love energy that can come to you at times like these. Allow your natural circadian clock to bring you out of it within an hour (It won't be off more than five minutes one way or the other). Note the impressions that colors, bouquets, and odors leave with you. At the end of the period write them down. Particularly note the impressions you received in the last hour.

4) *Spend at least four hours of your fourth day as a mute; don't speak at all.* Don't call out. Don't sing. Don't hold any conversations. Don't whistle or aum. Just be silent and let that loss of voice become a part of you. After your four hours are through, note the sensations you felt. Make a conscious record of how you sounded to yourself when

you first spoke or sang. Was it a relief? Or did you sound as if you were someone apart from yourself; different somehow? Note the contrast and how it made you feel.

5) *On your fifth day, re-trace your steps from the previous four days, spending one hour doing each of the four exercises we have outlined.* But this time, undertake them in a slightly different order: *First* do your intermittent deep breathing exercises, remembering to breathe in positivity and breathe out and away any negative thoughts, emotions or feelings. *Second,* go into the silence. Block out all extraneous sound, and try to meditate for at least twenty minutes of that time. *Third,* put on the blindfold for an hour and reexamine the sensory heightened world of complete darkness. *Fourth,* become speechless again. Give no voice to your thoughts and hold only the most positive thoughts inside you. After you have finished the final day, make a note of each hour period and compare them to your experiences on the first day. We also recommend that you continue with this five-day exercise for one week out of every month for at least six months, and chart your progress in having done so.

What we find you will often experience during this five-day plan is a gradual reintroduction to your intuitive nature. In the beginning, you can expect to experience some fears, doubts and discomfort. That is when you are challenged most to trust those pauses in your busy mental process; you have to allow yourself to surrender to it, and not fight it. After a while, sometimes an hour or two, you invariably start to become clearer and more receptive to Love Matrix energy. And through that perception, your realignment with your Great Universal Truth(s) will inevitably follow. It is the inevitable calibration of the individual with his or her higher self.

It was meant to be. It is a part of your destiny. The rest is a matter of timing; of how and when you choose that sublime moment of rediscovery. And that, as always, is your choice to make.

A Final Note: A Triumph of Heart and Mind.

"Where the heart lies let the brain lie also."

—Robert Browning
"One More Word."
Men and Women

Just as they serve us at times, clichés all too often hold us in check, and by their very natures become self-limiting. In the win-loss scenarios of our lives, one of the misconceptions we've constantly been fed is that we must pit heart against mind. Telling someone "you're letting your heart rule your head," by tradition borders on insult and invariably comes as a kind of admonishment.

It is a way of telling others they have no way of controlling their passions—that they are impassioned, and therefore out of control.

If you will remember, the term *passion* is one word that took its place on both sides of the Love/Fear Matrix. It was deliberately juxtaposed there for a couple reasons. The first should be obvious: Passion, without the governance of reason, is an unguided missile in the field of human dynamics. Unbridled passion knows neither discretion nor consideration. Impassioned lovers kill their mates. Passionate debates can end in fistfights. And passionate political causes often spawn terrorism. All these elements, by the way, carry with them such qualities as jealousy, rage, resentment, and revenge—the accouterment of the Fear Matrix.

On the other hand, passion that cooperates with universal Mind, with the oversoul, is the true nectar of life. It feeds our poetry. It is the source and flow of our drive to achieve great things. It is the wand of our wizard, the higher self. But it can only work once the mind has accepted the unconditional love that comes in behind it. The question that remains for us is whether or not we human beings are capable of attaining unconditional love. Even in our most splendid moments, is it too divine for our meager resources? It seems so, and yet, like the Holy Grail to which we have alluded before, it is not the attainment of high objectives but the seeking of them that ennobles us to our cause.

Success in life is understanding the marriage of heart and mind. By striving to achieve that balance, we are honoring the quest. We are doing our best and, in the process, becoming the best we can be.

Whenever we undertake to do this, even the effort sings inside us. It resonates. It points us back toward home. That is music of the GUT. That is the consummate sign that our Divine Multi-sensory Compass is back in tune again.

Chapter 7

Great Timing! (And How to Get it)

Your timing sucks!

If you've ever been told this, consider it a compliment. Because in the delusionist's codebook of near misses, there have probably been occasions where you have come so close to the fire of truth that it has nearly burned you. The experience, the fear of failure or rejection has been so strong, so overpowering, that you hit upon the perfect plan for never getting near it again. You have entirely miss-timed your approach to the body of your desire.

What a gift you have been given. How near you are to creating the sublime precision you were intended to enjoy! Think about it for a moment: If you can get it that wrong, then your timing is somewhere on the verge of becoming impeccable. The issue we want to address here is why it isn't already.

Of course we have experienced those seasons in our lives when our timing is flawless. From the perfect comment at the appropriate moment in a conversation to knowing when to send flowers to your significant other, you have struck the high note in the cosmic frequency; you have done the right thing.

We acknowledge that there is no specific data to support our theory. We also believe that a little extrapolation is good for the soul. Nevertheless, we're willing to wager that your timing, our timing, anyone's timing, is going to be better when there is less at stake. It's easier to time the smaller games of life. For one thing, they are more familiar to us. For another, they do not carry with them the pressure of expectation; we're not afraid of the impact our decisions will bring to bear on the outcome.

Once again, Fear enters the equation, and inevitably our GUT feel will also play the pivotal role in the timing scenario. If you've undertaken the disciplines that we feel will help you to improve your contact with your Great Universal Truth, you will have been able to excise a good many Fear Matrix implants and replace them with the Love energy that better senses the flows both of our universe and the microcosm of your immediate world. In that way, the Fear (in all its forms) that does slip into your midst will be recognized for the gift it is: as a warning device that there is something out of synch either with your decisions or with the opportunities for correctness that are being presented to you.

Knowing your GUT feel and trusting in it will help to imbue you with a sense of timing that is both acute and flawless. You will learn to respond to the meaning of *now* with both recognition and delight as well as understanding that the sudden, seemingly inexplicable agitation in your GUT is a cosmic lock that you occasionally need to turn in order to bar the door against certain unreliable choices.

Of course, none of us is going to make all the right choices all the time. There are occasions, seemingly unavoidable ones, when we entirely miss the mark about a prospective relationship or person with whom we interact. Such mistakes are a part of the process of thriving in this complex process called life. When such missteps do occur, almost always these events serve us as teachers in the classroom of higher discernment. And our relationships, either personal or business, that prove to be flawed serve us equally as valuable lessons in finding the truth of ourselves. What it helps to remember at times such as these is to review the circumstances, to look at the turning points in our judgment, and to find the places where we failed to observe correctly.

It is at these times when our *higher awareness* and our *insight* will serve us well. But a word of caution here: make your evaluations objectively. You are human, after all. And sometimes we make mistakes because, at some level of belief, we choose to make them; perhaps, if no other reason, than to learn.

Nevertheless, an intelligent dispassionate evaluation of your circumstances is as essential as it is helpful. And it will not only help you fine tune your GUT feel, but also hone your sense of timing as well. More than that, it is important to recognize that timing is a gift; it is not something you force. Your timing is dependent upon your recognition of trends in human dynamics, the flows of energy surrounding any situation, and the subtle shifts in movement that your GUT is meant to properly interpret. But timing, like the GUT feel with which it is so often interdependent, is certain to be refined—provided you have integrity of intention. If you are certain of your goals and are able to temper them with working toward the greater good, time is already on your side.

A Matter of Integrity. Time Rewards the Just Heart.

Conviction is the preamble to excellent result. It forms a large part of the substance of one's mission in life. But conviction can only hold together if one is certain of one's dedication to high intent.

We're probably sounding loftier than we intend to. And yet we all have to look into the mirror and face the eventualities of why we're here. In a way, the rules are simple. And again it sends us back to our one and two-word questions in Chapter 3, questions to which you alone have the answers. If you keep the integrity of your true intent (and we believe everyone's true mission is to make a positive difference in this world into which we have all come), then you will succeed. You will find your GUT feel, and your sense of timing will reward you accordingly. If not, if you choose to play nothing but the lesser games of life that serve only the minor pursuit of selfish aims and little pleasures, if you play the zero-sum game that comes at the expense of others, you will fail. And no amount of timing will serve you well. In fact, quite the reverse—it will turn on you and betray you in the end.

An astute sense of timing is an acquired skill to be sure. Oftentimes it can serve us simply in the course of the common allowances of maturity and experience. We learn. We do. We master certain skills, and with them the necessary timing to carry them through successfully. It is practiced. It is refined. And by virtue of repetition alone, it is often mastered.

Ultimately, however, mastery takes a different form. And one's sense of timing, like the servant it is, serves the just master with greater celerity. There are historical accountings by the score of those who have been gifted with a phenomenal sense of timing but who, by betraying their true intention, have seen it fail them in the end.

By the same token, people who keep their covenant with their mission in life, those who believe in the correctness of what they're doing, will find that timing rewards them. All they need do is be at one with the degree of their rightness, pursue it relentlessly, and be willing to wait for its inevitable completion. Patience accompanied by a sense of purpose is always the best measure of success timing, as well as it is of time itself. But timing is best illustrated by example. And it is here that we would like to offer an exceptional illustration of timing, both good and not so good.

That Magic Moment

There is a tide in the affairs of men that,
when taken at the flood, leads to fortune.

—William Shakespeare
Julius Caesar

The quote from Shakespeare's *Julius Caesar* has more than occasionally been raised as a rallying cry for opportunists looking to "seize the day" in today's international business climate. We note, yet again, the irony of quotes such as this, because when you pry away the paint and glitter of this famous exhortation, you'll find it is actually given by the Roman senator Cassius to enlist his compatriot Brutus in a plot to assassinate Julius Caesar. In truth, Shakespeare's classic five-act play is a running commentary on the pursuit of power, the madness that often accompanies it, and the critical uses of timing that inevitably come to be born out of it. Under scrutiny, it is a parade of folly and an acquittal of the virtues of vigilant patience.

Brutus, perhaps Julius Caesar's closest friend, is terribly upset about Caesar's having risen to become Rome's first Emperor, and perceives it as a pernicious but well-timed seizure of absolute power. Brutus disapproves of the assassination plot to kill Caesar, yet refuses to do anything to stop it and is, by virtue of his silent complicity, irrevocably drawn into it. In fact, it is Brutus who strikes the final devastating blow that brings his friend down. Caesar (according to the scenario based in *Plutarch's Lives*) suffers from some wretchedly poor timing of his own, since he is warned not only by an old soothsayer to "Beware the Ides of March," but also by his wife Calpurnia's prophetic dream. In it, she sees Caesar, bloody and stabbed to death on the floor of the Roman Senate. That is precisely where Caesar is headed on this morning of March 15 (the Ides of March!) in 44 BC. But rather than pay heed to any of the warnings he has received, Caesar forges ahead for his first official meeting with the Senate as Rome's new emperor. After all, he has just been urged on by the record crowds of citizens to accept the mantle of leadership, has used that mandate to abolish the Roman Republic, and been made a god in the process. Feeling immortal, he struts through the Forum, and arrogantly displays himself at the floor of the Senate where he is promptly turned into sushi by Cassius, Casca, Metulus Cimber, Brutus and a host of other disgruntled power brokers. By now these senators, their appetites and blades whetted for more such political cleansing, converge upon Caesar's protégé, Mark Anthony. But

Mark Anthony appropriately sidesteps any confrontation, asking only to be extended the courtesy of being able to present Caesar's battered body to the people of Rome and have it burned (the Roman burial tradition for great leaders of the time). He will do so, of course, only after the other Senators have been able to address the Roman citizens and explain their actions.

Ignoring every law of timing, logic, and mass psychology, the other Senators agree. And of course, Mark Anthony follows Brutus' somewhat tepid moralizing acquittal with a personal eulogy, the energy and eloquence of which equals any in political history.

Having learned well from his mentor Caesar that whoever held sway over the Roman mob held sway over Rome, Mark Anthony plays the crowd like a harp and uses that splendid moment to drive his adversaries into hiding and eventually down to defeat. Cassius loses his head. Brutus falls on his sword. And Anthony gets to give another brilliant soliloquy about Brutus having been "the noblest Roman of them all." Thus perishes honor in the uncertain man. So, Mark Anthony, more calculating than pure, sees his stock rise to new heights—all because Caesar, Brutus, Cassius and others fell victim to possibly the worst epidemic of self-sabotage that had ever been exhibited up to that time.

Of course, it didn't hurt Mark Anthony in the least that he was a gifted orator and a crowd favorite. He also recognized that in all our lives there are moments—epic ones—upon which such opportunities only pay visitation once. Mark Anthony saw that moment and seized it. So truly, the tide in the affairs of men applied more to him than any of the characters in Shakespeare's historical play.

Unfortunately, Mark Anthony was totally out of synch with his higher self. Power hungry, ambitious, arrogant, an obsessive carouser, Anthony became so convinced of his own invulnerability that he too had caught what could only be described as "Caesar's Disease." So, his downfall too was only a matter of time.

In truth, the only figure who was able to rise from this historical farrago with his power base intact was Julius Caesar's nephew, Octavian, who knew enough to remove himself from the currents of public frenzy until the time was right to seize control. Having relinquished the governance of what seemed to be a majority of Roman conquered territory to Mark Anthony, he sent his triumvirate partner off to administer the Eastern Empire headquartered in Egypt, while he played "caretaker" of the old Empire headquartered in Rome. Meanwhile, he used his blood ties as Caesar's nephew to wend his way through the most politically treacherous atmosphere in recorded time. Allowing Mark Anthony's brash instincts and Cleopatra's unbridled ambitions to alienate them to the Empire, Octavian remained in Rome to catch the downdraft of consequences, all of which he had contrived to fall in his favor.

No chain of events in history better illustrates the ebbs and flows of fortune and the inability of what appeared to be that world's most capable leaders either to cope with them or to time them correctly.

Let's review the turning points from Julius Caesar's assassination to Octavian's ascension as Augustus Caesar, Emperor of Rome.

First, Julius Caesar, who had made much of his career by following his heretofore flawless GUT feel impeccable sense of timing, suddenly disregarded both and rushed seemingly pell mell to embrace his own martyrdom. In other words, he seemed almost deliberately to sabotage himself. Once having slain Caesar, his assassins, who had laid the perfect trap, suddenly lost all contact with reason, logic, and common sense. Instead of seizing political initiative, acting decisively, and immediately securing the power they felt Caesar had corrupted, they turned the rest of the day over to Caesar's most loyal lieutenant—and then decided to run for their lives. Mark Anthony, who knew his own magical hold over the mob, lost sight of the fact that this kind of momentum was a monster that constantly had to be fed. Relying on his longstanding popularity, he abandoned his power base to chase his personal fantasies, and left Rome in the hands of the one man who seemed to have mastered the art of timing in all its aspects.

Upon examination, Octavian was the only man of his era who never once lost focus on his objective. He was clear about his heritage of leadership, was relentless in his pursuit of it, and understood the factors involved—especially the caprices of the mob and its role in history. His timing was exceptional because he remained aware of it while others did not. He recognized its fragile nature as well as his own while others, including his Uncle Julius, made assumptions that it would always be theirs to regain. Whereas Julius Caesar felt obliged to force the bonds of circumstance, Octavian was willing to wait. Rather than drive the current of events, he was willing to bide his time and let them unfold before him. As a result, Octavian—an eighteen year-old kid when the whole rigamarole began—would see himself elevated five years later to become Augustus Caesar, the second emperor of Rome, who would govern that empire for the next thirty years.

Augustus was also the one individual who shared Julius Caesar's conception of Rome's potential, a destiny he dedicated the full force of his time on Earth to bring to fruition. Cassius, Brutus, Mark Anthony, Cleopatra and the others were fixated with the balance of power but failed in their attempts to understand its virtues. They were not prepared to deal with the responsibilities that came with it and were swamped under by the very tides of fortune they claimed to understand.

So what, in this historical parable, are our lessons about timing? How does one recognize those magic moments in our lives, and know to seize them?

First, we immediately acknowledge that there was a bit more at stake in the Rome of 44 BC than one might find in the average scenario. The government of the greatest empire in the world to that time, world history, the political futures of the individuals involved, a moral compass for the world of that time, not to mention their careers and their very lives—all were factors that weighed upon the decisions of the principals in this life's play. So they were, to say the least, under pressure to conduct themselves intelligently. We also note that all their Fear Matrix endeavors such as scheming, power plays, intrigues, ambition, greed, lust for supremacy, mob psychology, and assassination—all bore great weight on the outcome. This is typical of such tumultuous periods in history but, we are grateful to observe, not of our daily lives. Our approaches to good timing are generally of less historical significance. The challenge that awaits us, then, is the fact that there are times, entirely too many of them, when we treat them as if they were. That kind of self-induced pressure, that kind of Fear energy, blunts our initiative and undermines our enjoyment. And yet this takes place, unwaveringly, for two reasons.

First, too many of us still view life very much as the ancients did—as *a zero-sum game*.

Originally popularized by economist Lester Thurow, the zero-sum philosophy of human dynamics states that for every winner in life there must be a loser, and the degree of loss will be in direct proportion to the degree of the win. In other words, it is universal balance achieved in a way that favors someone *always at the expense of someone else*. It has traditionally been the philosophy that drives most global politics and all international economics. It certainly drove the ancients, but is becoming outmoded in the world community of the new millennium.

The theory behind the zero-sum society is what is known as an *either/or* technology, when in today's society we recognize that *both/and* is not only achievable, but desirable as well. In other words, those things we desire in life do not have to come at the expense of someone else, if for no other reason than there is a shared understanding of the delicate ecology of today's world, as we know it. In today's global village, our fates—political, humanitarian, economic, and environmental—are tied, one nation to the other, one individual to another. This commonality of purpose makes the pursuit of a win-win objective not only advantageous but also essential to our progress.

There need be no victims in the success scenarios of the 21st century. And because that element of inequity is removed, another block to our decisions about life and the refinements of timing necessary to them has been removed. By virtue of both the new technologies of business and a new wave of human consciousness, we have come to recognize that "win-win" is not only the best scenario, but also achievable in all aspects of life, including sports and other arenas of human competition. We will explain this shortly.

Before we do, however, we need to address the second issue that daunted the ancients, that still confronts us even in this newly enlightened age: *the intoxicating issue of power.* Common historical perceptions of power have proved to be deadly. Tied to the zero-sum philosophy, they are invariably accompanied by an inclination to self-destruct—to self-sabotage.

Raw power is like an enormous rock, a rock that is constantly growing. By the sheer force of physical law, a rock of any size becomes a burden to the carrier. One cannot hold onto the rock for long. It must be released, either by flinging it away, by hurling it at the object of your desire, or by passing it carefully on to another. The best use of power, of course, would be to set down and use it as a foundation upon which to build something of value. But that requires a special sense of the rock and an appreciation of its intrinsic value.

The challenge for most people is that they don't know what to do with the rock, yet they refuse to let go of it. So, what has made them powerful eventually becomes the weight that drags them down into the sea of events, where they ride the rock to the bottom, never quite understanding its nature yet refusing to let go of it.

In such instances, their fear has blocked them to their integrity of purpose. Love is lost in the obsession, and one's sense of the ebbs and flows of human nature go with it. They sense the win; they sense the loss, yet lose their hold on the moment. Their timing has left them, and someone has pulled the plug on their resolve.

Winning, success, achievement, the realized ideal—all become so encased in fear that we lose all access to them. We feel the weight of the zero-sum game and sense that we have succumbed to it. Rather than recognize it as a temporary setback, we sense we are the cipher. We are no longer in a state of becoming; we have become the loss.

What a waste of time it is to succumb to such things. And yet, our training, including generations of attack-and-defend societal strategies, have left us feeling this way.

What we need to resume is our understanding of the sheer joy of the game, that life is meant to be won by simply obeying the integrity of our dreams. Recalling that, we can come to realize that *by winning, we help everyone win.* We live by example. We flourish by setting examples. That's why competition, which may seem to be a zero-sum game, becomes the universal prize in and of itself.

We have said it before in another way, but the sentiment remains constant. It is not the score, but the pursuit of excellence that ennobles us. Once again, by questing for the light we in fact become the light.

Click!

Muscle Memory.

The term is often applied to various performance endeavors, many of them attributed to sports, when in truth muscle memory was first advanced as a theory in the field of music. The belief, one that is often challenged, is that constant repetition of the same skills during extended periods of normal rehearsal will enable a set of muscles to respond automatically to the same sensory impressions, even when placed under such pressures as the strain of intense competition and the stresses created by fatigue.

In the areas of high performance, it is known that constant practice and application of the skills learned during that practice will impart such an indelible message to the memory of the cell, muscles, and motor nerve system that they will—even under absolute stress—take over and fulfill the task assigned to them. No matter what negative impact the mind brings to bear during such moments of pressure, one's muscle memory will simply take over and see the task complete. That, more than any cognitive application of the art, is often the final determinant of the depth of the virtuoso's achievement.

In elementary terms, it might be said that repetition is the mother of skill. But in this case it is an oversimplification of what actually occurs. What occurs, under its own volition, is an exquisite expression of timing. Every reflex, every instant is so eloquently timed that knowledge is complete, and that completion is accomplished with the brain and yet entirely out of it. In other words, *truly superb timing is accomplished when you are virtually out of your mind.*

Of course, you never are out of your mind. But what you allow to happen is a state of what can only be described as *flow*, or *flow momentum*. In the last chapter, we referred to the young man in example 8 of our GUT-feel case scenarios as being in a state of flow momentum when he "just knew" he couldn't lose at blackjack. In that state, he had released any contact with fear. He was in the sheer joy of the experience. And though the dynamics of risk dictate that it probably wouldn't have lasted, he was experiencing flow momentum, at least for the time being.

A virtuoso performer such as classical pianist Van Cliburn experiences flow momentum when he is at the top of his concert level performances. It is a unified consciousness born of eventual surrender to his muscle memory and the trust he places in his entire being to be at one with his music. In preparation, he has spent hundreds of hours of practice at the piano, several hours a day. So his timing, every shade and accent of it, is flawless.

It is beyond mental. It is beyond physical. It is a consciousness that is the sum of both, and the addition of what amounts to a psychic body of activity. It is a synergism that creates a kind of magic—the magic moment, if you will. Not one that is contrived or set in place by a series of events, this magic moment comes as a spontaneous force that one can see and feel. That is timing, indeed.

It is no less significant to see the splendid displays of timing of an Olympic figure skater such as former gold medallists Peggy Fleming and Dorothy Hamill. Once again, the hours of practice, the years of discipline, come to an explicit expression of excellence that neither judge nor critic can ignore. It is the pure joy of accomplishment, free of fear and the traps of mental strain. It just happens. That is timing indeed.

When Michael Jordan, after scoring nearly fifty points and hitting seven three-point shots in one NBA playoff game, declares he was "just in the zone" on this particular night, he is articulating a period of almost sublime contact with his already unearthly command of the sport of basketball. It is now common knowledge that Jordan was, in his sophomore year, cut from his high school basketball team. What may not be known is that this rejection brought him to a new level of dedication. On his own time, he practiced several additional hours a day to perfect his skills—something he continued throughout his pro career—until he could not fail. We grant you that his exceptional talent would have eventually shined through. But one only has to ask to what degree? His timing on the court, which seems psychic at certain moments, is a result that comes in direct proportion to the degree of his dedication.

San Francisco Giant centerfielder, Willie Mays, whom many including Ted Williams—thought was the most talented baseball player who ever lived—appeared to hit, field, and run the bases with such ridiculous ease that everyone declared him a "natural" at the game. In truth, Mays was one of the hardest-working athletes in any sport. Daily, after his team had quit practice, he would spend two and three hours working out on his own—hitting, fielding, running, into the darkness of night. So the flow of perfect play that he created was in part illusion. His muscle memory and was attuned to such a level that it could take over in clutch situations. Yet his personal disciplines, focus, and dedication to his field of endeavor had formed the foundation for the superb timing for which he was known.

Each of these paragons of pinnacle performance enjoy a number of factors in common. First, we note the clarity of intention of each virtuoso performer. They set their goals and objectives. They focused on them relentlessly. They practiced the skills necessary to achieve optimum levels of skill, and they did so with maximum joy and minimum anxiety. Their achievements, in other words, were an act of love. They were in the joy of what they were doing; they *enjoyed* it. Their muscle memory, cellular memory, motor nerve memory had all been so finely tuned that their entire performance went beyond the mind and the body, forming instead a total *flow of consciousness* that could neither be denied nor entirely defined.

In the process of such high level of achievement, something else happens: there is no way to lose. That, in the highly competitive world of art and athletics, appears to be a contradiction in terms—an oxymoron, a delusion. After all, sports in particular are predicated upon a win-or-lose, attack-and-defend strategy. A competition of any kind is the quintessential zero-sum game. Those are the rules; those are the boundaries.

But let's reexamine that concept for a moment. Does anyone who performs at optimum levels of excellence ever lose at anything? How many professional team athletes, when serving in a losing cause, observe that all they can do is perform at the best level they know how? Even as recognition-motivated as most competition athletes are—and though they are driven, even obsessed, with the glories that accompany first place—there is an eloquence of expression and a grace in movement they have created, even in defeat, that has an excellence of its own.

Dr. George Sheehan, the renowned guru of long distance-running, once observed in his performance classic *Running and Being* that, "Winning is playing the game in your own rhythm."[11]

In his book entitled *Flow*, Mihaly Csikszentmihalyi refers to the magic moment that is in all our capacity to create in this way:

> Flow helps to integrate the self, because in that state of deep concentration consciousness is usually well-ordered. Thoughts, intentions, feelings, and the senses are focused on the same goal. Experience is in harmony. And when the flow episode is over, one feels more 'together' than before...[12]

Someone who truly loves their work, their sport, their chosen field of activity, is already in the flow of such reward for effort that they have already won. There is no zero-sum for them and therefore no fear. Where there is no fear, there is no sense of loss, and therefore no losing.

So, if in any activity to which you are wholly dedicated there is no fear of loss, imagine what happens to your sense of timing. It only gets better with time, practice and application.

Can athletes "tank" on a given day? Can concert musicians give a disastrous performance? Do great competitors choke? Of course they do. But only if they let their mind get in the way. In every case it is because they started thinking about the outcome, about technique, about the opinions of others—about the zero-sum that awaited them as the loser, about the power that would be lost if they failed. So, they let the possibility of failure enter the equation.

Memory serves us painfully to recall how the sports world agonized for Greg Norman when he blew a six-stroke lead on the final day of the 1996 Masters Tournament to lose by six strokes to previous winner Nick Faldo... or in 1995 when perennial tennis bridesmaid Jana Novotna choked her way out of a 6-2, 5-0 Wimbledon Championship and ended losing to (then) five-time winner Steffi Graf... or when World Chess Champion Garry Kasparov made a disastrous miscalculation and became the first ever Grand Master to lose a tournament to IBM's "Deep Blue" computer, Kasparov was not in the flow of his game; he was in his head.

In each of the illustrations we have offered (and there are dozens!) these brilliant athletes and grand champions had lost the mind-body-spirit connection—the flow of consciousness—and became "head cases" instead. Fear froze their timing, and they became the zero in the zero-sum game. In the midst of their splendid—flight toward achievement, they had pulled that forbidden red lever and self-destructed. How very much they had in common with the ancients of Caesar's time. How very unnecessary it was to do so.

In some of the illustrations of timing we just gave, we grant you that pressures at very high levels can be extreme. The difference we note between those who thrive under pressure and those who succumb to it once again becomes a matter of consciousness. Those who know the click of the perfect drive, the swish of "nothing but net" as they drain the three-point shot, the applause of the audience that is the exclamation point for their excellence in the moment—they are the ones who know the gift of timing at its most eloquent and immediate expression. It is no less than Mark Anthony felt as he read Caesar's will to the masses or Augustus' sense of satisfaction as he unified the disparate forces of Rome, settled civil strife, and left his legacy for an empire. They are no more than our personal awareness of a woman who has designed a better computer program for her company or a father who has taught his son a sense of values in his life.

Timing can be instantaneous or gradual. It can dazzle in the brilliant moment or glow slowly over the graduation of time to be as durable as gold. Like the precisely attuned gifts of intuition and GUT feel that are so strongly interactive with it, a perfected sense of timing is best gauged when some one is able to evaluate their own position in relation to it.

The Best of Times. The Worst of Times. Pick the Top Three.

To begin this brief section, we invite you to scan your personal data banks and remember six different occasions that you feel best marked your sense of timing. *First pick three occasions in your life when your timing was flawless.* Everyone has good timing at something, or even during certain periods of their lives when everything just seemed to go right. Tap into those memories and pick three of the best.

After you write down any of the magic moments in your life, those occasions when your timing seemed flawless, we ask you to note the circumstances surrounding them. Were you engaged in something you absolutely loved to do? Were you in the flow of your integrity of intention when you did so? Was your good timing spontaneous or related to the flow of consciousness that comes in a performance or a sport? Or was it the result of a gradual acquisition of skill? Was simple dumb luck involved? If you feel so, what were the circumstances surrounding such good fortune? Did your seemingly uncanny timing come either as a result of something good you had done, or was it a preamble to it? Did it come at the expense of someone else? Did your good timing have a major influence in the outcome of your life from that point, or was it over a less significant issue? What was the final result of your good timing? And did your GUT-feel play a part in it?

We place all these questions in your path once again to trigger your thinking. And we encourage you, if you feel so inclined, to make a larger list, and then narrow it down to three occasions; not necessarily occasions that are of the grandest import, but ones in which your timing was the most flawlessly executed. It could be a spontaneous occasion such as the perfect round of golf. Or it could be a career-changing decision. The issues are ones of both quality and clarity.

Second, remember three different occasions when your timing was flawed (or even horrible). As in the explicitly superb examples of good timing, remember at least three occasions when it couldn't have been worse.

Giving equal time to three occasions during which your timing was less than perfect, ask some questions that parallel your perfect timing scenarios. For example, what was your sense of correctness in what you were doing? Were you in the flow of your integrity of purpose? Or were you trying to shortcut to achieve a result? What was at stake when your timing was off? What was the result of that bad timing, and how might you have corrected it beforehand? Was your act intended for a good purpose? If so, whom was it to benefit besides yourself? When you made the decision were you playing a zero-sum game? Or was it to be a win-win equation? Did your ill-timed action result in self-sabotage? How did you feel after you had done it, and what did you do to make it better? How was it finally resolved? And what did you learn from it?

Please understand that in the delusionist's code of conduct, there are no "bad" decisions—*unless* they are born of bad intentions. Sometimes we learn more from our failures than our triumphs. The secret of engaging in any folly is examining the nature of it and learning not to repeat it. That is valuable indeed and, if properly understood, will often hone our timing into something finer.

Once again, we reiterate. If you keep your integrity of intention, if it is aligned with your higher purpose in life, you cannot fail. Time will serve you, as will the ends that it brings. If you are able to place upon it your Love Matrix principles and attune your consciousness to the flow of joy in what you are doing, the ebbs and flows of timing will become your willing accomplices. When you pursue with both enthusiasm and discipline those dreams you hold closely to your heart, timing will become so much a part of your psychic force, your cosmic muscle memory, that your success will be assured. It is at these pivotal moments when you can recognize fear for the emissary of danger that it is. Embrace it as something that is apart from you, and look for the warning signs that it brings you.

Some ways to make it better.

By now, there are certain things we can say that apply universally to one's mastery of time and timing. One sentiment we hope we've been able to convey is that no one's timing is perfect all the time. We all have occasions, even runs of them, when every moment sees our choices flowing in a waltz of synchronicity, when all our timing is perfect. And yet there are those times when even our slightest movement swims against the current of events. No one is immune to such miscalculations. In truth, practically every event in the history of the Western world as we know it has turned upon calculations of timing that have seemed either divinely guided or catastrophically ill-advised. To illustrate, we detailed the events surrounding the rise and fall of Julius Caesar and the tumultuous ten-year period of Roman history that followed it.

What flowed out of it most assuredly was the understanding that timing is a gift that most often rewards the dedicated soul. He who keeps his sense of purpose will see his intentions rewarded, provided he is willing to allow the unfolding of events that will reward his initiatives. In a way, this flies in the face of the *Carpe Diem!* (Seize the day) force of circumstance, molders of destiny who so often grab history's headlines. When we take the time to examine the core of events, we often find that it is not the Napoleons and Rommels who write the final chapters of a period. Rather, it is the Talleyrands and the Churchills, the Gandhis and the Mandelas—those who are willing to take the long, patient paths to completion—who lay the issues of men and nations to rest.

We also made careful note of the fact that timing often becomes a casualty to the Fear factor. And the reason so many pivotal events in history are studies in folly rests with the belief that all aspects of human affairs are a zero-sum game. This was almost always true in ancient and medieval societies and even those of the pre-millennium Cold War. In the atmosphere of international harmony and global economic interdependence of the new millennium, cooperation is not only the preferred course of action, but may very well be essential to our survival as a planet. So, the win-win scenario may no longer be an option, but a necessity.

In our emphasis on timing, we have stressed the importance of the unconscious ease, the flow that is born out of dedication to a sport, art, skill or performance. So practiced is the dancer, so disciplined the runner, so finely tuned the virtuoso violinist or the cunning cricket batsman that their timing is a matter of mastery for us both to admire and emulate. They fall into the flow of their consciousness, and their mind-body-spirit connection. Virtually, they are out of their minds. And it is that very state of oneness with their endeavor that raises them above the level of merely winning or losing. It is only when the fear of gain or loss—the expectation of it—enters the awareness that losing even becomes a factor.

World-class athletes practice the same gifts of timing that and other masterful performers can be utilized by us whenever the occasion presents itself. And we can do so by putting into play the same skills on a daily basis. All it requires is a dash of discipline, a touch of courage, and an unbridled, passionate love of whatever you're undertaking. Begin with these requisites in place, and the rest is only a matter of time. Meanwhile, here are some other ways of refining your sense of timing:

1) Use the cosmic telephone. How many times have we all thought of someone only to have them call us within a matter of moments? And conversely: How many times have we called someone who was thinking about us at the very moment of our call? Even more pointedly, we have just gotten in touch with someone we know, only to find out that they desperately need our help. Or perhaps we spontaneously resume contact with a business associate who was just thinking about setting a project or assignment that fits our profile perfectly. Often, when such things occur in our lives, we are responding to the cues the universe has set for us through the cosmic grapevine that Carl Gustav Jung referred to as the *numinosm.*

This ties-in directly to our examination of GUT feel. And one thing we are all well served to learn about this delusionist's doctrine is the eminent connectability of everything. Rest assured, there are no accidents in this universe of ours. We are tied together for every grand purpose imaginable in the magnificent design of life. All we need do is feel it, heed it, and sense the energy as it flows to us. Nevertheless, it is most important that we do so in a timely fashion.

2) Find Your Chi. Chi is a Zen Buddhist term for your unseen energy center, your spiritual essence. It is most often articulated to us in the West in the form of a martial art—Tai Chi Kwan—that emphasizes a philosophy of universal balance and non-force as its exclusive form of expression. By going through a series of pacific movements, the Tai Chi student (and we are all students) is able to gather in the energies of heaven and earth and bring them into the self, where one can feel their currents, their ebbs and flows, their subtle shifts of emphasis. In going through the specific disciplines of Tai Chi Kwan, one's sense of rapport with the energies surrounding us becomes unreflected and yet inexplicably superb. The mind factors into the equation only incidentally, and only in its rightful place in the flow of movements. This kind of belief system is fodder for the urgent-agenda, instant-gratification Western mentality. And yet we make particular note of our personal experiences here to emphasize that one is actually able to come into contact with one's "ball of Chi" in a very substantive way.

Musicians, dancers, figure skaters, professional baseball players, and even NFL quarterbacks who have practiced Tai Chi claim better balance, smoother movements, a higher performance, and an even keener sense of the dynamics of scoring. What seems to be the entire nation of Taiwan looks to it as a customary form of morning activity as a means of tuning-in to their day. And Asian-based business groups in America who have taken up Tai Chi Kwan during break activities claim better productivity, improved company morale and fewer mistakes on the job.

Of course, the depth of your contact with your Chi will be directly proportionate to the degree of discipline you are willing to put in. And you may interpret Chi in purely symbolic terms and still achieve similar improvements in both timing and congruent uses of time. Such activities as yoga, transcendental meditation (TM) or simply stilling your thoughts for prolonged periods of time to let the energies of Universal Truth flow to you all work toward achieving the same superb sensory outcome— enhanced awareness of exactly when is the appropriate time to crack the shackles of limitation. What understanding Chi accomplishes for you is the ability to feel energy as a physical presence and bring its tides of time into your self. Then it becomes an element of living in the moment and realizing that the divinity of all timing resides in this.

3) Live in the moment. No advice in this doctrine or any other could be better given. It is at the core of the Buddhist faith, and yet no other belief system denies it. It involves a sublime kind of concentration on current activity in a way that glorifies both the moment as well as its participants.

This kind of focus precludes sidebars and extrinsic activity that take us away from our intended instants. When one is eating, for example, one is so completely at one with the food, its sources, the energy of its nourishment, that one can feel it, sense its every nuance. When one is in a relationship—whether it is one of intense personal love or demanding professional performance—one devotes unimpeded awareness *and positive energy* to that relationship. It is the same with basking in the light of a new dawn, watching the solitary flight of a bird, or picking a winning value stock. Absorption, dedication, commitment, intention, completion, fulfillment—all Love Matrix energies locked into the heart of the moment and permitted the fullness of time are certain to be realized. If you pursue these kinds of engagement with that sense of unity, whether you engage in the undertaking once or ten thousand times, you will be completed. To be sure, they should be accompanied by an intention to do good works. But your own pleasure and prosperity may also be included among them, provided they are not part of the zero-sum equation.

This includes competition in which the only true winning is achieving a sense of flow. Scoreboard tallies become incidental to such moments.

4) Learn and practice a sport or skill. As we have already illustrated extensively in our section on muscle memory and its role in the flow of excellence, a competition sport of any kind is the ideal training forum for refining one's sense of timing. We add to that list games of skill such as billiards, bridge, and chess, if for no other reason than the mental precision that is required in picking the perfect time to make one's moves—when to finesse, when to attack, when to maneuver. Competition hones our wits, to be sure, as long as we're able to remember that the game we play is just a game. It is not the unfolding of history or our personal *sine qua non.* Every movement we make in perfecting our skill, in tuning-in to our sense of flow, can be applied to the greater issues of life. By perfecting what we do and by giving every effort the greatest joy—by *en-joying* it—we can always win at our intention. Only fear can pollute our equation of exquisite timing—and yet even fear can be an aid to us, if we learn to time its arrival and use it against itself.

5) Fly into the face of your fear. By now, we should begin to understand that fear is an energy form of our own creation. As such, it is the seminal impostor; that is, when it's coming from us. When it makes its entry from outside of us, such as that which is generated by a mob (and therefore outside our ability to control), then it becomes our helpmate in a time of peril. The defining moment for us comes in our ability to differentiate between fear that may be founded and that which is generated through our own blurred perceptions of harm.

In such moments of indecision, it's best to remember that *fear is only justified if it is accompanied by a genuine potential for harm.* Physical harm—such as being in the path of a hurricane, an oncoming truck, or an enemy army of occupation—is fear that is entirely justified. Fear from such overwhelming extrinsic forces are best given over to our innate early warning system, our instincts for survival, and responded to preemptively—generally in the form of a quick, deliberate flight to safety.

Risk-fear, such as a fear of financial loss over a faulty investment decision, a change in career, or a drive through bad weather, is what might be called a *choice fear.* In these instances, make all your evaluations, use your intuition, and rely on your GUT feel.

If your initial GUT feel is good, then follow it quickly, and your timing will usually reward you. But you should always weigh the options, and remember: information is preparation.

Then there is the fear that comes from within, the most terrifying kind—the fear of rejection, the fear of failure, the fear of humiliation especially in the peer group dynamic. When you confront this kind of fear consider the source; then weigh the genuine potential for harm. In truth, other than the potential battering to your ego, there is none. In such times, let your focus, your intention, and your sense of joy take over. And realize that these are the moments of your greatest potentials for achievement and recognition. You'll also be able to recognize other opportune moments as well—such as relentless and life-changing trends.

This requires a unique understanding that there are forces at work in our daily doings that are so omnipresent that they become invisible. We disregard them, and we shouldn't. In their way, they have more impact on our timing than any other influence in our lives. They are crowds. And you cannot escape them any more then you can ignore them.

Some Additional Insights About Timing And the Madness of Crowds.

The gift of timing does not always belong to the swift or the fortunate among us. It belongs more readily to those who are willing to be aware. It is always important to recognize that there are elements outside our control—waves of momentum, movements of imponderable force, and the pandemics of madness—that we can neither prevent nor control. It is possible, however, to anticipate them and to recognize both their purposes and their source.

First of all, we begin by offering the theory that crowds are set in place to create extremes, either of love and celebration of spirit, or of fear and the violent emotions that can come from it.

Niccolo Machiavelli wrote in *The Prince* that the mob is a creation all its own and will always be manipulated either by appearance or result. He also went on to observe that in effect, the world is a mob. And though we hold a slightly higher opinion than Machiavelli of our global village, we do agree on one issue: The world is moved by appearance. It is also most dramatically affected by the group dynamic in all its presentations.

So what has all this to do with timing? Everything. Because the mind of the mass forms the intangibles of movement that we as individuals must deal with every day of our lives. And understanding them requires a code of conduct that we are all better served to learn from and profit by. With that in mind, we have observed that mass gatherings of human beings fall into four categories. We ask you to make careful note of all four of these types of crowds because, if you're going to perfect your sense of timing, you would do well to recognize the nature of all things in which your timing is a crucial factor:

Category 1 Crowds) Organized assemblies set in place for the preservation of order. These include armies, organized labor, legislative bodies, police forces and various government organizations. Usually, they are governed by strict codes of behavior and can be determined as generally predictable. In terms of Category 1 crowds such as the government and the military, you may deal with them in one of three ways: If you are actually going to be a part of them, it is best to remember that your success among them is born of a conformity to standards. Category 1 crowds are intent upon order and will brook no exceptions to their concepts of order. If one is not a part of them, the best recommendation for the individual in casual contact with them to become invisible. Armies are best avoided entirely. So are government bureaucracies. By their nature, these bodies are required to dehumanize everyone who falls under their influence. They are put in place for the efficient perpetuation of that group's welfare. And though they view themselves as beneficial, individuals who oppose them either get incidentally crushed by their obsessions with uniformity or singled out for elimination.

Category 2 Crowds) Mass gatherings put in place for a distinct occasion. This includes rock concerts, sporting events, church congregations, political demonstrations, theatre crowds, cocktail parties, and lynch mobs. These gatherings will both reflect and amplify the energy of their original intent and will only be predictable in direct proportion to the leadership that directs it. If there is no leadership or focus of energy, the crowd will be volatile in direct proportion to the absence of a central figure. In this form, it often becomes a challenge to both order and common sense.

Although nothing can be more uplifting than the responsive crowd dynamic created by a night at the symphony or a gathering to hear an inspirational speaker, any emotionally charged crowd is combustible. Especially when a group in protest for example senses that its objectives are to be opposed, a Category 2 crowd can become ferocious. And no force of energy can be deadlier than a mass demonstration where a revolution-minded Category 2 Crowd comes into direct confrontation with a Category 1 Crowd whose sole purpose is to maintain the status quo. Since the intention of one side is to disrupt order and the other to preserve it at all costs, any contact between them can spark an explosive synergy that is the square root of violence itself. One only has to look at the slaughter of students and Tienamin Square in Beijing in 1989 or the street riots during the 1968 Democratic National Convention in Chicago to gauge the degrees of violence that such emotional collision courses can create.

We point this out to note again that an intelligent anticipation of Category 2 crowd moods and movements is essential to your well being and occasionally even to your survival.

A Category 3 crowd amounts to what is known as the Occasional Crowd. This crowd is governed by the herd mentality and is only brought together for purposes of grazing and migration. As such, it is intent merely upon getting from one place to another. Such gatherings as mall crowds, airport crowds, and commuter traffic are only important to you in that knowing peak flow times can save you time, peace of mind, and a great deal of stress. In such instances, the true delusionist always knows when to beat traffic either by leaving for work at least an hour early or by working later until the flows of such constant masses have abated. Additionally, there are always contrarian means of travel through secret routes that every true delusionist knows. And anyone who's traveled will not only be able to spot them but also make use of them.

There is also another trick that all masters of delusion have learned when it comes to dealing with the herd: Keep your sense of humor, and don't take it personally. When caught in a herd with no feasible means of escape, find other productive ways of making use of your time.

(**Note::** It is important to remark here that Category 1, 2, and 3 Crowds are often best dealt with by some intelligent flak-zapping. Once applied with skill, zapping flak is all a matter of timing; timing laced with discretion. That means knowing when to transmit good will, love, and healing, and when to make an exit, and just get out of harm's way.)

Finally, we come to the firestorm of the mental network, the *Category 4 crowd—the Hidden Mob.* This is the crowd we overlook, the one we take for granted. The Internet, the floors of the Chicago Board of trade and the New York Stock Exchange—these comprise the "electronic herd" that Thomas L. Friedman so astutely identified in *The Lexus and the Olive Tree,* his book about the future of the global marketplace. These are the mercurial mobs, intelligent beyond measure, yet driven almost entirely by greed, panic, acquisition momentum and the gods of the moment. Armed with weights and measures and mixed perceptions of what the market should be, they claim to be seers into distant futures and yet their emotional instability can become an insidious link to chaos. Every sign in the road marks a crisis. And "research" and facts are only tools to turn the screws on incredible shifts in mood.

This is not a new phenomenon. It has been the nature of this beast since the beginnings of the financial and commercial marketplace. And yet its comings and goings remain a mystery to most of us, when in truth it shouldn't be.

In his sociological cult classic entitled *Extraordinary Popular Delusions and the Madness of Crowds,* author Charles Mackay, LL.D. made the following observation:

> In reading the history of nations, we find that, like individuals, they have
> their whims and their peculiarities; their seasons of excitement and

recklessness, when they care not what they do. We find that whole communities suddenly fix their minds upon one object and go mad in its pursuit...[13]

Dr. Mackay wrote his original manuscript in 1852 and cited a number of examples of such mass phenomenon as the infamous South Sea Bubble scam in London, alchemy, and even the Crusades of the 11th through 13th centuries. His crowning satire, however, was his accounting of the early 17th-century phenomenon in Europe that came to be known as "Tulip mania." Up to that time tulips, a native flower of Holland, would customarily sell for about 15 florins, or about one-half pound sterling in British coin. By the 1634, however, the craze for tulips became so obsessive that single bulbs sold for hundreds of times their weight in gold. In fact a small weight of tulips, only a few bulbs, would often sell for 5,000 to 6,000 florins or as much as 300 British pounds (a fortune at that time) for a single bulb. Somehow, this mania caught hold in the rest of Europe as well, and for nearly five years, tulipmania swept Europe and continued to maintain its hold in Amsterdam even after the rest of the continent had been cured.

According to record, "tulip mania" and the contagion of delusion surrounding it made several Dutch flower merchants quite wealthy. Those who were able to anticipate the sudden financial bonanza that spread from this mercantile mob frenzy were able to buy-in ahead of the curve, sell out at the peak of the market, and make a fortune. They had mastered their trade, understood the voracious momentum that accompanied it, acknowledged the short life of the bloom of such a singular market phenomenon, and capitalized upon it. In the open marketplace, there is no fault in capitalizing on a trend as long as one recognizes that all but a few trends are temporary.

In today's modern financial markets, "tulipmania" has become the metaphor used to describe the sudden frenzy that accompanied the almost blanket purchase of Internet stocks in 1998 and 1999. That mania, as all manias must, has suddenly redirected its terrible swift force and has become a purge of e-tailers in the year 2000, one that visionary investors long ago anticipated.

Out of the Mackay masterwork also emerged another catch-phrase that stays with us today—*the bubble economy* (named after the infamous South Sea Bubble of the 1680s).

That is the serial adjective that is used to describe the seemingly unstoppable prosperity momentum enjoyed in our financial markets recent adulation of tech stocks, followed by their sudden precipitous fall. As such, references to the "Bubble Economy." are invariably accompanied by a question mark ("Bubble Economy?") because in truth no one knows for certain whether the, "bubble has burst," as some believe, or whether the tide of this Force 4 event brought on by the Internet will propel us into eras of even greater prosperity.

Because it addresses the issue of prosperity and the mentality of *intelligent abundance* that accompanies it, we will cover this last aspect of timing in our Chapter 10, "Money Only Makes You More of Who You Are." We call it *Trend-spotting*. And it arrives in our lives as a by-product of personal clarity that most great prime movers of world market revolutions have in common. In equal measure, they all have one other aspect of timing that remains both inviolate and unchanging: That has to do with long term vision and the ability to sculpt a plan. Once you have set a long-term plan to form around your vision—and you stick to it—your timing in the short term becomes inherently more acute. And no mob influence, no matter how terrifying or alluring, can sway you from it or cause you to doubt its inevitable success.

...Before We Resume.

By now, as you advance in your study of the delusionist doctrine, certain patterns of awareness should be forming for you. One of them certainly should be an awareness of the inextricable interconnection of everything. In this chapter alone, we have been able to see how timing is predicated upon refinements of both one's GUT feel and the mind-body-spirit trinity that forms the flow of right action. We have also seen how timing affects the currents of power and how, inversely, power without intention will become time's casualty. These are all issues we have introduced to you here. And because of the depth and scope of them, we will resume our perspectives of them again in a more sophisticated context in Chapter 9, "Power Play." Understanding the value of both power and timing and the reliance of one upon the other is part of the delusionist's plan to help you refine and fulfill your destiny and become larger than life. This is not a pipe dream but a probability.

Just as we have come to approach a sensible, pragmatic application of unconditional love as a means of putting fear in its place and using fear as a triggering agent in refining the gifts of our Great Universal Truths, we are now ready to face the most terrifying prospect of all, our ability to achieve great things—not just our ability, but our responsibility as well. That is what getting larger than life is all about: taking responsibility for all the things we are truly capable of being.

Chapter 8

Get Larger Than Life

Were I the size of my potential, I could feed the world.

—Anonymous

The game of life is played on a very large board indeed. Yet most of us are intent upon controlling only one small square of it.

It is our most charring paradox that we are self-absorbed without having any sense of self, that we are narcissistic without understanding the true meaning of self love, that we have dreams and yet content ourselves with looking on while someone else plays them out. We want to make a difference, to help chart the course for what R. Buckminster Fuller described as "Spaceship Earth," but we're unwilling to undergo the rigors of becoming either pilot or navigator. Instead, we book second-class passage and hope that someone will take us along for the ride. Rest assured, they will. But be equally clear about this: The destination will be theirs and not our own.

Is it because we are lazy? Or do we suspect that beneath it all, we are ordinary? Indolence is nothing more than the consequence of fear – fearing failure for trying something that might show us our own potential. Teddy Roosevelt once challenged a nation by observing that "It is not failure but low aim that is crime." The question we must constantly ask ourselves is this: Where are we aiming our life up to now? Or are we aiming it at all?

Many of us never attempt anything of value because we never dare to test the hidden peril of that first step. We fear that even our verbalization of it will make us appear absurd. We feel the hot breath of criticism, and we wilt. And yet we ignore the obvious. To be excellent at anything, one must first be willing to be the fool.

French novelist Albert Camus once wrote that "All great thoughts and great deeds have ridiculous beginnings."[14] His apologia, appropriately entitled, "An Absurd Reasoning," serves as a manifesto for those who would dare to take parallax pathways to fulfillment. In truth, every success begins in small measures, with what the Japanese refer to as *kaizan,* little baby steps, and by acknowledging that we all take the path toward greatness by first choosing goodness – by choosing to do good things exceedingly well.

Persistence in pursuit of a cause becomes a cause in itself. And it is not our dreams but our determinations that make us what we become.

Nelson Mandela, one of the most influential political forces of the last fifty years, didn't start out to become president of the newly integrated South Africa. He was a young Bantu student from the Soweto projects of Johannesburg who addressed a great evil called apartheid with all the integrity of opposition he could give it. His focus made him heroic. His willingness to be abjured, to be arrested – to be ready to die for what he believed in – made him someone apart. Mahatma Gandhi describes his own amazement early in his life at seeing his position in the affairs of his nation beginning to swell like that of a brook rising to a river. Yet his own tireless dedication to the cause of racial and religious tolerance could not have seen his impact become less. Please don't misconstrue our examples here. We aren't suggesting that those of you reading this should try and become the next Gandhi, the next Mandela, or even the next Albert Camus. Then again, why shouldn't you? Why shouldn't we all step outside our comfort zone or at least push against the walls of our own limitations?

At least we all owe it to ourselves to strive for excellence in everything we do, to have a passion and pursue it with all our heart. But in order for us to do that, we're going to have to be willing to look at our options a little differently. For that, we offer a set of delusionist's guidelines for getting in touch with your greater self.

At this point, we offer them in two phases: one that encompasses the broader context of our delusionist philosophy; another in the more specific day-to-day applications of what you do in relation to whom you want to be. Please keep in mind that by now, if you've been diligent at all, you should be experiencing the benefit of your Love-Matrix training and are able to use both your GUT feel and your refined sense of timing as tools in learning how to get larger than life. If so, you may look upon this chapter as an opportunity for further development as well as a way to put into practical use much of what you have learned already.

Change-up. Change Down.

Change is the immutable law. And whether we choose to acknowledge it or not, we live in fulfillment of the second oldest philosophical argument in the western world—Heraclitus' Law that, "all is flux."

"Upon those who step into the same rivers, different and ever different waters flow," this Greek philosopher wrote in about 500 BC.[15] A true delusionist, Heraclitus found his arguments ridiculed in his own lifetime and by other philosophers for centuries that followed. But genius is best judged in qualitative terms, and a man is often measured by those who praise him. Eventually, Heraclitus would have found his arguments praised by Plato as being both solid and supportable, a belief shared by the Roman Emperor and philosopher Marcus Aurelius who, over five centuries after Plato, reiterated the belief that, "The universe *is* change."[16]

Change is something we now recognize as a life force—so much so that it has reached what was once referred to in *The Greening of America* as Consciousness 3, a belief commonly accepted in the public mind without direct awareness of its source. We all understand this, and yet so many of us continue to do the same things in life, to follow the same routines, trod the same paths, while somehow expecting something new to take place.

Rest assured that even by staying the same, by doing the same things, by following your mundane daily routines, you are changing. You are stagnating. Muscles atrophy from disuse. Machines corrode when not in motion. Dreams left unpursued will wither and fade from sight. We all know this, and yet we so abhor what we perceive to be change that we do nothing. This is the worst kind of change of all—one that leads us to *entropy*, a deathlike state.

For most of us even to be hit with the challenge to, "get larger than life" is terrifying. Part of this stems from an innate fear of change. In *The Ordeal of Change*, dockside philosopher Eric Hoffer advances the theory that we human beings are so averse to change that we will do anything to avoid it.* He articulates a laundry list of reasons including a fear of the unknown, the fear of failure, and dread of the consequence of doing something out of the ordinary. Hoffer also expanded the paradigm to a broader sociological scale, although we note the underlying reasons were always the same. To no one's surprise, all of the reasons (we choose to call them excuses) had bases in the Fear Matrix.

Rest assured, fear petrifies whomever experiences it; it renders them immobile. We fear change, and yet by the very act of fearing we are changed. Even as you read this, you are changing in some way. You are forming new opinions, making new decisions. Even choosing to do nothing at all is change of a kind. It is called decay. Knowing that change is inevitable is liberating

---

* Although in his later years he became a renown philosopher and best-selling author of such works as *The True Believer*, Eric Hoffer was a stevedore who chose to stay and work on the docks of San Francisco for the remainder of his career.

when you realize that you are always at choice as to what exactly is within your power to alter. So, you can choose to make changes for the better. *Think back upon five times in your life when you chose to make changes for the better,* and for your own peace of mind do not give them all the same weight of dramatic impact. You may select some occasion as trivial as choosing to change your hairstyle or as weighty as changing the course of your career. List those five times and reflect upon three things as you do so: the degree of difficulty surrounding the decision; the ultimate positive impact it made upon you personally; the positive impact it made upon others.

No matter how difficult the decision at the time, if it is made for the betterment of all concerned, if you truly believe that in your heart, then you can trust that the outcome will reward you.

Changes for the better are called progress. Changes that are vain, self-serving, zero-sum or mean-spirited are regressive and will end in no good long-term result. And rest assured that *change for the sake of change is not progress, but merely creates the illusion of progress.* And since there are no neutral thoughts or actions, consider the good result of making change, even if you begin by merely cleaning out your closet (not a bad way to start!).

Now, list ten changes you'd like to make—call them improvements—in your life. They may be small or great in nature and should vary in the degree of difficulty they present to you as well as the impact they might make on you and others in your life. We only ask that you follow the criteria we established earlier that the changes be positive, and that they have an outcome that is a win-win for everyone concerned. By all means, it's okay to have one or two superficial changes on your list, but take heed of the hidden dangers in change for the sake of change. If you truly intend to grow, progress and improve, most of your changes should make you reach, stretch, and pull yourself out of your comfort zone. It's good to feel the uncertain currents of uncharted seas and the tradewinds of new ideas. But in order to do that you have to take some chances.

Remember: *Fear is only justified when there is actual potential for harm.* Unless there are some hurricanes on your horizon, earthquakes beneath your feet, or freight trains about to run you down, the only true danger lies in staying in one place and doing nothing. That other trembling you feel is the temblor of unlimited opportunity to be something you've never been before. Face that challenge and feel yourself breaking out of your shell. Sometimes that requires perishing to all that you have been in order to become something else again. It requires both surrender and sacrifice to the degree that you must lose part of what you have in order to make way for what you desire.

It is scrubbing out your vase and cleansing the receptacle for the new self that will grow from it.

Be Willing to Die.

When we alluded to this quality shared in common by all those great souls who were willing to go to the limit to virtually become larger than life, the metaphor probably seemed extreme. Perhaps it seems less so now, because it implies a devotion to go the limit, to die unto oneself. This does not require that you fall on your sword or go through some drastic personal crucifixion in which there is nothing left but shards of your former self. It does mean a commitment to the core of one's integrity—to the one and two-word paragon that comprises your soul's contract in this lifetime. And it does mean making some changes—at times, major ones.

To every personality construct there are labors that need to be laid to rest and self-images that need to be slaughtered. These are the little deaths to the personality ego whose only peril lies in the terror we feel when approaching the white-hot fire of our dreams.

If you are working in a job you hate, and the capital of your destined nation is in another profession, you cannot merely wish for the change to take place. You have to work toward that end—even at the expense of your own comfort, physical stamina, and financial stasis. You have to pay the price, undertake the schooling, put in the work, risk the pinpricks of pain and chagrin that come with the clumsy process of learning. It is risking to appear the fool while learning to become a prince.

Mozart notwithstanding, no musical prodigy ever played the perfect song from the moment he touched the keys. A thousand sour notes are always struck while finding the flawless strain. No one ever parred a golf course on the first round of their lives; myriad hooks and slices and shanks led to the epic moment. How many times has the skater fallen on the way to her perfect 6.0? And the revolutionary computer program was born through an infinity of crashes.

Rest assured, if you truly want to live larger than life, you will have to die a thousand times along the way. You have to be willing to try and fail, and then to try again. Do it once, and the second attempt will come as second nature, and you will see the light of your own potential grow brighter with each pass. Lives of quiet desperation, though often led, are usually unnecessary. We are all at choice to constantly renew that spark within us. And once we do we'll realize that every little death brings with it another resurrection.

Be Willing to Be Born Again.

Just as Eric Hoffer was able to articulate that our human nature so abhors change that we will do anything to avoid it, we propose a counterpoint: *Containment eventually smothers the organism.* And we only need witness the process of birth in any vertebrate to behold confirmation of it.

Any creature that is egg born dwells for a brief time in the perfectly self-contained environment. It nourishes itself in the climatic perfection of its shell and the protein of the fluids inside it, until eventually it becomes the proteins it has consumed and so fully develops that it must burst out of that shell in order to survive. For illustration of this, watch a baby bird or reptile as it pecks and chews its way out of its egg; note the desperate sense of liberation it displays, the vulnerability of its discovery of a new life. The same principal applies to any mammalian fetus, and most strikingly to that of the creature *Homo sapiens*. The human embryo spends approximately nine months in a divinely designed ecosphere known as the womb, growing all the while into the perfectly developed fetus. Finally, in such time as the host mother can no longer contain it, the fetus must burst free from that ideal environment and breathe the air of a new life. If it does not do so, it will perish.

That instinct is cellular and carries over into the adult human being. We have mentioned earlier the scientific axiom that the cells of our bodies completely renew themselves about every thirty days. So we maintain that our instincts for renewal—for being reborn—are far stronger than the habits of conformity and the safety of sameness. So our proclivities to grow and develop, literally to be renewed, are cellular in fact, and as such are the more relentless of the two urges.

There are scientific tests in legion to show that confinement enforced upon so-called lower life forms causes severe depression, immuno-deficiency, and early death. We know what incarceration, especially solitary confinement, does to human prisoners, and yet such limitation does not have to be evidently dramatic or incessantly oppressive to be felt.

In the now infamous 1994 "Biosphere" project, eight people including two couples contracted to spend an extended period of time, about 30 months, in what was carefully designed to be a perfectly contained geodesic terrarium environment. Atmospheric pressures and temperature levels would be maintained at ideal levels. All plant life, water and foodstuffs available to sustain them were stored inside the compound, and they would be able to grow certain fruits, vegetables and crops both to test the dome environment and to gauge their ability to flourish within it over a protracted period of time.

Within ten months, the Biosphere experiment was called off due to what were purportedly logistical snafus and technical glitches. Insiders reported that there were other forces at work, not the least of which was an oppressive sense of propinquity, or the stress of living in close quarters, that the inhabitants of the Biosphere collectively experienced. Considerable feelings of claustrophobia and a general inability to cope with their circumstances were also said to have plagued these modern inner space cadets, not to mention a few personality conflicts.

We accept these declarations of frustration and add some observations of our own. The Biosphere experiment failed in part because it was the attempt of some very accomplished people to get smaller than life, virtually to reduce and contain the natural flows of their own behavior. Millions of us, in our way, live in "Biospheres" of our own creation. We stifle our movements and clamp down on our ambitions in order to fit into a more orderly, contained universe that we have set nicely down for ourselves. We become "Truman" in *The Truman Show,* but without the eyes or the interest of the world upon us. We find safe havens in sameness when our very cells, constantly restoring themselves, are crying out to be free.

We invite you to become born again. The term "born again" often carries with it a fundamentalist religious connotation. That's not all bad, because we note in the reborn religious proselyte a kind of personal zeal and contagious enthusiasm that we should all feel about every aspect of our lives. Spiritual faith, tempered with a little tolerance, can be a good beginning, but there is so much more to being reborn than we even consciously imagine. Lovers often speak of being born again in their newfound romantic involvements, and people with new careers in professional dreams finally realized often speak of having found a "new life" vis a vis their improved professional associations. Almost weekly, we see people in the fields of entertainment, sports, and politics get born again, their careers renewed, their momentum for achievement regained.

We have seen actor John Travolta's career, for example, resurrected to the extent that he is now a billion dollar box office legend. Heismann Trophy running back Marcus Allen was described as "buried" on the bench with the Los Angeles Raiders, only to be "reborn" in an NFL Hall of Fame career at the Kansas City Chiefs. British Prime Minister Winston Churchill saw his own career in politics "written off as dead" by the British press only to become one of the fifty most influential figures of the last millennium. We use these examples because they are dramatic, and show us at any level that perseverance is the secret of any success.

We also note that these personal rebirths did not come, at some point, without some derring-do, or without some constant focus upon one's dreams. But one does not have to be a world figure to accomplish such things.

Someone somewhere has to be willing to step outside the safe designs of their life and grow again. After a fashion, they have to blast their way out of their personal Biospheres. Although we understand the psychology of remorse that often accompanies such acts, especially at a sociological level, personal change is often not as difficult as it might seem because for most of us it will happen sooner or later in our lives. The act of doing so only becomes pathetic when the decision is made later in one's life—often too late. Then again, we must ask the question. When is it ever too late? Renewing oneself does not necessarily have to be an act of profound magnitude. We can be reborn in little ways and, in so doing, remember that it is by those small steps that we progress most emphatically.

A woman of our acquaintance, a film company comptroller during her day job, has a remarkable way of getting reborn every year on her birthday. On her 31st birthday, she announced she was leaving the production studio early that day to celebrate her anniversary by going bungee jumping. When we expressed our surprise and delight at her show of adventurism, she blithely observed that she had celebrated her 30th birthday the year before by skydiving, and her 29th by scuba diving off the Great Barrier Reef in Australia. In fact, she told us she had undertaken this kind of intrepid self-renewal by learning a new skill every year since her 21st birthday. Since that momentous occasion, she had done everything from skiing in Chamonix to becoming an Aikido master, and would do so every year on her birthday until she left this plane of existence. She was not an especially striking personality or what one would think of as dynamic, but she had taken it upon herself to become a Renaissance woman, and in so doing found a way to become larger than life. Rest assured, we would never perceive her in quite the same way again.

Growth is a force of Nature that cannot be denied without eventual erosion of the entity in denial. Containment spawns atrophy. If you doubt that for a moment, we encourage you to recall the last time you left a plant too long in its original pot or box. After a time, you realized that the plant was—by its very nature—growing roots out of its planter. At some point you had to realize that you either had to get the plant a larger pot or there was a very good chance this living entity would become depressed, wilt and die. To the extent of our needs to grow, we are no different than our plants—with one major exception: we have free will. We can make the necessary choices to step outside our box. Or even better—to be bigger than our box.

Become Bigger than Your Box.

Many leading motivational consultants define problem-solving behavior as "thinking outside of the box." In fact, thinking outside of the box has become the universal rallying cry to the creative nature in all of us. But in its way it limits us as well, because though thinking outside your box is a positive first step, it still leaves us physically and situationally inside the box. The implication is both pointed and simple. "The Box" defines the life we have created and the world that we control. It also determines the set of conditions that control us, and oftentimes the only way we can become bigger than our box is when we are confronted by the challenges that life hands us.

Success coach Tony Robbins refers to the circle analogy (taught him by another counselor) and uses it to illustrate the challenges presented us. By drawing a simple circle on a piece of paper, we are symbolically able to define everything in that circle as our sphere of influence—that which we contain, control, and hold mastery over. It is, in other words, our comfort zone. Any problems presented us are shown as a dot outside us, an extrinsic force put outside the perimeters of our circle and therefore beyond our comfort zone. According to this personal enhancement design, those dots represent opportunities, because the only way to deal with them is to expand our circle and bring them into our sphere of influence, expertise and power. By rising to meet the challenge, we cause our circle to grow and increase both our grasp of life and our sphere of influence. This is another way of saying that all problems (or challenges) that we meet and master offer us our best opportunities for growth.

Whether we speak in parables of circle or box, the defining moment for us comes in our willingness to deal with the challenges set before us, and in our ability to recognize them as a chance to get larger than life. Failure to deal with them makes us smaller than life and diminishes us in all the ways that matter. We stay inside our box, and we begin to die.

Our mind tells we are defending ourselves, while our heart is aching to fly free. If we listen to our hearts, all of us—without exception—will be at peace with the truth that challenges are set in our path to make us better, stronger, and wiser. Like the tree or plant, we were meant to grow. We were meant to be larger than life.

Be the Light.

Some people come into your day and transform it on the spot. They greet others at the core of who they are, relate to them, bring everyone they contact into a sense of personal validation, and implant some glow of indelible positivity into the moment. It is a piece of the sun that shines in the room even after they've left it. It doesn't happen often, but when such moments occur, you never quite forget them. They "radiate." They're "luminous." They are very special individuals who seem to carry purpose around them like an aura. They may be someone famous or someone you've never seen before, but they all have one quality in common: They have got "the magic."

Occasionally we witness this kind of incandescence at a celebrity event, and as such it is usually manufactured—the illusion of presence in the presence of illusion. But more often than not, like the fantasies they manufacture, the magical auras we behold are those of energetic moments and the extensions of our own deep desires. Nevertheless, we watch them intently because they serve a purpose: They show us the potential of possible worlds.

Almost all of us spend a large portion of our media experience in search of the light as it shines through others. Academy Awards, Grammies, Super Bowls, Olympics, star-studded concerts, coronations of kings and queens, royal weddings and inaugurations of presidents—all these occasions capture our close attention because they reflect a radiance we suspect in ourselves, they speak to our proudest moments, and they show us the best that we can be.

That is the ultimate allure of mind candy, because for a few minutes we see ourselves somewhere in the mix. We even become part of them ourselves. We slip into a realm that is larger than life and feel the breath of transformation upon us, the urge to be something better. We witness them, relate to them, and if only for an instant, believe we have it in ourselves to be this way as well.

We have news for you: you can be in this moment. In your present circumstance, whatever it is, you too can be the light. You can radiate positivity and give to others the gift that comes at no cost to you other than your effort to relate in a positive way to them.

Begin by looking for that child in others and recognize their beginnings. They, like you, were born in the light of their highest potential. All you need do is readdress it, and ask yourself the question: What can I do to bring the light to this situation? How can I make it better or brighter?

It doesn't have to be some monumental achievement, but it does take a little cosmic logic on your part. First, be aware that we are, to our marrow, heliotropic. We all lean toward the sun. We are all heaven-bound. Even in our most dismissive moments, every one of us is looking for the light. And the best way we can find it is to bring it in ourselves.

Begin by taking your focus off yourself and placing it upon others. Reach out to them. Relate to them. Grasp that elusive moment that might bring a ray of joy into their day. It can be a simple gesture, a simple expression of interest, or a brief act of grace that will enlighten them in their awareness of what matters. It might be a smile, a pleasant comment, or an offer of assistance at a key moment in an encounter. You might want to acknowledge someone for an act performed on your behalf, or simply show them the light of their own potential.

In our personal experience, we each have our own system of being the light for others. Paul's method comes in the simple act of carrying a pocketful of buttons that contain the slogan "I Make a Difference." As simplistic as it sounds, it never fails to make a positive impact on the recipient and crack even the hardest shell of resistance. On one occasion, Paul remembers giving the button to a concierge in a New York hotel who had labored tirelessly to acquire him an extremely precious pair of theatre tickets. Along with a generous gratuity for his efforts, Paul pinned the button on him, and was perhaps a little surprised that the gesture actually brought the man to tears.

"No one has ever done that for me before," the concierge confided. "Money can't buy the kind of feeling you get from something like this."

Precisely. Even in a city as tough as the Big Apple, we can draw down the sunshine.

Robert has his own formula for reaching out to others called *The Second Smile Phenomenon*. It's his favorite means of zapping the flak, and it happens in one of two ways. The first is to smile at the people you see, wherever they are, whatever they're doing. It doesn't have to be assumptive or invasive; it just has to be pleasant, a sincere effort to share the joy that is in you. When you do, it is virtually impossible for anyone else to ignore this extension of humanity—even if it is one of resistance, of paranoia, or of facial muscles that distort in an attempt not to respond in kind. In an overwhelming number of instances, the person to whom the smile has been extended will smile back. And it is a constant source of amazement for us to find that the man or woman with the most soured, self-absorbed expression or agonized scowl will, upon receiving our smile, blossom into a grin of such radiance that they become like a flower opening to the dawn.

The second kind of smile in the second-smile phenomenon is a bit more complex, but promises an even more durable degree of impact. That comes with encounters in which you are able to get to know someone— whether it is a counter clerk or your orthopedic surgeon—and tap into the light that shines in them. It requires for a brief time that you be a listener rather than a talker. Rather than try to impress someone with who you are, be impressed with who they are. Listen to how they speak. Learn about their dreams. Then nourish them either with an encouraging word or an observation that will empower them in whatever it is they're seeking to do. Leave them smiling about who they are and the bond of humanity you share. Then see if that smile awaits you the next time that you see them. Usually, you'll find that it does, and that you have made a difference in how that person sees his or her universe. By beholding the light in them, you have shown your own. That is the second smile, the one that makes another's life a little brighter for your having been in it.

That kind of light can spread more broadly and in even greater depth to those with whom you are involved more closely on a day-to-day basis. In those cases your gift of humanity, caring, and personal empowerment can be given as effortlessly yet with as much sincerity as a smile. And yet the positive influence you exert can last for the rest of their lives, and can make them feel their own potential to become a part of life's greater games. That is flak zapping at its most effective—simple, seamless, and always at the level of the higher self.

In all of these instances, we are all blessed with the additional opportunity to learn about the people in our lives, to tap into their dreams and help them achieve them. That does not imply the need to meddle in their affairs. What it does mean is that we are supportive of their aspirations and their desires to accomplish new things. Whether it is a professional contact, a constructive insight, or a simple act of encouragement, we have shown them that we care enough about them to want them to succeed, to thrive, to be fulfilled.

If, in your profession, you are in a position of power, lead by example, never belittle others (especially in front of their peers), and always be willing to reveal the positive pathways to solutions.

If you're in a support role in your job, your social activity, or your team function, then truly be supportive. Strive for excellence to such a degree that the truth of your achievement cannot be ignored. And trust in your angels enough to know that accomplishment of a pure and honest labor is a covenant with success. Give it everything you have in terms of work ethic, encouragement, and personal loyalty. Remember that loyalty is the measure of who you are even more than what you accomplish.

Whatever you do, don't take your bright light into dark, hostile places unless you are absolutely certain of your transformational powers. Often in our attempts to relate to others, we find ourselves having allowed them to drag us over into their personal imbroglios, up to their coffee bar conspiracies, or down into their scenarios of gossip, complaint and conniving. Be aware that even your unspoken presence in such a situation implies both complicity and accord. To be sure, there will be those times when you have the opportunity to uplift a situation by encouraging others to find the goodness in their concerns. However reluctantly, they might join you in a chorus of praise and reconciliation, and you will enjoy the bonus of letting people know you stand in your own truth. But you can also expect some measure of resentment if you do. And playing the peacemaker in a hostile environment only serves if you entirely comprehend the risk involved.

Under those circumstances, you have to rely on your GUT feel to determine whether the danger offers genuine potential for harm. And be willing to cut your losses and move quickly out of harm's way when such dangers are real. In all instances, to be sure, you may apply your Love Matrix and Master Class skills in dealing with others. But sometimes getting larger than life is a matter of being discreet. Knowing when to stay out of someone else's nasty business not only conserves your light, it also enables you to have more of it to put to use at those times when your shining can truly do some good.

Remember that Jesus, as great a master and teacher as he was, admonished us to "cast not your pearls before swine, lest they trample them under their feet, and turn again and rend you." *(Matthew 7:6.)*

Rest assured, it is a part of life's merciless certainties that trouble, in some form, will find you soon enough. When it does, we humbly submit a possible solution for that as well.

Be the Eye of the Hurricane.

On this unstable plane of existence we call life, there are times when madness is as inevitable as it is pandemic. It is, however, only contagious if you let yourself get caught up in the storm. In the human metaphor, storms of controversy come on waves of personal emotion, and part of the lesson of becoming larger than life is learning the skill of never becoming part of it yourself.

Whether it is a corporate power play, a political squabble, a dispute between neighbors, or a family calamity, the best course of action to take at the outset is to take no action at all.* Too often, we rush into the fray of

---

* The obvious exception is any situation that involves a life and death personal emergency, in which case swift and decisive measures need to be taken.

unwelcome moments only to be tarred by them, when it is often best to wait them out.

There is no question that haste is the mother of all folly, and the worst thing anyone can do in times of crisis is to overreact. And yet that is exactly what people who are ordinarily wise often succumb to doing.

For the true delusionist, we offer this contrarian point of view: The more violent the storm around you, the more calm you should become.

One constant of human energy is that it always seeks redemption. Even at the nadir of its violence, it swirls toward reconciliation. Even if you are being directly attacked, do not retaliate. Instead, be calm, be still and wait, for time will relentlessly labor to heal itself.

If we convey no other message in this book, let it be this: that in the bold new universe we propose, neither attack nor defense are ingredients for survival. In fact, they assure us all of a string of iron conflicts and the perpetuation of loss.

All conflicts and all crises have their roots in the Fear Matrix. And the only way to overcome them, at least in the beginning, is to do absolutely nothing at all. What you most often find is that the worst case scenarios in a conflict seldom get played out. Certainly when they do, it is best not to become a partisan in them.

Instead, sit in the Silence. Calm your mind. And once you have stilled your thoughts, place these four considerations before you: *1) How did it happen? 2) What is the best of all possible outcomes that can be achieved? 3) What is in my power to do to bring it to its highest potential? 4) Let me be sure that I let go of my attachment to the outcome.*

Give the situation time. Let it incubate—an hour or a month—until it reaches its climax and begins by the force of natural law to clear itself out. Then simply put the question to all parties by offering this healing entreaty: What can I do to help?

A proposal of help, sincerely put, almost always zaps the flak. It is an irresistible force. Without pressing upon the nerve centers of the issue in conflict, it is an assumption of personal power, a revelation of probable solutions and, above all else, an answered prayer. Even the most jaded partisan will find it difficult to resist your offer. And you will have accomplished all positive outcomes by never getting involved in the first place.

You will have solutions of your own, of course, but it's best not to rush in to offer them. Rather, it is better to ask compassionate, intelligent questions—the kinds that can guide others to the right solutions on their own. That way, they will feel some sense of authorship and will more readily embrace them. You will have accomplished both resolution and result, and will have done so without drawing undue attention to yourself. You will again have helped empower others. And anytime you can do that, you are growing larger than life indeed.

It is here that we again stress the most emphatic law of timing. Let the world unfold before you. Let it have its little say before you have your own. Once the crash and run of negativity plays itself out, as it is in its character to do, it will leave the solutions in your charge. When they finally find their home in what you've become during the wait. Remember, the best actions to take are those that mend and repair. The wisest words are those of healing that are always spoken last; they're best remembered and seldom held in contempt.

Don't let the World Get in Your Way.

It's true, as Socrates said, that, "The unexamined life is not worth living."[17] By the same token, an overexamined life might well be the next worst thing. Scraping around in the dark corners of our past inevitably conjures those little demons of denial that continue to cause us pain and stunt our progress. So please accept this admonition to the wise: Nothing holds us back more resolutely than the tethers of past resentments, so, don't dwell on them. Focus instead upon those things that will empower you in the present.

Forgiveness is cardinal to the evolution of your Love Matrix capability, and it is essential to the quality of forgiveness that you are able to forget past grievances. We covered this in Chapter 4, "Love and Fear." But it bears repeating again that all of us, to some degree, have experienced levels of abuse, neglect, or offense either from family, peer group, or in our professional activities. Holding onto them bonds you to those negative experiences just as surely as if you were chained to them; the stronger your resentment, the stronger the bond, and the more they hold you back. To help you release your ties to them once and for all, we suggest a physical act of flak zapping that works surprisingly well:

Make a list of everything, past or present, that constantly upsets you. Write down every last item. Take the list to a safe open space like a fireplace, strike a match and burn it. Of course, you'll toss this list into the fireplace, because if you don't—if you hold onto it—you will be injured. Understand the power of that metaphor, because it's precisely what you've been allowing to happen with past resentments all these years. Now, the act of burning it and throwing it away can set you free. As you do, see every issue that has plagued you visibly go up in smoke. Watch it vaporize and release all connection to it. Feel the freedom as you do it.

So many of us not only let past resentments get to us, we also let present obstacles become our Nemesis. Most setbacks we experience in life are little more than bumps in the road, yet we so often let them take on the dimensions of brick walls. We may set our course during the day in good spirits and high intention, only to have the slightest imbroglio throw us completely off balance. An insult from a stranger about our weight or style of dress, a cross word from a loved one, a traffic jam, a dun notice from the IRS about an underestimation on our 1099—the little bumps and bruises to the ego occur, and our day has gone off kilter. We get into states, when we need to be mindful that we are the states that we create; we are their authors as well as their interpreters.

Certainly living in the Love Matrix and focusing on being the light are means of overcoming even the most challenging of situations. Once you are able to be mindful of these gifts that you naturally possess, you can use them at will and transform any occasion.

Remember that every challenge presented to you is nothing more than an opportunity for transformation—a genuine chance to zap it. The choice is up to you. You may transmute and uplift any situational flak if you apply some of the delusionist's skills we have set forth on these pages. And of course, we grant you that there are times when, even in your most enlightened, love-centered, make-it-better moments, you simply get overwhelmed and may need a little help. When those occasions to arise, change your attitude. You can do so like flipping a switch, if you keep mindful of some things we have discovered and actively put them into practice.

Actions and behaviors create attitudes and beliefs. Of course, we are customarily taught the opposite—that attitudes and beliefs create actions and behaviors; certainly they can. But in this world of cause and effect, we have also come to realize that effect becomes cause, that means become the ends, that there is little separating one from the other. As we are connected one to another, so our every thought, word and deed is linked in continuum and can readily become both the intention and the result, the cause and the effect.

Just as depression can cause us to slump and weaken the timber of our voice, just as panic can provoke psychogalvanic reactions in us that make us involuntarily sweat and tremble, just as stress can raise our blood pressure and cause us to hyperventilate, we can change it all by using the revelation of physical expression to turn it around.

Life is not a prison. And we were not meant to be trapped in dispositions that implode our potentials for joy. Merely by shifting the dynamics of our activities, we can alter the emotions that bombard us. The simple act of deep breathing—slow, deep breaths—can both calm and pacify us as much as any Prozac or St. John's Wort. By throwing our head back and smiling, by speaking in a firm voice, we can empower our point of view as well as the way we're perceived. Neuro-linguistic training teaches the degrees of energy that can be created by motion and stance, the subtle behavioral nuances that virtually transform the ways in which we're perceived, as well as the ways we come to perceive ourselves.

Anyone who has ever played a competitive sport will acknowledge the fact that no one dares take the field with timid or tentative behavior. We prep. We loosen up. We breathe. We do calisthenics. We cheer. We flex. We strut. We hold ourselves proudly and celebrate the glory of our endless practice and forthcoming expertise. We rehearse our rituals of success if we intend to win at all. Why, then, would we even consider taking on the game of life in any other way?

Every day is a game, a joy to play. And with the right preparation, certainly a win is in the offing. The world does not intend to get in our way. It simply exists for itself. What we do in the midst of it, is make it a better place.

Think Great Thoughts!

"Our life is what our thoughts make it."

—Marcus Aurelius
Meditations. Book II

Volumes have been written on the power of positive thinking and of how liberating higher thought can be. And yet the majority of humankind remains enslaved by its own consciousness.

In Chapters 4 and 5, we examined the power of positive attitude and emphasized that we are the sum of every thought, word and deed. Of the three, thoughts are the most powerful and the most frequent forms of energy, and yet we toss them around like pennies without regard for their value. It is estimated that we perform several hundred different acts a day, from brushing our teeth to creating scientific equations. Depending upon who we are and what our professions may be, we speak anywhere from 500 to 10,000 words a day. However, from all calculations to which we have been exposed, the human mind is estimated to entertain between 60,000 and 90,000 thoughts during its waking hours. What's more, our thoughts—because we believe they suffer no tangible consequences—are free to roam the realms of boundless possibility.

We have already determined what attack thoughts can do and what kind of negative impact they can help create—especially as a sword turned inward against oneself. We also understand that, by clearing our mind of Fear Matrix influence, we can open it to a banquet of boundless possibilities. Surely we already do, but the question remains: To what degree do we think positive thoughts? How magnificently do we dare to dream?

Since it is our devout belief that every thought carries an energy all its own, our highest thoughts as well as our most positive dream scenarios should be given both the weight of frequency and the force of conviction. The secret is to truly desire them and to set a plan for their achievement. If your desires are those of service and achievement, you may accompany them with all the perks of prosperity you desire, for you certainly deserve them. The main issue with positive and goal-directed thoughts is that you don't have to limit yourself.

Of course, it's natural to experience negative images from time to time. We've been programmed to have limiting beliefs, so much so that self-reproach is a part of our mental processes. Ultimately however, it is not that we are invaded with negative thought forms; it's how we deal with them that takes final measure of who we have become. We have noted their inevitability Chapter 4, "Love and Fear." And we add here that negative thoughts come in two forms. The first is the *accidental negativity* that occurs to us—the evil thoughts or ugly events that creep around the fringes of our consciousness but do not come from us; they just happen. Treat them as you would a foul odor or an unsightly scene along the road. Speed by them quickly; give them scant notice and no energy at all.

The second negative thought form is the *core negativity* that comes in images conjured from our Fear Matrix. These too should be zapped. Weigh their actual potential for harm and then flush them from your awareness. And do it with ruthless speed. The more quickly you release them, the less hold they will have on you. Put them behind you.

Let the future be filled with your most daring notions. And don't stop at just dreaming and planning. Talk about it. Tell others about it. Share your visions. Enlist allies both on this plane and others, and do so actively.

Put into application what Napoleon Hill referred to in *Think and Grow Rich* as your "mastermind" team of experts. Enlist others, all successful in their way, who have been cleansed of the dross of petty envy, and who are what Abraham Maslow referred to as "self-actualized" human beings. And don't be afraid to ask them to participate. There is no harm in asking; no one has ever been killed by a rejection—but many have died slow agonizing deaths while dwelling in doubt.

Once you have gathered together your "A" list of achievers, it is not merely desirable but also essential that your inner circle be those who are attuned to your highest standards of ethics and ideals. Use them both for feedback and alliance. Share your beliefs, and act upon them. Because it is only by taking positive steps toward achievement that your highest thoughts will be realized.

In his *Gnomologia,* William Fuller wrote in 1732 that "The man who does not believe, does not live according to his beliefs."[18]

Thoughts without actions are songs in a storm. Their beauty is buried in the roar of current urgency. If you have a great thought, give it life. Begin by speaking it first. Say what it is, and it will find a way to keep on breathing.

Speak Your Heart.

"To express great thoughts, you must be heroes as well as idealists."

—Oliver Wendell Holmes Sr.

Valedictory Address at Harvard University. 1886

Behold again the brilliant audacity of the small child. Flush with purpose, imbued with the belief that all things are possible and that nothing need ever be denied him, he declares his intentions to the world. She announces her desire to be the next President of the United States. He plows through a row of Teddy bears and, scoring in some end-zone of his contrivance, shouts that he will be the next all-American quarterback. She, upon tending a marginally tolerant cat, bandages its paw, announcing her intentions to become a doctor. He, arrayed in paints and crayons, lays out a rather abstract masterpiece and declares his dedication to becoming a great artist.

Those adults among us—doting friends, parents, aunts and uncles—listen to their fervent claims upon greatness and wink at one another with knowing glances. Of course, we console ourselves with the understanding that these children have set the mark a little high; no one really becomes these things in the end. But then, like a jolt of divine intervention, we tip our hat to the benediction that their naive courage seems to shed upon us all. We shrug and tilt our heads, and bring our credulity to the fore, if only for a moment or two.

"Could be," someone utters, hopefully.

"You never know," a mother echoes. "In this life, all things are possible."

We grant them a stay of dream denial, and pray that silent ode—that they may achieve the fantasies we no longer entertain.

Somewhere along the way, we stopped talking about it, because we were taught it couldn't happen. How dare we do such things to ourselves? It simply wasn't meant to be that way.

Yet to get back those bold notions of our potential, we have to redesign them, give them voice, and finally act them out.

In his highly effective "My Navigator" series, Los Angeles-based success coach Paul Roth teaches his students (whom he calls pilots) that if they're going to achieve anything in life, they first have to "speak it into existence." Mindful of that very important aspect of "saying is believing," Paul Roth has his students tap their dream machine for the one achievement to which they most passionately aspire. Then he gives them the assignment not only to design and write their self-described dream but also to speak it aloud in no uncertain terms. Whether recited or read, his students must have a statement of being and say it with conviction in front of the entire class.

The reading aloud is not required but is strongly recommended if the student is going to achieve his or her objectives. And the only resistance comes at the outset, when the strategies are written but not yet spoken. The greatest fear the students express comes not from creating the strategy but at the recitation of the goals—for fear those who are listening will think them deluded for giving voice to such lofty ambitions. What happens instead, is a quick determination that everyone in the class shares similar dreams and desires, but with practical plans for achieving them carefully laid out and expressed.

Thus far, the results achieved in "speaking your intentions into existence" have been remarkable. Students claim a marked surge in confidence as well as a sense of responsibility to pursue and accomplish what they have finally dared to articulate to others. According to Paul Roth, "The results have been exceptional; more than 65% of the students achieve their spoken objectives within a year of issuing them."[20]

Whether this kind of result can be achieved every time is even more directly proportionate to the energy of dedication we give it than the designs we draw for it. In other words, it isn't enough to have dreams. We must also work to make them come true.

This goes beyond prayer or affirmation, because it is a pledge, a commitment to oneself and to others to achieve your objectives, to have a plan and to give that plan an effective forum for realization. As thought spawns speech and speech prompts action, action generates results. On this linear plane of life it is proof of what works.

Do it—And Do it Daily!

In spirit, we abhor the constant scorekeeping that makes up so much of the act of living. In practice, we acknowledge physical, demonstrable planning, list making and preparation as essential tools for getting larger than life. In the first place, every successful person within our sphere of experience has undertaken this regimen and recommends it. Second, it works, certainly if not infallibly.

Statistics abound to reinforce this observation, but let us regale you with one for the time being: A Harvard student survey in 1967 indicated that about 3% of the graduates of the University's four-year undergraduate program had actually written down their goals and objectives—a life's plan, as it were. A revisitation to the Harvard Class of '67 about 25 years later indicated that the 3% who had written their goals had accumulated hundreds of millions of dollars more in personal wealth than those who had not. In other words, they had kept their higher consciousness on course with a design for their lives as well as a resolution to achieve it.

Resolution is the pivotal issue here. And most people fail to plan their lives because they're afraid to take that first step. So in order to help you develop the resolution that you may need, we recommend that you make three "Larger than Life" lists.

We acknowledge that we've asked you to make lists or follow regimens of some kind in almost every chapter. What we hope you'll also pay attention to is the high probability that, as you go through this delusionist's course of study, your lists will begin to change both in nature of content and quality of aspiration. To give them point of reference, however, we send you back again to your one-and two-word core definitions in Chapter 3. Although you may alter them at any time, in all probability those self-definitions reflect your soul's desire and will vary only in degrees.

The Larger than Life lists we now suggest that you make are more practical in nature and have to do with the day-to-day conduct not only of what you are becoming but also of what you desire most to be in the following areas: *1) career enhancement, 2) prosperity potentials, 3) physical health and fitness, 4) mental growth, 5) family and quality of life, 6) spiritual growth and development.*

We ask you to make two lists: the first a very extensive list, the second a list with only one preemptive goal for each aspect of your life.

We ask that your *Larger than Life List 1* include everything from your wildest fantasies to some aspects of your life that you are successfully undertaking now. We do this because we have found that, in stating their goals and objectives, people often focus disproportionately on the empty spaces in their lives and forget to acknowledge the little wins that have already propelled them successfully along their way. And, in focusing upon things they want, they often start to place blame on what they don't have. We have all succeeded in so many areas, it is important to examine those and realize that we are more complete than we might imagine, and that all goals attained form those little steps toward the attainment of the larger dreams in our lives. Keeping lists that only contain unrealized ambitions tend to tar us with an unjustified sense of inadequacy.

Your *Larger than Life List 2* comes in the form of a mission statement and should include only those single issues that are an indelible part of your life's plan—the ones that, forsaking all others, you would hold to your highest level of aspiration. Those are core issues, ones you won't compromise for anything. In a way they are the ones that truly matter, and yet if you drew up only this short, one-item list, it could prove to be a tyranny of desire that would stunt your opportunity for growth. High aspirations are only as valid as their potentials for achievement. And it is a tendency for many people to put objectives on this list that are so lofty they couldn't attain them no matter what. In all cases, it is best to set as your goals those ideals which you have at least taken some steps toward achieving. In other words, they should be one of the principal destinations in your flight plan as well as being in tune with your core one-and two-word destinies.

It also helps to remember that the true measure of success comes in the transformation that takes place during the quest—not necessarily in the attainment of the perceived goal. Success in terms of personal impact can be measured in so many ways. Don't set your standards so high that, by their very nature, they bring you down.

Julius Caesar, when he turned thirty, is said to have wept because at his age Alexander the Great had already conquered the known world. It is also said that Alexander the Great, upon turning thirty, wept because there were no worlds left to conquer. Both men, larger than life, ultimately short-circuited their own destiny by pulling the red lever on their lives and eventually self-destructing. In so doing, they became smaller than life in fact, if for no other reason than their obsessions were with power for power's sake. In becoming larger than life, you will soon come to find that, from our delusionists' perspectives, all power comes through us and, as such, endures only as long as it serves others.

Our *Larger than Life List 3* entails a recommended regimen for getting the most out of your life's plan on a day-to-day basis. What we have found is that people will make resolutions. They'll even write down lists and have good intentions for them. But if they don't set certain disciplines for themselves and carry them out on a daily basis, the initiatives fade almost as quickly as they are put in place. So by taking some small steps every day, each of us will sense an increased capacity to make a difference in our own lives, and to move toward that larger game to which we all aspire.

For the purposes of this regime, we are using the six criteria we set in our first two lists, but we are doing so in what might appear to be a random order—the kind you would experience in the course of a normal day (in this case, we hope to make it an extraordinary day). We do so with the full understanding that these are recommendations only. You may have a system and a list of priorities, something of your own design you would prefer to follow. What this format does is submit a superstructure for you to work around and reshape as you see fit. It is a program that has worked for us, and offers optimum flexibility within its own design.

As you begin this, you will notice immediately that many of the disciplines we recommend here have been included in developing various skills in other chapters. As we emphasize the interconnectability of all things, we underscore our belief that the mind-body-spirit correlation forms the synergy that enables us to become larger than life. In truth, it is life at its most abundant.

1. Breathe in. Breathe out. We emphasized this in Chapter 6, "Go with Your GUT," but cannot emphasize it enough here. The simple act of breathing—the act we take most for granted—holds the secret to so much of the good that happens to us. So many self-enhancement courses now teach deep breathing as an integral part of their health regimes. Many aerobics courses and all yoga classes begin with deep breathing as an introduction to the start of exercise. In his *Creating Health,* Deepak Chopra describes *breathing* as a process of *intimate connection with the universe.*

"In this sense," he adds, "breathing is literally an act of sharing. It is a biological process that puts us in touch with the past and the future of our own species, and with all other living beings as well."[19]

Merely by practicing breathing in the present moment, you can empower yourself and feel a true sense of unity with the world around you. If you take long deep breaths in the morning, it will help you wake up more quickly. If you take long deep breaths at night, it can help you fall asleep more quickly and sleep better once you do. And you will find it will let the natural flow of thoughts come into their proper perspective.

2. Go into the Silence. In a silent room or outdoors in front of an imminent sunrise, you may meditate, pray, or simply still yourself and feel the slow certain surge of clarity come through you. Undergoing this process will put you in the moment, and help you to clear your thoughts for the day ahead. You may do this for five minutes or for an hour or so, as your schedule allows. Time is not as important as your ability to release the busy traffic of your mind. For many people, this extended serenity can be intimidating, but slowly they start to feel hum of urgent events slip from their focus and the power of higher thought slowly slip into their awareness. The silence helps heal the cacophony of conflict and gives you new perspective of whatever has been set before you. When accomplished in tandem with deep breathing, the Silence helps put you in the present moment, and in so doing attunes your sense of timing for the world about you. Time begins to be something you can hold in your grasp. Days slow down for you, and you actually find yourself accomplishing more with less effort.

3. Learn Great Thoughts. You have already been admonished to think great thoughts, and to understand the value of role-modeling or emulating those who have set standards for us all. At least part of this comes with studying the great thoughts of those who have gone before us. Rather than starting your day with broadcast news of gang wars, school shootings, wars in Eastern Europe, and traffic jams, spend your time in upliftment by reading from the teachings of Jesus, Buddha, Mohammed, Plato, Emerson, or Krishnamurti. If our thoughts are precedents for our actions, then the more elevated we keep them, the greater our potential for achievement.

In his handbook for higher thought, *As A Man Thinketh,* James Allen observes the following:

> A man's mind may be likened to a garden, which may be intelligently cultivated or allowed to run wild; but whether cultivated or neglected, it must, and will, *bring forth*. If no useful seeds are put into it, then an abundance of useless weed seeds will *fall* therein and will continue to produce their kind.
>
> Just as a gardener cultivates his plot, keeping it free from weeds and growing the flowers and fruits which he requires, so may a man tend the garden of his mind, weeding out all the wrong, useless and impure thoughts, and cultivating toward the perfection the flowers and fruits of right, useful and pure thoughts.[21]

As silence empties the business of the mind, the cultivation of the realm of higher thoughts puts us in position to make the most of every day and to get larger than life in the process.

(**Please note:** These first three elements in your "Larger than Life" daily design can be accomplished in no more than half an hour to forty minutes each morning. But if you're pressed for time on your way to getting about your day, you can always listen to audio books and motivational tapes played at the same time you're dressing for work and driving. Part of being larger than life is making the time to do things. Desire opens the face of the clock and slows the sweep of the hands.)

4. Don't forget to say thank you. We have emphasized earlier that gratitude is the grace of angels, and yet it is the first admonition everyone forgets.

In truth, we live in the most bountiful period in this young planet's history and in the most abundant civilization in recorded time. We live such lives of privilege, yet find in them the causes for feeling a sense of lack and deprivation.

Rest assured, we grow larger than life in direct proportion to the extent of our embrace of what life is and in the recognition of the blessings it already bestows upon us. Every moment we live is a privilege, and just as we should have the social etiquette to say "thank you" to someone who holds a door for us or presents us with a gift, we should possess the spiritual etiquette to thank our Creator for the gift of this exceptional, abundant life and the doorways of boundless opportunity held open for us at the dawning of every day.

5. Eat and run. In our longing for longevity, two factors constantly emerge that are viewed as essential not only to living longer but also to having a better quality of life while you are doing so. They are diet and exercise.

It is a source of constant amazement to us that people will spend hundreds or even thousands of dollars on a suit or a dress, and yet want to buy dirt-cheap processed foods to put into the only suit of value that must last them a lifetime—their own bodies. People will spend hours a night (3 1/2 on national average) watching television, but won't take the thirty minutes or so three times a week to undergo the exercise and build up their endurance so that they may have more energy to take on the life they so desire to master.

There are hundreds of healthy diets that have been designed for concerned individuals, but most of them have several qualities in common. What we have found best is to eat all natural foods, as few processed foods as possible, and diets that are at least 70% water-based foods—such as fresh fruits and vegetables. Many health gurus such as "The Juiceman," Jay Kordich, recommend juicing and drinking fresh juices from fruits and vegetables at least twice a day, every day. And there is increasing information to support the hypothesis that fresh food, high-fiber, low-fat diets are the best for total health, heart health and longevity. Beware, however, of the "non fat" label on foods, and eliminate as many processed foods as possible from your diet. If fat that naturally occurs in a food has been removed from that food, then sugar, salt, or some flavor-enhancing chemical has more than likely been inserted in its place and will have long-term toxic implications that far exceed the potential harm that any fat could create.

The measured benefits of moderate to heavy exercise now exist in studies in legion. Any aerobic exercise—jogging, swimming, cycling, aerobic weightlifting, tennis, racquetball, squash, hiking, any number of active team sports—undertaken at least three times a week improves lung strength and respiratory proficiency, oxygenates the blood, enhances efficient consumption of calories, and relieves tension that often leads to stress. It is also now believed to be a key element in anti-aging and life extension.

It is no longer an issue of *whether* you should exercise but rather *what kind* you should undertake—and how often you should do it. The crucial issue is to pick an activity you do like, stick to it, and do it often.

6. Take one new step. Most people can't seem to get larger than life because they believe it will take some Herculean effort to do so. In truth, all great things are achieved by taking one small step at a time in the direction of your desired objective. That's why it is important on a daily basis to take the six criteria from your larger than life lists and make one small, real new step toward accomplishing each of them every day. If you're working toward your prosperity criterion, you might read a business investment article on portfolio management, make an actual on-line investment or set up your own 401K plan. If your criterion is physical health and exercise, let this be the day you take that first twenty-minute power walk. If you want to grow spiritually but are feeling blocked in your attempt, let this morning be the first one in which you simply sit in the silence for five minutes and let your angels do the talking. The issue is to take your small steps every day, and then review at the end of the year just how much you've been able to accomplish. You will be amazed at the growth you will have experienced.

We might even recommend, here, that you keep a log or journal of those daily steps—just a note for each—and refer to it from time to time, when you feel you might not be making the grade, or just to provide that jolt of encouragement to perceive just how far you have progressed.

7. Make it better. This is the cardinal law of flak zapping. Remembering to be the light, you may use this criterion for every task you face, for every challenge that confronts you, and for every situation that presents itself to you: "Was I able to leave it better than I found it?" What we don't often realize is the exceptional power we possess to improve everything and everyone we touch merely by bringing the light of our goodness to it—and doing it every day! From performing random acts of kindness to bringing business solutions to our corporate environment, if we can truly transform each moment by seeing the perfection in it and bringing our own perfection to moments that require it, we can make this world a better place with every undertaking. It costs so little to see the light in others, to perceive the good in all things. And realize that there is so much good you can accomplish that you can actually measure it at the end of every day—weigh it like the gold it is. Even in those times when you've fallen short of your objectives, you can review them, and upon that reexamination realize how you can amend the mistakes and make the situation even better next time. It is only by that continuous caring and constant review that we can make every moment a demonstrable success. And by feeling that success, we are inspired to continue to do great things.

8. *See, be, and share your abundance.* Prosperity is a consciousness. It does not require great fortunes, but it does demand a certain abundance of spirit. If wealth abundantly flows throughout our lives, it should first come from within. Homes, cars, planes, yachts, elaborate trappings of wealth—all these are superficial manifestations of who we are, and are in their way illusory. To be abundant, we must be expansive in our relations to others, give to those in need, share both of our time and our wealth.

By doing this, you are more than tithing (or giving 10% of your wealth). Although tithing is important, to be sure, and part of the laws of manifestation, by giving equally of our time, our love and our community involvement—and by doing so every day—we truly show ourselves to be larger than life. It is coming at last to the realization that we can look for heroes nowhere outside ourselves. One cannot look to others to make a positive impact on the world. Not only does that absent us from responsibility, it also creates expectations. And expectations—those burdens placed upon occurrences outside the self—carry with them the baggage of disappointment. All changes for the better are up to us in the moment, and will commence upon the moment of our decision to take charge.

We will touch more on these issues in Chapter 10, "Money Makes You More of Who You Are." For now, it is important to remember that it isn't the grand sweeps of largesse but the small gestures of good will that can and should come as easily as the act of breathing.

9. *Revise and Delight.* One of the great mistakes that people make when they set their life's plans, whether it is a Larger than Life list or another, is that they feel that they are somehow indelible—that they can augment but never change them

Your designs for your life are not commandments from God etched in stone; they are the good intentions of a human being that come with their own eraser. We are convinced that the reason so many people don't follow up on their resolutions is because they change their minds and fear the loss of power for having done so.

One of the things we will point out in our Chapter 9, "Power Play," is the fact that you never lose power by changing course. You only lose it if you refuse to change course. Change is the mother of evolution, and it is only by evolving that we become larger than life.

So, we not only encourage you to reexamine and revise both your mission statement and your lists of goals, but also that you do so often, if not daily. Look at them. Recognize the magnificent creation you are, and know that your noble intentions will be fulfilled. Then put the list down, put it out of your mind, and do it!

And don't let the world get in your way!

Go Public. A Summary.

Getting larger than life, like life itself, is a progression of steps. And the final step is this: You can't grow to be larger than life if you hide from the world. You are the light. You are a good person making better a world in search of greatness. So it serves no good purpose for you to grow into your fullest potential and then retreat from your proximate universe. Not only is it counterproductive; it is virtually impossible.

By growing larger than life, you have already proclaimed to the world that you are taking your rightful place in its mainstream of functions and events.

It doesn't mean you have to be a great statesman, a celebrity, or a public figure. It does mean that you choose to make an impact and to bring to your immediate world the light of your abundant spirit. That often entails no more than putting your higher self in place of your ego and seeking that kindred higher self in others.

Whether you are involved in a community environmental project or working to help the handicapped, whether you are involved in community theatre project or just involved recruiting others in your neighborhood to join a local recycling program, you are out to make a difference. You are following your daily criterion of making better every situation you encounter, and you have decided to do so in a grander scale than before.

Of course, it takes more energy and commitment to take part in your world, but that is what being larger than life is all about. It's about finishing your day with a sense of accomplishment, of contribution, of having made a difference, and of knowing the glow of positive human contact. It is about taking power over your own life and passing that power on to others, knowing in the fullness of each moment that you have tasted the freshest fruits of life, and that the more you do, the greater will be your rewards—and all the richer all your moments of rest.

Waste no more time arguing what a good man should be. Be one.

—Marcus Aurelius
Meditations. Book X.

Chapter 9

Power Play

Life is a search after power; and this is an element with which the world is so saturated—there is no chink or crevice in which it is not lodged—that no honest seeking goes unrewarded.

—Ralph Waldo Emerson
"The Conduct of Life"
Essays and Journals

Tread carefully, seeker of truth. Poison lines the cup of gold that power represents. It is our most terrifying obsession. We long for it without truly being able to give it definition, and yet fall away when it approaches because we dread its consequences—the consequence of having it even more than being denied it.

We know the clichés about power. But, without definition, they are nothing more than that: clichés.

Henry Kissinger, while serving as U. S. Secretary of State, repeatedly offered the seductive if trivial observation that "Power is the great aphrodisiac."[22] We know that one, by now; it has become idiomatic if not axiomatic. We also know Lord Acton's reference that "Power tends to corrupt, but absolute power corrupts absolutely."[23]

We note as well that Lord Acton hedged his bet on power. Power *tends* to corrupt, we agree. That doesn't mean it is compelled to corrupt. And it is our delusionist's contention that absolute power in the human condition is a virtual impossibility.

By all appearance, the play for power dominates every species in the animal kingdom, and perhaps even some plants. From the obsequious allegiances paid the Alpha pack wolf to the frenzy surrounding Queen Bee in the hive, violent ambition and an almost self-destructive striving for "power proximity" defines every creature on earth. But this is a power of a singular kind that has everything to do with societal dominance and little to do with the individual to whom power is bestowed. It is not surprising, then, that this planet's ostensible conqueror, humankind, has perfected the worship of temporal power into a perverse kind of art form, again by understanding only the illusions of what power represents.

The illusion of power is the high castle. Everyone is possessed by the desire attain it, yet few believe they can find entrance or stay inside without penalty. Perceived power is the mirage of achievement against which all other tangibles are measured. It prompts the madness of striving. And those who strive without stopping to love are among the most miserable creatures in the world.

True power is the cosmic Eucharist. Its Truth is unyielding. Yet our longing for it is very much like staring into the sun. We try in vain to see meaning inside it until we are finally struck down by it. Our perceptions blurred, we are even blinded for a while until we realize that, no matter what we do, we will benefit from its grace—its warmth, its light—without its ever changing the essence of itself.

We are that sun in small. We contain the light and the warmth. We contain the truth that the blessings of power run through us all, through every living part of us. And it is merely by comprehending how to tap into that source that we can attain its true meaning.

This is the delusionist's greatest triumph: both the understanding of true Power and mastering the ability to use it as intended in the divine plan of our lives.

Part of it lies in defining the difference between the individual's power in its proper context in the stream of creative consciousness, as opposed to the madness of crowds. It is also a lesson of how great individuals are able to create intelligent interactions even with such monstrous apparitions as the hidden mob and the hideous force it represents.

Make no mistake about it: Understanding the true meaning of power—and its Source—can be the redemptive difference in our lives. The challenge comes with acknowledging its spiritual base while learning to differentiate between its physical manifestations.

That is up to us.

Power Defined.

The Random House Unabridged Dictionary has twenty-two separate definitions for the noun, "power." The modern *ENCARTA World English Dictionary* has fifteen. From the dynamics of primitive atomic structure to the launching of spaceships, "power" is a meaning not only used on its own but also coupled with hundreds of other words to define the ability of any cell, energy unit, force or living complex organism to have life beyond the confines of its initial state. In its essence, having power is movement, life and the very nature of ascendance over the one's physical environment.

Lambs or calves develop the power to walk, even on the first day. A fledgling bird eventually comes to take flight under its own power. Human beings perfect the power of speech. Fossil Fuels power our cars and airplanes. Electricity provides the power for our appliances. The heart is referred to as the body's "power plant." And civilizations flourish ostensibly because they have achieved the power to harness the forces of nature. Every force of nature and every exertion of an energy unit are defined in terms of the power that they emit.

If this focus upon power appears simplistic, it is to drive home a very important point: Our strivings for power go beyond our perceptions and deep into our cellular consciousness. So much emphasis is placed upon the concept itself that we are convinced by force of culture to attach to it a significance that extends far beyond ego. It is a striving of the life force that is in us—so much so that the very mention of it triggers responses in us that transcend mere explanation.

At basic levels, power is accepted for the necessity of survival that it expresses. As such, it generally has a positive connotation. But it is at the more sophisticated contexts of usage—the societal, political, scientific and even spiritual uses of the word "power"—that its valence becomes mixed and its role ambiguous.

Common phrases such as *power struggle, "power tripping," power politics, power plays, power suits, power lunches,* and *power walking* have become so much of our international character that one would be hard-pressed to expunge references to them from daily usage. Not all of the terms carry positive implications, to be sure, and it is here in that indefinable mindscape between practical experience, personal lust, and spiritual longing that our universal sense of Power becomes both contradictory and confusing.

Forces of Darkness and forces of Light come into play. And only one certainty about power remains: No one wants to be without it.

To be without power, in the human mind at least, is to be without either validity or base. We all must have power over something; that is our common illusion, and the Original Sin.

> "To reign is worth ambition, though in Hell.
> Better to reign in Hell, than serve in Heaven.[24]

John Milton's Lucifer makes his vain pronouncement in *Paradise Lost.* And later in the Garden of Eden, this original fallen angel (in fact, he was an Archangel), disguising himself as the serpent, first convinces Eve and then Adam to partake of the forbidden fruit from the Tree of the

Knowledge of Good and Evil—a power known only to God and his angels. Of course the two succumb, and we've all been paying the price for that indiscretion ever since.

Guess what? The lust for power has laid low the entirety of our species. It is a specter that rises up again in the mythology of a thousand different cultures. And so we are taught to fear power while longing for it at the same time. It is revealed to us time and again as the seminal temptation. And none of this resolves the issue that the need for power is instinctive in the species—all species!

If we merely tap into our core beliefs, each of us can see that there is and always has been a way for us to have our power and also hold it in the highest possible light. It is neither unnatural act nor Original Sin. It is the Truth of who we are that sits behind the mask of who we think we're supposed to be.

Perceptions of power in all its manifestations could easily send us off on a tangent that would drag the rest of our focus along with it, and take them off the issues that truly matter here. History, politics, entertainment, and the plots and schemes of personal aggrandizement are replete with tales of power, struggles for power, and accompanying self-sabotage that would titillate us terrifically while teaching us little that we didn't already know.

What is important at this point is to define power as it applies to us (first) and how we use the power granted us to interact in all other aspects of our lives. That is the issue of personal power.

Personal power, in the delusionist's definition, is the ability to positively influence all other aspects of our lives without having to control them.

This brings us again to the supreme paradox, because all primary definitions of power describe it in terms of the ability to control others—other people, other circumstances, other outcomes within one's sphere of involvement. As of this writing, there are hundreds of titles listed with both Barnes & Noble and Amazon.com that bear the word "Power" somewhere in the title. Over the years, books with such titles as *The Power of Positive Thinking, POWER/ How to Get It. How to Use It* and *Personal*

Power have sold millions of copies. People are currently being taught about *The Power Within,* shown the way to find *48 Steps to Power,* and being educated into the ways of *Power Imaging.* Without exception, these are noble attempts to empower others to "take control of their lives," and say so in no uncertain terms.

Our terms are less certain and more explicitly to the point that these are almost always appeals to the ego, when it is our belief that the power lies with the individual's oversoul, and that the issue is not so much power as it is a word that needs to replace it. That word is *mastery.* And all true power begins and ends with the mastery of self.

The Ego and the Oversoul.

Half the harm that is done in the world
Is due to people who want to feel important.

—T.S. Eliot
The Cocktail Party (1949)

First, let us give some strokes to the ego, because no concept in our common vernacular has been more frequently misapplied, vilified, and bastardized. In daily application it has been made the metaphysical scapegoat for everything that is wrong with the human condition. People are denounced for being egocentric, for "ego tripping," for having their ego out of whack, for being all ego, for having "an ego the size of a house," and (in less pejorative terms) for having a healthy ego. Over time, the ego has fallen victim to easy usage by people who understand only shards of its total meaning.

In its original context, *Ego* is a Latin term meaning "I am," and represents the first words God uttered to Moses proclaiming his divine presence as the Creator of this universe, as well as the first utterance of the first commandment: "I *am* the Lord thy God…" (Exodus 20:2).

In later scholarly usage, the *ego* came to embody the complete unity of mind and spirit. And it was only in the early 20th century that Sigmund Freud, the father of modern psychotherapy, came to popularize the ego as the regulating factor between the *id* (our selfish animal instincts) and our interactions with society as we know them. In other words, the ego's original function was as a kind of behavioral traffic cop between our base desires and our higher self or oversoul—what Freud chose to call the *superego.*

Carl Gustav Jung committed the ego to another role as that of spiritual arbiter in the collective unconscious. And it was only later that the ego, in combination with other syndromes, came to take on the villain's role. Such terms as *egoist, egotist, egocentric, ego-alienated, ego-obsessive,* and (of course) *egomaniac* started dressing the ego in ever darker colors, making it more of an enemy to the human expression of self than it was ever intended to be.

Before the ego came along as the behavioral stigma, we were saddled with less complex references such as "pride," "vanity," "conceit," and "arrogance" as depictive of our lower nature.

In truth, we have many egos: the mind ego, the body ego, the personality ego, the cellular ego, the visceral ego. And, because they are all egos, each believes itself to be the center of the individual's need for well-being, and each makes its own demands not only for attention but also for dominance.

What we are saying is that the larger ego, the *ego-major,* is not one, but a compendium of egos, each one vying for supremacy and longing to drag us off to its own agenda. Anyone who exercises frequently will tell you that if they lay off working out for more than a couple of days, their endorphins will nag them to heed their needs; and in a splendid kind of addiction, the individual responds by running or working out in order to trigger the serotonins needed to satisfy the body ego's very positive cravings. When someone's personality ego gets out of control, it may prompt them into an illicit love affair, a marital infidelity, that will have inevitable repercussions later. Against the outcries of the GUT, the mental ego's awareness of folly, and even the advice of friends, the personality ego entertains the illicit passion and lusts for satisfaction of itself. But it is the satisfaction of that vain self-image—that narcissism—that the ego-major, what we choose to refer to as the "self-ego" tries to put into balance.

Rest assured, that the self-ego will do whatever is necessary to create that sense of balance on its own. But the ego-major is in truth the smaller self that is helpless unless it surrenders its power to the higher self—to what Ralph Waldo Emerson perfectly defined as the oversoul.

By definition, *the oversoul is the spiritual self*—the higher self—that drives us to the truth of who we are and what we are meant to be. It is the *Creator connection* that each of us possesses, the one that is waiting to guide us if we can recognize it for the truth that it holds. It is the voice that sang to you when you addressed your core questions with your one-and two-word answers in Chapter 3. It is our angelic awareness.

The self-ego longs for this oversoul connection, because at the nexus of its understanding it knows that it was not meant to command but to serve the purposes of the higher self. And the only way it can truly bring all the rampant egos of itself into harmony is by surrendering to that angelic awareness—to that oversoul. That is perhaps an easier thing to acknowledge than to accomplish. But acknowledge it we must if we are to survive at all.

Give it up!

We begin this section with a categorical declaration: *It is the unguided ego's destiny to self-destruct.* We advance this theory as being axiomatic, because history supports us in this, and so do the chronicles of every arena of human behavior.

Everyone from Napoleon to Richard Nixon, from Martin Luther King Jr. to (actress) Ava Gardner, from Evita Peron to Henry VIII have fallen victim to the inability of their self-ego to control their ego selves and have sabotaged themselves in some way. Whether it is hubris or hidden sexual appetites, whether it is trenchant paranoia or insatiable desires for pleasure, there are figures in legion from the fields of entertainment, politics, business, arts, letters, and the sciences (especially military science), who exhibit those same self-destructive tendencies. Historical figures such as author Ernest Hemingway, actress Marilyn Monroe and painter Vincent Van Gogh self-destructed in fact; they presumably took their own lives. Others have taken a slower route and often let the force of circumstance do it for them.

The net result is the same, and invariably each of these cases of self-sabotage deals with issues of power, and the inability of the individual ego to cope with it. In chapter 7, "Timing is Everything," we gave numerous examples alluding to the fact that the quest for power without intention—power for its own sake—eventually destroys the holder. The individual in this case is merely metaphor for the ego, and intention is merely metaphor for the divine guidance that is required in all things.

We also acknowledge that, in all of the above cases, the individuals we pointed out as being self-destructive in some way were chosen because, almost perennially, their actions and behaviors dictated their attitudes and beliefs. As such, they were caught in a vicious cycle of one predicating the other. Almost invariably, we insist, they did so purely out of the self-ego's inability to regulate its other egos. And we hasten to note that they are in the vast majority. Few of us are immune to the fall-out that comes from the lesser egos' endless power struggles with the self-ego. It is something to which not even the most enlightened soul is immune.

"I claim not to have controlled events," Abraham Lincoln confessed in a private moment, "But declare plainly that events have controlled me."[25] Characteristically self-effacing, Lincoln still managed to disregard the more than forty purported assassination plots against his life during his presidency and sat unguarded and alone in the theatre on that tragic February night in 1865. And what level of ego imbalance prompted John F. Kennedy to ride unshielded in an open motorcade on that fateful November day in Dallas? Or Julius Caesar, despite the warnings, to go to the Roman Senate on the Ides of March?

No one consciously courts his or her own martyrdom. No one intends to self-destruct, yet almost everyone self-sabotages dozens of occasions in their lives, and some of those instances of self-sabotage involve dire consequences—all out of the ego's collision course with the various aspects of itself. Yet we declare certainly that these conflicts are avoidable—if one is willing to surrender, if one is willing to regard one's angels and simply ask for help, if one is willing to tear through the veils of ego and embrace the oversoul that always stands inside us to be our servant and our guide.

The self-ego, the mind that obeys it, functions with flawless efficiency if it is allowed to serve in its capacity as second in command. It is the spirit—through the oversoul—that must assume all power if our destination is to be reached. The oversoul is the captain of the ship of self, and joyous is the ego that embraces it. Rest assured, it will do so, but only if it learns the meaning of surrender.

This implies a trust that only true delusion can bring—the understanding that we are not in control—that there is a God with a divine plan for us all. Just as it is the unguided ego's destiny to self-destruct, it is the attuned ego's sole *raison d'etre* to serve the divine plan that has been passed on through the oversoul to us.

It does not require religion to find this. It does require faith: the faith, the belief that our Creator has a plan for us, and the conviction that it is not only our ability but also our right to achieve it.

But discovering the right to fly to our destined nation—our true power—does not guarantee that we will do so. We begin by giving up the needs of the ego-self to control the outcome of events. By the same token, it is required of us that we remain vigilant in our pursuit of the seminal truth that is in us, the one that is meant to guide us through this nebula of life.

The Seven Powers.

Let us begin by observing that once you have tapped into your higher purpose you already have all the power you will ever need.

That is the soul's desire that your higher self holds out to you, the core of your belief system, and the standard your oversoul has set for you. With that awareness comes focus, intent, commitment, and an understanding that no power on earth can deter you from achieving your dreams. No false prophet can lure you off your path. No mob can overwhelm you. No storm and stress of world events can put you into a panic. No skeptic can sway you from your conviction, because you know its correctness.

By recognizing the liege of your oversoul, you have already acknowledged that the power comes through you from a higher source— that you have no power, and so you become as powerful as any human being on earth.

Knowing this enables you to have mastery over what would otherwise be the rampant energy of your lower egos and allows you to place them all in context, under the domain of the oversoul. In so doing, you transform the "power struggles" of your egos into the perfect coordination of what we call the Seven Powers. You don't have to be a prince to possess them, or a head of state, or an Olympic caliber athlete, or a business tycoon. But you are best served with the understanding that power is also a perception. And if you stand in your own convictions and the truth of your personal vision, you will always bring power to every equation in your life.

Many of these powers have already been introduced to you in the context of setting forth the delusionist's course of action. What we want to accomplish at the moment is to "en-courage" you—to fill you with the courage to bring them into fruition, to make them a part of you. What is required of you after that is diligence and constant practice of the principals set forth in them. It means knowing how and when to take action, and then doing so, acting swiftly and without recourse to failure.

That is the power that is in you—to know the Truth, to bring it through you, and to pass it on to others.

1. The Power of Love. As in our Love Matrix references in Chapter 5, we emphasize that the love to which we refer is *unconditional.* Love that comes with condition of any kind is not about love; it's about no control. Control is the consummate condition and condemns the relationship to failure. To love unconditionally, we acknowledge that all things positive on this earth come from the Higher Source of all Love. It is the recognition of our ability to use love's power to transmute, uplift, and carry on the wings of angels all our intentions. It is both preceded and followed by the Power of Forgiveness and through that forgiveness becomes power unleashed through the freeing-up of negative attachments that chain us to past limitations. When you embrace the power of unconditional love, you bring that power to your relationships, to your work, to your intended higher purpose, to your destiny. And this Love Power—the most irresistible force in the universe—acts as a colossal magnet for all the positive energy this life can provide. And since the source is unlimited, the very act of our embracing even one small part of it brings us the limitless universe of our inevitable success.

2. The Power of Thought. We have emphasized the power of thought often before, but feel that it is something that can never be stressed enough. Because thoughts flow freely through us like rivers through a continent of intent, we can never control their ebbs and flows. Nonetheless, we are both their tributary and estuary. And their sum and direction will be directly proportionate to the energy we give them. Upon first glance, it appears to be a tyranny for us to command that we think only positive thoughts. More accurately it is a commandment; and more than a commandment, a Truth.

In his *As a Man Thinketh,* James Allen offers the observation that in all our thought processes doubts and fears should be excluded, and that it is not only to our benefit but is our responsibility to remove them from our thought vernacular:

He who has conquered doubt and fear has conquered failure. His every thought is allied with power, and all difficulties are bravely met and wisely overcome. His purposes are seasonably planted, and they bloom and bring forth fruit which does not fall prematurely to the ground. Thought allied fearlessly to purpose becomes creative force...[26]

Again, we stress the fact that our thoughts are the staging area for all our outcomes as well as our actions. Like the vase, if we do not clean them out from time to time, they will surely clean us out.

3. The Power of Faith. It is a testimony to the power of faith that it is the whipping boy of intellectuals and the dread of all tyrants.

"Faith," H.L. Mencken cynically observed, "is the illogical belief in the occurrence of the improbable."[27]

We answer with a reposte by adding, "but with an unwavering anticipation of all that is possible."

In truth, faith is the glue of our positive imaging and the acknowledgment of the universal justice that awaits all high intent. True faith is marked by gratitude; so, never does it beg. It simply becomes a part of us, like breathing in and out. Once it does, doubt dissipates and a new bracket of potentials manifests that we once would have denied ourselves. But for that to happen, belief must become us as well as the flame of certainty. That is what burns away all doubt. And faith is the salve that heals it.

4. The Power of Inner Peace. We see it in another, and we marvel—that quiet fire, that sense of correctness that knows a higher source. It is only found in those who have worked to tap into the master within, to go into those silent spaces between the ridges of thought. Those who have know secrets about themselves and work a secret knowledge of communicating their wills to others without ever giving voice to them. Out of the soft unspoken nuances of thought and deed, they empower others. They bring reason to their efforts and solutions to their challenges. Those in possession of inner peace never trumpet who they are. One just knows upon the experience of them that this is a power from the center, one that comes from the spiritual core of what they have become. Ego never enters into our consideration of them. They are what we aspire to be, and what we already are *if* we find the notes in concert that harmonize with the oversoul.

5. *The Power of Truth.* Nothing is more powerful than the truth. And no individual is more influential than the one who embraces it for exactly what it is. Truth is both hands of the clock at midnight. And speaking it is like telling time. One should do so with kindness but never with error, because there is a vestigial instinct in all of us that knows when the hands have fallen away from the mark. And those who have attuned themselves to the higher self that contains them have refined that GUT that tells them when truth is being misused.

It is the delusionist's conviction that we are, as a species, developing such acute levels of awareness that eventually, no one will be able to lie. Our thoughts will be seen and heard before they are ever given voice or power of demonstration. That is the truth and whoever embraces it, though they be the slightest of beings, will hold the Titan of life in the palm of their hands.

6. *The Power of Laughter.* "I will laugh at the world," sings forth the pronouncement from Og Mandino's *The Greatest Salesman in the World.*[28] It comes not as a declaration of ridicule but one of welcome to join in the laughter—that the life we lead is meant to be shared not in fear but in the unavoidable rush of the joy that comes in every moment we breathe. Laughter is the cure-all, the proven life extender. Modern therapies are given in its name, and at least one study has shown that levels of cancer growth have been slowed in patients who experience entertainment that, over time, induces regular bouts of laughter.

Laughter strengthens the facial muscles, helps reduce wrinkles, and apparently can even help lower one's blood pressure and stabilize the metabolism. It is a trait shared in common by many species of animals, and the most important point to stress is that it is a gift that any of us can possess upon demand. And if one doubts the power it can convey, we stress the fact that, since actions and behaviors do determine attitudes and beliefs, laughter is the tonic to set right the body electric and to do so with both speed and all deliberate care.

Laughter by any other name is *joy.* It is both its mother and its offspring, as much effect as cause, and so we are all the more joyous in both our anticipation and our expression of it.

We might add that it is the other side of gratitude and carries the face of fulfillment. To be fulfilled with joy and laughter is to be in a state of grace. It is like praying without ever having to say a word.

7. The Power of Positive Passion. This is the summary power because it contains all the drive and deliberation, all the commitment and caring of the soul in quest. As we noted that it is enthusiasm that is the fuel for our destiny's flight, we emphasize further that passion is its parent. Enthusiasm comes in moments. Positive passion is enduring. Once discovered, once the torch is lit, it remains eternal, unwavering, and resolute to drive us—to our dreams, to the end of our days on earth.

Once we are in tune with our passions for cause—once they are acting in concert with the oversoul—they serve us with obedient zeal; they are the flying horses of our heart. So great is passion's force, so boundless is its energy that it can drive us up through the envelope of our expectations. It is the source of all intention and the will that gets it through. But it must be tempered with an obedience to our higher selves.

"Only passions, great passions, can elevate the soul to great things," wrote the French philosopher Diderot in 1746.[29] In his *"Pensees Philosophique,"* he spoke to the heart of democracy in an age of monarchies when personal freedom was a distant ideal.

We emphasized earlier that passion is the triumph of heart and mind, and our greatest ally to success. Naturally it belongs as a power, but one of power's manifestations. And as such, it can only be embraced by recognizing that all powers come from the same higher Source—and that source runs through us, not from us.

Usually, what comes from us—from what is driven by mind and ego without tribute to the higher self—is doomed to lead us back down to incorrectness, to reversion to the chaos of the egos' plays for ascendance. For that reason, we must be diligent in our obedience to the truth that the oversoul gives so freely of itself. If we are not, if we have tried to attune ourselves at all, our GUT will warn us first—and, failing that, we will know somewhere that the music we hear will be less harmonious than before.

And never underestimate the separate egos' desires for their own separateness. After all, power is at issue; and they will split it if they can. Even their attempts will disturb our harmony and challenge our perspective. So, let's be mindful of the warning signs and recognize them as they occur.

Seven Ways to Lose Your Power.

Don't give this laundry list of little lies too much force of energy. Too many of us have perfected this section already. We might also have titled this section *Seven Ways to Get Smaller than Life,* for surely they are formulations to assure that folly as well.

But if this work has taught us anything, it is that all our thoughts, words and deeds combine to make us greater than or lesser than the world we have chosen to live in. And they do so on a daily basis. So the nasty misbehaviors we indulge in also apply. And most of us, if we dare to be truthful, have employed them from time to time.

Still a dis-ease, if left undiagnosed, can pollute the noblest system. And we are devotees of prevention even more than of cure.

1. Disempower others. Disempowering others is the zero-sum game at its worst, and yet it is the most frequently and insidiously applied. It is the telltale of the charlatan and the last desperate act of the disenfranchised bully. There are people around every corner—from religious charlatans to political hacks—who make their mark by convincing the guileless that they possess powers others do not have. And none of us should be so conceited as to think we can call them all out. From the stockbroker who, rather than inform them, bullies his clients into thinking he knows more about financial markets than they, to the doctor who knowingly counsels a woman to a hysterectomy she doesn't need, there are those who would challenge the power in us and use it for their personal profit.

And it is our constant delusionist's plea: Please think for yourself! Anytime your GUT turns over, it is telling you to take back your own power—to take command of your own decisions and let both time and its daughter, discretion, lead you to the correctness of alternative thinking. Consider all your options. Don't make decisions in haste. And whatever you do, don't become one of those insidious saboteurs yourself.

The parent who answers the child's interrogative "Why?" with a brusque "Because I said so," the pet owner who punishes a companion animal without first trying to communicate at its level of understanding, the careless remark that brings a friend down, the phone call that isn't returned—all these things, however subtle and unreflected, are cheap uses of power. They are attacks against others that bring them down, usually in order to raise ourselves up.

We do it out of habits born of fear. And more often than not, we do it because we were taught or role-modeled in very much the same way.

But being a delusionist is not about accepting what exists. It is about daring to break old patterns and set new standards. It's about taking the power of love that comes through you and making it the entirety of who you are. It's about empowering others as the consummate means of empowering yourself. Otherwise, the opposite effect can and will come into being.

2. Disempower yourself. It is often our greatest failing that in times of stress, times when we most need to take charge, the first thing we do is give away our own power to someone else.

Much of this occurs by inculcation, often through the infusion of false information. We have had acceptance of authority, often blind acceptance—drilled into us since conception—most of it, we were told, for our own good. We are taught to give away our power, and most of us never learn to get it back. In youth, it may be expected, even demanded, of us. But when we mature, when we come of age, we are at choice with what we do.

Giving up your power is not to be confused with giving it up to your higher self—to your angels—to Universal Mind. It is giving it up to another person or group who convince you they have powers you do not possess.

Most cult groups are notorious for taking people already preconditioned to give up their power and convincing them that they must be obedient to some order or other. For this we offer a foolproof remedy, especially to the young: Never doubt the wisdom of your individual need for self-expression. And never let anyone else sell you powers that they tell you they possess and you do not. If you are operating from the oversoul, if you have tuned into your higher path, no one need ever shake your resolution.

3. Hypocrisy. It seems self evident that this would be an obvious behavioral toxin to avoid, and yet it remains one of the great plagues of human nature. The national politicians, the televangelists, the personal enhancement gurus, those who preach the moral high ground and yet live lives of moral depravity and marital infidelity, define hypocrisy, and yet we tolerate them, even praise the broad base of their work apart from their personal behavior. The morally upright presidents of major corporations who sell foods, beverages, alcohol, drugs and cigarettes to the consumer that contain known toxins, poisons, sulfites, and harmful chemical processes, embrace hypocrisy as a form of professional practice and then search for plausible data to rationalize their actions. Individuals who claim to be a friend and then denigrate or betray another at the next given opportunity, practice hypocrisy as daily fare. So do nations who claim to be champions of liberty yet resort to torture as a matter of government policy. So do parents who preach morality to their children yet practice immorality in front of them such as shady business practices, violent behavior, personal abuse, and social cynicism.

If this all seems painfully evident, we point out these aberrations because they have become a part of our national character, and worse: because we tolerate them in others even as we lament them to ourselves. And by our tolerance of hypocrisy we become accomplices to it. Should we wage war upon it? The answer is decidedly, yes. By the same secret ways it has pervaded our world, we must disavow it—by becoming living examples of its diametric opposite. It is only through our adherence to the truth and our upholding of that truth, that even the meanest of lies will starve and die away.

4. Abuse the power you have. In the summer of 1999, an auto mechanic in Los Angeles (we will call him Henry Smith) was arrested for shooting his cat because it hissed at him. Upon questioning the man, the police discovered that Mr. Smith not only had a rap sheet for disorderly conduct, public brawling, and simple assault, but also one for spousal and child abuse. In fact, his wife had already left him. His sons had grown and could now fight back. So he had no recourse against them. So, the only power he had left over anything in his life was his cat. And, in one final desperate act, he had finally erased that last small expression of himself.

We use that rather pathetic tale to illustrate the fact that, in order to validate themselves, even the most disenfranchised among us try to exercise power over something, often in a forceful way that leads to abuse or denial.

That is fear's most desperate offspring and the beginning of the end. And we point out with certainty that any exercise of power, once abused, will inevitably start to erode, until it is taken totally from the abuser. It may take a millennium—as was the case with ancient Rome—or mere decades as occurred with the Soviet Union. Or it may happen to punish a million trivial cases of individual corruption, as in the case of Henry Smith. But power abused is a double-edged sword and will slay us in the end. Their end, though brought on over time, is usually both violent and swift. And no one will mourn their passing or the loss of what they became.

5. Lose your credibility. Making commitments that you don't live up to, promising aid and then withdrawing it, not keeping appointments, not following through on promises, not acknowledging others through simple courtesy—these all seem like minor vices. And yet they are termites to our credibility and end in our invalidation and the decimation of our house of self. Our power is only as good as our word. Once we start to break it, we invalidate ourselves and eventually find no franchise for our efforts. As ever, it comes to issues of integrity, and we emphasize again that integrity is at issue in everything we do. From our most casual interaction with a companion animal to a major business transaction, all energy we project carries with it a measure of integrity that implies our ability to do what is best for all concerned—to bring it to its highest possible level of fulfillment. When we do this, we can sense a resonance inside us that completes us in the moment. When we fail to honor that higher command, when we fall short, our integrity begins to drain away. And our credibility is the immediate casualty to it.

Another absolute way of losing your credibility is by taking credit for everything good with which you are associated. Bragging, boasting, speaking loud and often of your accomplishments is an open declaration of weakness and an open invitation to countervaluation. Confidence can be conveyed without ever speaking a word.

There is a Japanese saying that "He who boasts shouts in an empty house." And yet there is the compulsion among too many people to leap to the fore to take credit for everything that happens around them. As if sharing praise for an accomplishment will strip away their power, they rush to assume the limelight when nothing would enhance them more than acknowledging others for their contributions.

None of us exists in a vacuum. We are fellow travelers in all things bright and bold that are done in this world. Giving credit where it is due, and especially acknowledging that all good comes through us as well as from us, is the tune that is heard most clearly and, even in noisy rooms, is relished by all.

6. Obsessions with "control." All our earlier protestations to the contrary, this remains the most controversial ground we will trod if for no other reason than that, to the mavens of conventional thinking, control is power's most immediate issue. Every book, tape, course, and power philosophy emphasizes that for us as individuals to succeed, we must take control of our lives. We are told we need "to take charge" of our jobs, our personal responsibilities, our diet, our time, our finances.

To all of these admonishments, we agree wholeheartedly. We also offer this caveat: Like so many other aspects of empowerment, we tend to overdo the issue of control. So many of us, by "wresting control from others," squeeze the trust out of every relationship and, by abandoning trust, risk the loss of everything. There is no more noxious social definition awaiting us than to be adjudged "a control freak." And yet many of us embrace the epithet as if it were a badge of honor, believing that beneath the resentment we have created—the disempowering of others, the loss of validation, and the abuse of our position—we have managed to maintain our power. By doing so, we have let the ego declare that it is still in charge. Yet by pursuing this path of lies, we have shown faith in nothing, love for nothing, and empowerment to nothing except the echoes of our own fear.

Just as our God and our angels have delegated their trust to us to follow our divine path, we must delegate to others with a special kind of faith. Trust is the greatest show of power—the letting go of need, filling our thoughts with faith and knowing that the rewards for it will be both forthcoming and inevitable.

7. Conformity. This comes as a broader aspect of issue 2, *disempowering yourself,* but its implications are weighted differently. In our reflection upon cults and the loss of identity in them, we approach them as being, by nature, pathological. More often than not, the rational mind possesses at least enough sense of self to recognize them for what they are and resist them.

Conformity is far more insidious and answers a social need. And the need for acceptance—for validation, for recognition and praise—is as overwhelming as it is instinctive. In some ways it is part of the social order and presents no problem as such; it is simply the cost of living, as it were. But social conformity—especially in the peer group—can be as irresistible as it is oppressive.

It is here that we must caution you to always be wary of the dynamics of large groups of any kind. It is our basic animal nature and very often our flaw that we are drawn to the crowd—to the flock, the herd, to the congregation, to the welter of mass-mind thinking. We rely on it for validation when, more often than not, it drives us away from the essence of our own truth. No illusion of personal validation can be swifter, for example, than the poor disenfranchised ghetto youth who joins a gang. Instantly he experiences a rush of validation, of acceptance, of belonging, and perhaps his first-ever sense of power. What the youth has done, immediately, is give up all his power to the collective. To the youth, the gang represents the mirage of perennial power when, almost without exception, it is the agent of fear.

In his play, *An Enemy of the People,* Henrik Ibsen makes the delusionist's cry of outrage against the madness of the crowd when his protagonist, when facing the violent opposition of mediocre minds, cries out, "The majority is never right!"[30]

The outcry here is not against democracy but a warning against the monumental danger of the herd mentality. Crowds, as we have noted, carry a madness all their own, and even the best of them are driven by fear. To that degree a crowd is more certain, more predictable, and in its way more terrifying than any of which the human nature of an individual can conceive. Still, we are drawn to them. Even as they change us into something other than the rational being we would be if left to our own devices, we succumb to their seductive clamor and the madding whorl of their numbers. Whether it is the wild passion of a rock concert, the coerced levity of a political rally, or the wild momentum of a stock exchange floor, we behold the crest of energy, and only the bold among us dare to see the chum of turmoil behind it.

There exists in everyone's life those dissonant moments when the solitary path of the seeker of truth appears lonely, dark, and foreboding, and the allure of the collective appears irresistible. It promises the synergism of cooperation and the preponderance of good things. It promises a power to which the disempowered soul is drawn. But what is the nature of that power, and what is the price to be paid? That is the issue that so few of us dare to foresee.

Remember that once you have tapped into the true source of your own power, the higher Source, you need look for it in no other quarter than yourself—your higher self. In it is contained the strength of conviction and the surety of all intent. And you can be calm and sure of yourself, even as the world goes mad around you.

If you can serve without demanding of others service in return, if you can speak the truth without rage and never dread the opinion, if you can heed your own counsel and rouse respect even as you do, you control your destiny; you command your own life. No one can be wealthier than to stand alone and, gazing in the mirror, say without fear or vanity, "I like what I have become."

Your Day as Emperor of the World. A Summary.

By now, we trust this study will have left you with at least two conclusions: The first is that no individual can possess absolute power beyond total mastery of self, and that can only be approached by coming into unity with one's oversoul and the divine plan it carries from our Creator to our ego. The second is that power, once attained, is a trust that requires a certain degree of moral governance. One has to be diligent in the maintenance of it as well as being aware of its potential for making an impact on others.

With that in mind, we now bestow upon you the title of "Emperor of the World," with absolute power over the world as we know it.

This comes with a catch, of course, and the stipulation is this: You only get to be emperor for a single day. You have unlimited wealth at your disposal, boundless influence over governments and nations, and every initiative you set in place will be carried out beyond the extent of your limited tenure.

The rest is up to you. You may spend a day in mindless pleasure and unrestrained wealth-gathering. You may follow your life's dreams and put in place the initiatives to assure it. And you may select a number of means by which to make this world a better place—by reducing world hunger, working toward environmental reparation, and mandating equal rights for women throughout a world so desperately in need of them.

This is not an either/or scenario. These options are not mutually exclusive. But you are limited by the merciless issue of time. That time is both linear and real. And you are, by those realistic constraints, obligated to prioritize. So, for the sake of realistic achievement, we invoke one additional restriction: You are limited to five choices in total. List them, and briefly describe why you feel them to be important and the kind of impact that could be made with them.

Finally, we ask you for a second list. This one is to contain only one priority for the ultimate expression of one day of your omnipotent tenure— the one you would exercise if you were only allowed a single choice for the statement of who you are and what your legacy would be to the world.

In the aftermath of your list, we make no value judgments other than to ask you if you considered all of the ramifications of what your alternatives would be. And by asking, we might give you some food for thought.

For example, one inclination of the exercise of power might be to overthrow all the dictators of the world. But would that change anything? Are corrupt leaders, ruthless governments, and expedient social systems the cause of public consciousness, or an extension of it? By changing leadership, would we merely be changing the personality of corruption, and not the substructure that created it in the first place? Then again, is bringing harm to anyone else—a nation or a human being—ever a proper exercise of power? And the dilemma persists: how far does anyone's individual power truly extend?

By taking initiatives to end world hunger, even as Emperor of the World, could you do so in a stroke? (After all, you're a human being and not a god.) And if you mandated such a dramatic initiative, wouldn't you have to design a plan to make it work? Or would hunger not best be ended by teaching indigenous agrarian peoples how to use modern technology to properly plant and harvest crops? Is education not a more *powerful* tool than welfare?

And what about the world ecology? Where would you begin? Can it be a global blanket initiative? Or does each nation have its own delicate issue of checks and balances? Would the same environmental initiatives that work for one country not possibly undercut the precarious economy of another?

These questions are rhetorical and lead us to a point: Power, though we long to possess it, carries with it a weight of tremendous responsibility. An emperor for a day can mandate world peace. And as an abstract concept, nothing could be more admirable than that. But it is the enforcement of it that falls upon those who follow.

The assumption of power at any level of existence is never entirely a matter of thinking good thoughts and issuing spiritual mandates. It requires training, diligence, passion, and a relentless focus to attain a mastery that has to be truly inspired. That is power's challenge to us and why, though we long to own it, that we dread it for the obligation it incurs.

The secret of owning power of any kind comes with the understanding of playing within life's rhythms. It is both pathetic and at the same time a very human failing that we fantasize about having total power without ever taking a single step toward achieving the personal authority that is within our grasp.

Success, leadership, wealth, acclaim—all belong only to those who become their students and who share a passion for their attainment. Such manifestations of power only underscore the consciousness of those who lay claim to them. And it is through their achievement that people are able to show themselves for who they truly are.

That is perhaps everyone's greatest fear—the realization that they will be more publicly visible, that their actions will be noted every step of the way, that they will be held more accountable for what they do.

Some people even fear that success, wealth, and power will change them—that they will become someone else again, someone they don't like. It is our finding that quite the opposite is true: The greater your wealth, the greater your influence, the more it will reveal the truth of who you are.

To some, that is the ultimate terror; to others liberation—that we will be known for who we are and that our power will finally be called upon to fully express itself.

Chapter 10

Money Only Makes You More of Who You Are

When reason rules, money is a blessing.

—Publius Syrus
Moral Sayings, 50 BC

As we members of the new economy step across the threshold of the 21st century, we do so with a sense of economic fearlessness that we have never experienced before. For many of us, prosperity has become an assumption of entitlement; we intend it to be a part of our lives. And attitude has the power to create abundance.

We make this observation, because recent estimates indicate that more strongly than ever before in history, we have taken control of our financial future. A survey in a March 2000 issue of *Newsweek* found there to be approximately 4.5 million homes in America with a combined net worth of $1,000,000 or more, more than 35% of them growing out of the meteoric rise in the stock market since 1994. Granted, many of these have been paper moguls, and fortunes are prone to alter considerably when financial portfolios start to vaporize as they have in the months of tech carnage and the NASDQ collapse preceding this writing. But the truth remains to face the fire. Prosperity has become a part of our national mindset and will continue to be so for decades to come.

With the establishment of a Force 4 event such as the Internet, potentials for the perpetuation and expansion of our wealth are solid indeed. Not only has the Internet altered the entire course of world markets through e-commerce; it is also predicted to be the significant factor in the minimization of such cyclical economic scourges as inflation and recession. This flies in the face of the prediction models of all economic fatalists. And yet all of us stand in the new millennium with the awareness that all things are not only possible but also at our fingertips.

Being dedicated futurists, we say this despite the recent spate of tech chaos in the financial markets. We believe that rampant prosperity will regain its momentum all the way into *The Roaring 2000s.** We already live in the era of the virtual corporation, where it is predicted that in the next ten years nearly 60% of the U.S. working population will be operating businesses out of their own homes on either a full-time or a part-time basis. Out of this, a new kind of plutocracy is already springing up—one filled with its own perceptions of social responsibility, one that may not be as easily read as it was in the past.

Many of today's cybermillionaires are under thirty-five, have a different set of personal value paradigms, and are prone to a sense of cocooning and hyperprivacy. Some not only do not care for interaction with their proximate communities, but also feel inclined to avoid it. Others will not only come forth to do so, but also understand that their wealth is a master key to their rise to heightened awareness and social responsibility. As we have insisted that power solely for power's sake will finally crush those who try to possess it, it is also our delusionist's belief that abundance, by its very nature, is determined to be shared. If it is not done so immediately, the of the world marketplace in the new millennium. wealth

---

* *The Roaring 2000s* is also the title of a book by Harry S. Dent Jr. on the future

that is created—even by the most avaricious and greedy individuals—will eventually benefit the public and fall to those in need. And those who do not consciously make this contribution immediately will make it later by means of legacy, heritage, or simple punitive taxation.

Other than our theory that wealth will ultimately be appropriately distributed to benefit all of society, we understand that when it comes to the attainment of it, it is a triggering agent for neither virtue nor corruption. It has no sense of right or wrong.

Money only makes you more of who you are. The truth comes in deciding who you are in the beginning, perfecting your higher self, and understanding that sooner or later wealth becomes your cosmic magnifying glass. It will show you for what you are and everything you are not. It's all a matter of determining your own consciousness and deciding whether yours is abundant or impoverished. And money, as you soon will see, has everything and nothing at all to do with what you make of it.

The Return of Arête

Without a rich heart, wealth is an ugly beggar

—Ralph Waldo Emerson
"Manners"
Essays: Second Series, 1844

Many historians believe the Greeks of the ancient city-state of Athens brought their society to flourish through a concept called *arête*. There is no true direct translation of arête. The closest definition is one that signifies *courage*. Courage in any context is laudable, but in the Greek definition, it often signified courage of a different kind—the courage of one's convictions, a noble spirit. In a liberal translation, arête might well be interpreted as "the cup that runneth over." It addressed the issue of the complete human being—the Renaissance man, as it were (women were excluded from any notable function in the societies of ancient Greece).

Having achieved fulfillment in one's own lifetime, the man who had attained arête could, abundantly and with little effort, see the grace of his life's work flow into every aspect of his proximate world, giving freely and fully of his professional expertise, intellectual acumen, wealth, and personal influence to the betterment of society. It was high cachet to his accomplishments, and more; a kind of a social contract, one that proved to be as much of an obligation as a distinction.

One of the critical understandings of arête is that it was an abstraction. Like charisma, you either had it or you didn't. It wasn't subjected to weights and measures or extracted from the individual by means of tithe or public demand. Instead, it occurred as a consequence of that man's natural abundance. Like an estuary of good works, it simply cascaded into society, serving that body as both an ordination and a fulfillment.

In the beginning, this code of individual abundance did not always imply material wealth. Personal character, intellectual property, the wisdom of training and skill at a given art or craft were often paid homage as well. But in time, it was monetary riches and political power that seized the concept of arête and took it for its own. Arête became the calling card of the influential, a kind of prestige that culminated with the amassing of wealth and power. Even then, a man had to extend himself beyond personal riches to be considered a valuable citizen. He had to be able to grasp the significance of success and the honors that came with it—a realization of personal achievement, a sense of contribution to community—and convey it to others. It was a show of prosperity consciousness, an abundance of spirit that others would both admire and endeavor to emulate.

Alexander the Great, prince of the royal house of Macedonia—the poet, the learned student of Aristotle, and eventual conqueror of the known world—would certainly have been perceived to have achieved arête. But it was Pericles, the "first citizen" of Athens in the fifth century BC, from whom the concept of arête found its archetype. An accomplished man of letters, a student of music, and a brilliant political visionary, it is Pericles who instituted the first formally structured democracy in history. Imbued with a vision to place Athens at the cultural center of the world, he spearheaded the fulfillment of the Acropolis and the building of the Parthenon as Greece's cultural and political centers. Even in ruins, they stand as architectural marvels that have inspired such achievements as Jefferson's designs of Washington D.C. and virtually all of the architectural monuments of ancient Rome. An expansionist, if not an imperialist, Pericles spread Athens' sphere of influence throughout the ancient Mediterranean. Yet he did so without ever placing undue burden on the citizens of Athens. Motivated by an innate sense of social responsibility, Pericles was the embodiment of philanthropy. At the end of his life, he bequeathed his estate to the people of Athens and was said to have remarked upon his dying bed that "No Athenian has ever put on mourning through any action of mine."[31]

Since he died with his nation perched on the edge of a disastrous campaign against Sparta, we tend to think Pericles protested perhaps too much upon the virtues of his peacetime accomplishments. Yet history acquits him as having been a noble visionary as well as for having been equitable, egalitarian, and gifted with a powerful sense of civic responsibility.

Given such qualities, one could never be poor. And yet in the face of achieving them one becomes humbled in the awareness of how we have come by such things. Granted, success and the wealth that it carries create its own kind of invulnerability and the sheer joy of its own expansiveness. And yet it is incomplete if its light is kept hidden. Shining that light does not imply a gross display of riches. It does, however, insist that your abundance be conveyed to others, not through some coerced altruism but as it flows progressively through you. In that way you, as a river coursing along its path, refresh the hope of others through the natural ebbs and flows of who you are.

Prosperity vs. Poverty Consciousness.

Wealth spawns its own special kind of creature, and there is no certain formulation for how it affects people who attain it.

As we shall soon illustrate, some of the most mean-spirited people in history have, at the exclusion of all else, developed a knack for acquiring incalculable monetary wealth, while others found their wealth to be born of a prosperity consciousness. And even though financially bankrupt at times, they were never without it.

This brings us to two entirely disparate schools of thought (and there are supporters in legion for both) where perceptions of abundance versus lack come into conflict.

One comes from the *Old Testament* and more explicitly from the *Torah,* And that is the belief in *kinahara,* or the *fear* that Jehovah would punish (or strike dead!) the spendthrift, the sybarite, or even those who wantonly displayed their wealth.

It can be charted all the way back to Genesis 41, and Joseph's interpretations of Pharaoh's dreams, warning him of the seven years of famine and the need to prepare for them by setting aside a portion of one's bounty. Such "plague years" were predicted and planned for periodically throughout the Old Testament of the Bible. And a good thing too, because all the prophesies were fulfilled.

By many interpretations of the Old Testament, Jehovah was never too happy about gross displays of wealth in any case, because it seemed that everyone from Joseph and his coat of many colors to Job were always being punished for flaunting their opulence, for being grandiose, or even for being economically favored. Since there are at least 47 different references in the same books about His desiring abundance for His chosen people, this created a paradox that carried over into the Christian faith, because for centuries the rather well-healed Catholic church taught both its priests and parishioners that poverty was a virtue and, along with humility, one of the certain passages to heaven. Meanwhile, even the most impoverished peasants were, in peril of their souls, expected to tithe.

The Hindu teach that its highest of five castes, The Brahmins, must renounce their its worldly wealth and return to sparse surroundings, meager circumstances and modest clothing—virtually a beggar's existence—in order to be freed from their place on the wheel of life and ascend into Nirvana. And of course, the Buddha was a prince who abandoned his heritage as the future suzerain (or king) to pursue the path of the mendicant priest, living in the moment and off the charity of Nature.

All these were religions that reconformed cultures to be set at odds with themselves for even enjoying a few moments of material pleasure. And yet by the very teachings of those same faiths, impoverishment too is thought to be abhorrent, either a sin or a karmic debt of unwashable proportions.

"A poor man's wisdom is despised, and his words are not heard," comes the warning from Ecclesiastes (9:16). The peasants, the coolies, the untouchables, have always been believed to carry ignorance on their brows and disease in their pockets.

That leaves so many of us with a tradition of the tepid middle path, that gray unspectacular life that garners neither praise nor blame. We build those little boxes for ourselves, line them with worldly comforts, slip inside and snap the lid shut above us. And doesn't it sound familiar that we must turn to other representations of who we are to reinforce our feelings of purpose, our sense of accomplishment?

Of course, in modern times, we have at last evolved into the perfectly manifest material society. And yet there is the carry-over belief—and the residual guilt that goes with it—that wealth in itself, without the integrated gratification of spirit, is certain to be lost. And so we plunge again into the materialist's *Carpe diem,* seizing every day with all the pleasure and physical goods we can gather.

Karl Marx's precept that "Religion… is the opium of the people,"[32] has been slowly but certainly superseded. Entertainment has taken its place. Amusements, things, "Sharper Image" executive toys, SUVs,

DVDs, soap operas, multi-media feature films, and cheap vacations to Maui have become the mind candy that seems to sate the spirit. And though they speak nicely to us, they do not speak well of us. Diversions change. New designs come out. They update. They modernize. They tantalize. And all of us must keep up. We have to have the latest models; our peace of mind depends upon it. Lost in the cycle of acquisition—of more and better of everything—we continue in their pursuit, until we arrive at the realization that we have become the collection of our collections. Like the mindless vagrant who wheels along his shopping cart piled high with someone else's discarded necessities, we have come to be owned by that which we possess without noting or even remembering the preponderance of trivia they bring into our lives.

This is a poverty consciousness in the extreme, and yet it is our own rebellion, a way of fighting for our right to individuation. We reach out for acquisitions because, for the moment at least, they make us feel greater than we would be on our own. Somehow, we indulge in the hidden delight that we are flouting social tradition by doing so. Meanwhile, we feel overriding guilt, because at the same time we are hammered with the virtues of the *Millionaire Next Door** and the belief that financial success can be cultured in increments and be guarded like buried treasure. We are also told that we must economize our enjoyment, must sock away our abundance to fend off the tarnishing edges of our future; the rainy day, the seven years of lack. And it's actually good advice.

Frugality is to be admired at times. It buys us that imponderable element known as security. And if we are leading our lives inside the box that has been built for us, it is assuredly an element of survival. The question that comes to us is, why are we just surviving? The answer would be, because we've been taught to do that first—to take care of the basics and grow our dreams of spirit out of what passes for our spare

---

* *The Millionaire Next Door* is a bestseller by Thomas J. Stanley and William Danko about how average people are able to create exceptional wealth

time. That is the safe play. And yet from the outset it impoverishes us, because it teaches us limitation. It coaches us to play for our inner directives on the side as if they were some childish fantasies. Indeed they are. But living without them, however carefully we plan, impoverishes us so that wealth—true wealth—can never be ours to hold. Meanwhile, our rightful franchise, the powerful potentials within us, are left to waste away like vestigial glands from which our body of circumstance no longer requires a service.

Denying your full potential creates as much poverty of consciousness as does stinginess, niggardly hoarding of worldly goods, and a denial of your humanity to others truly in need. Unless you are fulfilled in who you are, unless you are committed to that secret code inside you, no amount of wealth will assuage the sense of lack you will feel. Power shopping every week won't do it. Buying three cars or your fantasy yacht won't do it.

There is only one answer to finding the prosperity in your life, and that lies in acknowledging that you already possess it. You have it within you to achieve your own level of arête. And when you do, all wealth, prosperity and sense of completion will flow abundantly from you. First, however, you will have to determine the kind of wealth you desire: wealth of spirit, arête, the conviction of the committed soul; or pure monetary gain and all the power that implies. To answer the unasked question, "no." They don't have to be mutually exclusive. But they tend to be. And as is the case with all things in life, we have some choices to make.

While you are making them, we cannot emphasize often enough that abundance is a state of mind. As we have so carefully noted, it is one of the pivotal means of getting larger than life. If you are physically, mentally, emotionally and spiritually balanced, if you live and breathe abundance, you are rich already, and you can never be impoverished.

The Mentality of Thriving. The Moguls' Secrets.

All exceptionally wealthy people appear to have at least a few qualities in common. Whether they are likable or despicable, whether they are visionaries or opportunists, whether they are passionate industrialists or simply devoted to the gathering of fortune, they all share specific values when it comes to a sense of the greater vision, to spotting trends, and to understanding the maintenance of personal clarity in the midst of the madness of crowds. They also possess an uncanny knack for the administration of what we call *intelligent abundance*—that is, the application of generosity in ways that reward all concerned.

We cover these unique qualities shared in common by so many of the well-to-do with a clear understanding that this is not a "how to" attain financial security, a primer on ways to take charge of your finances, or "the millionaire's (billionaire's) secrets' of gathering wealth. From *Think and Grow Rich* to *Seven Steps to Financial Success,* there are enough books on techniques of enhancing one's prosperity potentials and building one's financial portfolio to fill a business library. Of course, we can all benefit from financial planning, success planning, savings strategies, tips on how to succeed in real-estate, insights to investing, and techniques of masterminding with others smarter then we. But those provide the mechanics of acquisition; they are techniques. And though many of them are admirably clever and often effective, they deal with surface strategies and not the true potentials of the individuals they instruct.

What we are offering here are aspects of a "prosperity consciousness" that we believe all great moguls have in common. There are dozens of proliferations of each, yet like the truth itself, invariably all aspects of success have simple underpinnings.

1. A sense of the greater vision. Most truly wealthy people have both a sense of vision and a passion that drives them beyond all else. If it is not all-consuming, it is energizingly clear. The best measurement of success is a love of, and a faith in, your chosen field that goes beyond the mere attainment of money. Almost invariably, it carries with it a rampant sense of plenitude that demands to be shared, and a broadness of spirit that makes the pursuit of riches resolutely contagious.

"I would have every man a capitalist," John D. Rockefeller Sr. declared. "Every man, woman and child. I would have everyone save his earnings and not squander them, own the industries, own the railroads, own the telephone lines."[33]

He made this passionate declaration upon setting his trust fund and stock-sharing program for all the employees of Standard Oil, the company he founded. He possessed a vision and a commitment to see it fulfilled. And yet John D. Rockefeller once became noted for the misquoted statement, "The public be damned." Actually what he said was "public opinion be damned," in reaction to someone's unfounded concerns about a Standard Oil's apparent monopoly. Still, our misunderstanding of him was our legacy of press-engendered "facts" that simply didn't apply to the truth. The Rockefeller foundations and institutions he left behind set the stage for a sharing of wealth that has become synonymous with philanthropy.

A sense of the greater vision transforms the seer, often beyond the passion of his or her personal commitment to it. That is the ultimate expression of wealth that money becomes *manna,* or heaven's rain, and the legacy is something that remains for all to share. That's what visions are about. The best among them come divinely inspired; the worst, divinely directed. The best come early in one's career and sweep the visionary along in the currents of his or her own potential. The worst come as a final act of contrition, an expiation of sin, and yet explode like a gigantic sigh of relief that erupts from the cosmos itself.

"The man who dies rich... dies disgraced," Andrew Carnegie was once quoted as saying.[34] A hard-driving, often ruthless industrialist, he never once lost sight of his vision that the distribution of his wealth was part of his plan for being on earth.

There are examples by the score of wealthy men, whose personal virtues might otherwise be held in question, yet whose vision for creating wealth and abundance went far beyond the mere expansion of their own empires and extended to every aspect of society itself.

That is a part of recognizing that the prosperity power that is in you comes with the ability to know that you can, through your own desire to become larger than life, grow into the game of wealth. Soon, you come to realize, as many billionaires do from the outset, that by extending your vision for abundance to go beyond your personal wants and needs, you expand to fit your prosperity mission; you become the wealth that you foresee for everyone else around you. Once you come out of centering on yourself and start to think of your skill, service, or abundance in terms of serving others, you will find that success comes more easily to you.

It is the universe's way of saying 'thank you.'

You will find that, even though your circumstances may appear dire in the beginning, fear will no longer have a stranglehold on you. A sense of accomplishment will synergize you, infusing you with clear vision that prosperity is not only available but also available upon request. That is the mogul's consciousness. And whether that consciousness comes in the form of a preordained spiritual awareness or simply the instincts of the street, it serves you well.

2. Personal Clarity. The power of "Trendspotting." Let us be categorical here: Power is instantly able to read fear. We also hold firmly to the belief that fear in the midst of benevolent power acknowledges that power is like an obedient dog, waiting to receive guidance and control as well a sense of direction. On the surface that is, once again, a paradox. So, let us elaborate:

We have already made note of the fact that every crowd is, at its core, driven by fear. And it serves one well to be able to discern the level of that fear and know either how to assuage it, how to avoid it, or how to capitalize upon it. This is particularly true of what we earlier referred to as the Category Four crowd—or the hidden mob of world financial markets.

In his *Age of the Moguls,* author Stewart Hollbrook makes a definitive evaluation of the great industrialists and financiers who, in the early 20th century, forged America's future. According to Hollbrook's model, the true visionary entrepreneur is the kind of master delusionist who can differentiate between the true Force 4 event and the "bubble" that often forms inside of it, and capitalize on each of them. Such mega-moguls as J.P. Morgan, John D. Rockefeller, Cornelius Vanderbilt, Andrew Mellon, and Andrew Carnegie, according Hollbrook, had two traits in common.

Their first common trait was an uncanny ability to time the moods of the mob. Having acquired the understanding that all world financial markets were driven by both fear and greed, the industrial prime movers of the turn of the 20th century were able not only to anticipate market trends but to manipulate them as well. Their insight into the instability of the fear-driven financial markets enabled them to operate in the calm of both short-term trading and long-term deliberations. Understanding that the unforeseen force of hysterical conversation of all financial markets could be used to their benefit, they could detect the difference between confident urgency and reactive fear. Because of that, they were not only able to stay ahead of the game; they had invented it.

The second quality all these people held in common was the power not only to recognize trends but also to set them. Without exception, they were inveterate futurists. As such, they could instantly differentiate between a one-time commodity Zeitgeist such as tulipmania and a Force 4 event such as the arrival of the Internet. This intuition can only be perfected when fear has been voided from one's spiritual vernacular and replaced by an understanding of destiny.

Astute evaluations of markets and events—we choose to call it *Trendspotting*—come as a result of an intelligent understanding of the group dynamic, both in the streams of positive thought at the high end of the collective consciousness and the madness of crowds that marks the lower resides of the awareness spectrum.

Streams of positive thought in the collective consciousness come in the sheer joy of formulation that individuals experience when they are integral in the development of a trend, when they are part of a movement that they know is going to change the way we conduct our lives for the better.

Such movements are given a Force Level ranking from 1 through 4, a Force 4 event being the one that engenders the highest level of impact. If our sense of timing teaches us nothing else, it should awaken us to the nature of true Force 4 events. By definition, a Force 4 event is an element, invention, or creation of technology that not only reflects the progress of an era but also alters the entire conduct of it, as well as all eras to follow.

The design and implementation of the internal combustion engine (such as are found in the locomotive and the steamboat) was a Force 4 event. The automobile was a Force 4 event. So was the electric light. So was the telephone. So was aviation. So was television. The invention of the computer and the quantum leap of life enhancements that have stemmed from it have made the 1980s and 1990s in particular the last Force 4 experience of the 20th century. Most experts already agree that the first Force 4 event of the 21st century will be the explosion of world commerce on the Internet.

It also logically follows in the procession of human history that the momentum surrounding a Force 4 occurrence carries with it the sociological impact of a tidal wave. Such power pervades it that its resonance alone attracts the madding crowd and all the fads, rages, and frenzies that so often unfairly stigmatize it.

Just as there was the lunatic fringe surrounding the beginning of flight, just as there were crackpots and failures in the age of invention that ended the 19th century and began the 20th, there is already the inevitable entourage of madness surrounding the development of the Internet. Each Force 4 event in history is rife with its own retinue of eccentrics, imitators, and scams.

During the 1920s that saw the heyday of the automobile, there were more than 200 car manufacturers in the United States who had presented designs, run advertising campaigns, and issued stock. Many of them were legitimate "players," such as Studebaker, Packard, and Nash. Others had little more than a garage and a single prototype. And yet they managed to find the "greater fool" to invest in their ill-funded, poorly planned, and often bogus enterprises. Today, eighty years later, there are three major U.S. manufacturers—the Big Three—and a handful of truck, tractor, and heavy equipment manufacturers.

The question is, in the wake of what was the arguably the most significant Force 4 movement since the automobile, who will survive the frenzy? The core truth at the heart of any Force 4 event remains inviolate. In time, the movement itself will strip away all extraneous activity and will do so with a calculated ruthless efficiency. Just as the Internet will change the course of world technology and communications from this moment forward, there are lies that wrap around it to confuse the unwary. They come in two forms. The first one says that the information superhighway is a Zeitgeist that is merely a precursor to the ultimate communications breakthrough that will follow. The second is that the Internet is a technology momentum locomotive, upon which any passage you book will guide you safely home. In truth, there is often more penalty invoked in coming too early and blatantly ill-prepared to a Force 4 movement than in coming too late.

In the midst of all this, there exists the perfect time for companies with vision, sophisticated technology and truly original concepts for Internet commerce to succeed beyond all previous means of measurement, one that will reward the savvy investor, the gifted entrepreneur, the business opportunist, and the astute consumer.

But how does one time such things? In trying to learn how to time the smaller games of our personal universe, how many of us ignore the larger games of life? How many of us believe we can make an impact in the wake of a Force 4 event when we failed to recognize it for what it was? How many of us were consciously aware of what a Force 4 event was or that we were living in a sequence of them? That is a part of the delusionist's challenge: to be aware of the world around us and be tireless in our vigil to behold the bright light in the clouds.

These skills have come as a result of constant focus. They also come with a warning: Never succumb to the moods of the crowd. Understand the mob. Note its ebbs and flows. Even learn to anticipate it. But never fall into it. To do so prompts the worst kind of conformity, one that can prove disastrous—because it takes away your power.

Always understand that any vision worth holding merits long term consideration. Short-term seekers of profit and loss and wild leaps into the maelstrom of financial frenzies are not investing. They're gambling.

The truth of one's vision is acquitted with time.

"Let us wait for the wisest counselor of all... Time," a very wise man once said. His name was Pericles.

3. The Law of Intelligent Abundance. It has become a factor in the just society that it is in the public interest to reward philanthropy. Living trusts have become the legitimate tax harbors of the rich, and practically every billionaire has long since predetermined the nature, structure, and degree of his or her giving. Foundations, libraries, trust funds, and tithing are established perhaps less out of personal magnanimity than for generous tax advantage; that is as it should be. Those who have worked hard to obtain wealth should be able to determine the direction as well as the velocity of their generosity.

Of course, that kind of mega-mogul largesse is both calculated and accordingly factored-in as being part of the overflow of superabundance. The Carnegie-Mellon Institutes, the Rockefeller Foundations, the Vanderbilt Universities—all are products of largesse that had to be given because not to do so would condemn their wealth and relinquish the control of it to taxation. In the new millennium, such benefactors as Berkshire Hathaway's mutual fund inspirator Warren Buffet and Microsoft Founder Bill Gates have given billions for their namesake foundations because their boundless wealth empowers them to do so at no virtual cost to them. That is the concept of arêté applied to modern times. That is a structure of social justice, and yet another blessing that stems from living in a republic.

But where does that leave the rest of us? We can become checkbook benefactors, contribute to charities, and organize our time to devote to the cause-group of our choice. Or we can understand that these very good acts are just a beginning, that abundance—*intelligent abundance*—finds its truest haven in the flow of who we are.

With little effort and without all the money in the world, we can be enriched in every expression of ourselves. Part of this comes with being the light and getting larger than life. Part of it comes with understanding that our passion for life is our power, and the greatest capital we can possess. The rest of it comes by realizing that every act we commit emits an energy from us, and that energy will expend abundance as fully as it is given.

It comes from doing a favor for a friend, from holding a door for a stranger, from giving a dollar to a beggar on the street without the extraction of judgment, or rescuing a companion animal who appears to be lost. It comes from taking it upon ourselves to go public with our lives—to get involved in our community and make sure others have an understanding of the goals we all share. It comes with setting out wild bird seed to help our feathered friends get through a cold patch in the winter. It grows out of our willingness to listen to others, rather than speak from the hollow room of our own self-image. It blossoms out of never forgetting a special occasion of someone close to you. It expresses itself in every tip you give, every gift you wrap, every time you do something to benefit others before you reward yourself. It also comes with remembering to be good to yourself, and by showing a willingness to receive as richly as you have given. Because when you flourish, when you take those moments to shine in your appearance, in the way you are, in the manner in which you prosper, you can be a beacon to proclaim to others: "This too can be yours." It comes by wearing your prosperity with both grace and gratitude. It comes in remembering to say "thank you," in acknowledging others in the little things they do that otherwise might go unnoticed. It comes through being good to your word, through answering your correspondence, by reciprocating good turns, and by speaking your mind when people look to you for the truth. It comes in allowing extra time for your family and those you love; because those who cannot give their time to loved ones are impoverished beyond the periphery of pity.

Intelligent abundance is the understanding that every act we commit, every word we speak, every moment through which we interact with others is an opportunity to give of ourselves, to let our deeds—without fail—follow our intentions, and to enrich the moments of everyone around us. It's nice to speak of; it's pleasant to contemplate. But unless we are abundant in deed, we are not properly pressing into service the bounties we have been given. It costs so little, and yet it accomplishes so much.

It has been our experience that the most successful people always find time to do these things. No matter how busy or important, they make it a part of their daily lives to address the needs of others—they see to the tiny kindnesses that the rest of us forget—because they comprehend the value of every moment we live.

Our actions and behaviors determine attitudes and beliefs—not only our own, but also those of others who observe us and the manner of who we are. If we speak of abundance, act abundantly, and are abundant in each expression of our selves, we become their lightning rod. We can set the spark in them that recharges that inner voice: "I, too, can become what I behold."

We are all one another's teachers, our role models for better or worse. That is why, to close this chapter, we have selected three examples of people who have revealed, by their actions, why money only makes you more of who you already are. Two of them are famous. And one, though well-known, has asked to remain anonymous.

In truth, we could refer to dozens of examples, enough to fill a book in itself. But for the purposes of this section, we point to three archetypes who are studies in contrast: one a terribly misperceived impresario whom history has only recently revealed to us in the total context of who he was; the second, a visionary billionaire whose historical impact is often misunderstood and perennially underrated; the third, a role-model "millionaire next door," a self-made millionaire whose life, conduct and success serves as an example of all that is possible for any one of us beyond the mere acquisition of wealth.

"Money is a hard master," P.T. Barnum was once purported as having said. Yet as we shall see, it never mastered him; in truth, he made it his servant. He understood abundance and lived it in everything he did.

P.T. Barnum. The Father of "Show Business."

No public figure ever received as much misrepresentation as P.T. Barnum, and yet no one would have appreciated the irony of it more.

Phineas Taylor Barnum is best remembered for two things: The popularization of the circus, and the apocryphal statement attributed to him in the press: "There's a sucker born every minute." It is doubtful that he ever said it. Yet this became the factual paradigm from which he was perceived by the public

In truth, it could be fairly said of Phineas T. Barnum that he virtually invented family entertainment as we know it today. He was the modern progenitor of what we commonly refer to as "show business."

Born in the first decade of the 19th century, Barnum was the son of a modest shopkeeper in Connecticut and never entirely abandoned his cultural roots.

Still, early on he beheld the light in the eye of the average person—the need to be dazzled, the need to be delighted, and the need to be entertained. At the time, when the world of entertainment was divided between the operas, theaters, the symphonies (avocations of the rich) and dancehalls, gambling, boxing and barrooms (the curse of the hoi polloi), entertainment as we know it now was practically an abstraction. And except for the occasional county fair and cattle show, there was virtually nothing for the modest family to do other than to parade through a stuffy museum or listen to a band of local amateur musicians.

As a very young man he acquired the backing to take over the dull, financially troubled Sutter's Museum in New York City and turn it into an affordable showcase of exciting events. Constructing a theatre built for "intellectual lectures," he reconformed it for nightly shows of family entertainment. He brought the masses culture such as the ballet and cloaked it as pure entertainment. He brought the public the glorified circus (The Barnum and Bailey) and expanded into three and later five rings, each filled with the most skilled, amusing, and fascinating acts available in the world—the general public's first ever multimedia experience, "The Greatest Show on Earth!"

Often thought of as deluded, he never demurred from his sense of vision, and viewed all adversity as a challenge to be something better. If one word could define him, it would be as a *positivist*. Credit part of this to his spiritual training in the Universalist church, and a doctrine which teaches that all events in one's life are for the best—a part of God's plan. That does nothing to detract from the generous spirit of the man himself. Nothing ever got P.T. Barnum down, and only prejudice and human cruelty such as slavery ever invoked his ire. When his investors high-hatted him and refused to acknowledge him socially, he praised their business acumen and paid them off early and with interest. When his prized museum burned to the ground, he looked upon it as an opportunity to build a new one on the same location on an even grander scale. When his wife lost a child at birth, he looked upon the tragedy as a sign to spend more time with his family. When his home burned to the ground, he saw that as a drive to build another, and to become more productive in his profession. When the Barnum Museum burned a second time, he looked upon it as a sign to change professions and brought the small-town traveling circus to such spectacular proportions that could only be done justice in an entertainment palace of his conception called "The Madison Square Garden."

Irrepressible, P.T. Barnum viewed money as the tool of prosperity and not its source. And though he noted some of his promotions as "a bit of a humbug," he never cheated the public out of fair value for its money. He never dishonored a personal contract, never reneged on a debt or went back on his word. He always paid off his creditors early and with interest, and was devoted to his wife until her death. Finally passing from this life in 1891, he had outlived most of his contemporaries and died, it was said, with a smile on his face while inquiring about that day's profit from "The Barnum and Bailey."

The least that could be said of Barnum was that he helped people learn how to dream again, and his legacy was a fanfare for the common man.

Ross Perot. The Billionaire Populist.

We begin this profile with a purely subjective but nonetheless firm conviction: Ross Perot almost single-handedly changed the face of modern American politics. In an era when public cynicism about our political leadership was at an all-time high, when our government was three trillion dollars in debt, and our national political morale was at an all-time low, this billionaire entrepreneur simply and effectively reinvolved the American public in their nation's business.

Perhaps it took a billionaire maverick to do it. But in a world where most of the super rich are concerned with the further acquisition of empire, Ross Perot saw his considerable wealth as an opportunity to create the leverage necessary to actually effect change. It was in keeping with his character as well as the patterns of his professional career to do so.

In his way, Ross Perot perfectly fits the delusionist's profile in that, like Henry Ford before him, he kept counsel with his vision of what could be done in his industry despite the tide of popular opinion. Just as Ford in the infancy of the automobile industry found a way to design the first assembly line and mass-produce cars so that everyone could afford one, Perot was one of the pioneers of computer technology. A top field representative for IBM in the infancy of the computer era in the 1960s, he quickly saw through the web of circumstance of hardware sales to the infinite potential that lay in designing systems software for the major computer manufacturers. Founder and Chairman of Electronic Data Systems (EDS), Perot later confided that the reason for his rapid rise to prominence, power, and personal wealth lie in the fact that no one else would invest in his fledgling company.

"In those early years, when we were starting up, I couldn't get anyone else to invest in us. So I had to put up most the money myself. And all I could take in exchange for it was stock."

It is a quality of true vision that it voids itself of fear, and those who succeed cannot afford to have doubt counsel their destiny. It is a perception men like Ross Perot came by early and kept as a conviction during the years that challenged their growth.

Brought up in modest circumstances in a close-knit, loving family on a small ranch outside Texarkana, Texas, Ross Perot pursued a boyhood dream and broke through the barriers of social privilege and political connections to secure himself a rare Senate appointment to the United States Naval Academy.

Self-empowerment counselor (and *Seeds of Greatness* author) Denis Waitley was a contemporary underclassman of Ross Perot's at Annapolis, served with him in the Navy and remembers him well: "You always knew where you stood with Ross Perot. He always came straight at you, always looked you in the eye, always spoke his mind and never once wavered from the truth of who he was. He always spoke to you, never about you. And never left any question about what his expectations of integrity would be. You had to respect a man like that. And you couldn't help but recognize that this was the kind of man who was born to lead."[35]

When EDS grew to be one of the most influential technology firms of their time and Ross Perot came to be one of the richest men in America, he immediately saw that wealth as an instrument of personal conscience and public statement. In 1969, he flew in the face of public sentiment against an unpopular war in Vietnam, and chartered two Braniff Airlines jets to carry a cargo of Christmas gifts to our POWs in North Vietnam. When, in 1979, the U.S. Embassy was seized in Iran and certain U.S. corporate officials were being "detained" by the new government of the Ayatollah Khomeni, Perot financed and spearheaded a successful undercover commando mission to get his people out, while the Carter administration floundered ineffectually, complaining that he had "acted rashly."

In the early '90s, when Ross Perot saw a rudderless U.S. economic policy, a national debt in the trillions, and a disaffected American voting public, he launched a grass-roots campaign for president that has since become a legend in American political history. His issues, as usual, were ones of character and of legacy to our children. With a slight build, cartoon ears and squeaky voice that were fodder for caricature, Ross Perot kept his sense of humor, kept his perspectives on the greater good, and launched a political stump campaign that went to the core issues of the American people. He spoke from the heart and opened them up to the best of all possible worlds, including reinstilling in them a belief in their own power to effect change. Out of that effort a new political party was born.

Many believe that, had his campaign not stalled by a brief unexpected withdrawal, Ross Perot might have actually been elected. That seemed to concern him less than the successful empowerment of the voting public, and the formation of a third party—the Reform Party—that experienced its beginnings in the 1992 presidential campaign.

It didn't even visibly seem to chafe Ross Perot when on the network televised three-way debates, Bill Clinton (the consummate political chameleon) eventually began to shadow all his policy stances and "me too" his positions on the economy. The only unrehearsed candidate in the debates, Perot's messages rang true and his purpose remained clear. And when he looked up at the gallery of students at Washington University in St. Louis, and said, "This election is not about us. It's about our children, and their children, and the generations to come. You up in the balcony. I'm doing this for you," the house came down with the eloquence of thunderous applause that no amount of rhetoric from his opponents could overcome.[36]

Ultimately, The Reform Party, the party Ross Perot inspired, expanded to embrace a broad base of political philosophies that tend to put principal above mere party politics. It has prompted a revolution in the political context of America, if for no other reason than now people who have a belief and are willing to passionately pursue it, have a forum for expression outside the network of politics as usual.

Rather than the continued pursuit of wealth, Ross Perot has always pursued issues of character and has often flown in the face of popular opinion to do so. His flawed campaign against NAFTA was a study in noble failure; and time has proved him right in so many ways. (The Mexican Peso has devalued, the Mexican worker has been totally disenfranchised, and our southern borders have opened to the largest flow of cocaine into this nation in three decades.) His railings against the lack of personal morality of public officials have recently seemed quaintly out of sync with the cynical times in which we live, and yet were still infused with an undeniable correctness of conscience. He has never hesitated to publicly risk derision as long his moral compass showed us the way to true North and spoke to the greater issues inside us. (And isn't that one of our definitions of becoming larger than life?)

Would Ross Perot have been able to make such profound social impact had he not been blessed with such considerable wealth? One has to suspect that, no matter what his circumstances, he would have given it his best shot.

Lucinda Z. The Millionaire Next Door.

Characteristic of her modesty, Lucinda Z. has chosen to have her identity kept secret, and yet is the first to insist that if she can become a millionaire, anyone can.

"For me, having abundance was not a choice. It was a necessity," Lucinda remembers, with a glint of determination that precludes debate.

Her reasons are well-founded and unwavering. Born the only daughter of a famous show business couple, she knew the taste of opulence just long enough to savor it before it was pulled away from them all at the ripe old age of seven. With their careers on the wane and their money squandered on bad investments, her parents

soon divorced, leaving her mother, Lucinda, and her two brothers to face a lifestyle that was suddenly in lack.

Seeing her mother having to carry on with no practical career skills and only one property (a small apartment house) as a source of income, the young Lucinda soon found her entire family facing a life of perennial deprivation. Barely able to make ends meet, and receiving little in the way of financial assistance from their bankrupt father, the young family barely eked out an existence.

But it was then that Lucinda decided that she would never be in lack again. Studying the "science of mind" taught in her Christian Science faith, she embraced the belief that she could, out of the power of her mental focus, draw to her the kind of abundance she had always wanted.

"If you don't see failure as an option, it eventually loses all its power," she observes, adhering to a very spiritual truism that has long been a guiding influence for her life.

When she grew into mature teenage, Lucinda borrowed money to get a car to get her to her part-time job (and paid the note off instantly), borrowed money to put herself through college and promptly paid off the loan, and learned how to shoe-string finance-troubled real-estate properties.

At twenty-one she blossomed into a stunningly beautiful woman but eschewed the lures of show business in lieu of a full-time career in real estate.

"There were simply too many uncertainties in that world (of film). You're at the mercy of so many people for so long," she remembers: "I wanted a career that would net you a proportionate reward for your efforts—where you could see immediate tangible results."

Along the way, even though she had no money in the beginning, she looked upon giving of herself as an essential part of her character and of the natural law of tithing. Whether it was bringing meals to an octogenarian shut-in, or finding a lost stray dog or cat a home (usually hers), Lucinda saw every act in life as a chance to make a difference.

"You may not always have money, but you can always find ways to help others. It always comes back to you in so many good ways; that's universal law."

Uncanny in her sense of value, she became a leading Los Angeles real-estate agent and wealthy in the bargain. The quintessential "millionaire next door," she sees even the most ordinary purchase as an opportunity for the acquisition of value—and through that wealth. Rather than buy furniture, she bargain-hunts for antiques. Rather than purchase a car that will depreciate, she buys a classic that is certain to appreciate. Rather than buy knickknacks for the house, she gathers *objects d'art* and never laments if one of them gets broken.

Having amassed several million dollars over the years, Lucinda has been able to build a home for her mother, a townhouse for her brother, purchase a home for her step-mother and was able to support her husband's foray into show business until he made it as a star in a long-running television series. Once, her husband struck it big as a television star, she was able to set up a pension fund that would provide for him no matter what kind of downturns came in his career.

Now, well into her forties, Lucinda has the glow and beauty of a 25 year-old (much of that beauty from within). She never forgets a birthday, never ignores a friend in need, and never hesitates to honor requests from others to participate in causes that make this world a better place. Having rescued dozens of cats, dogs, and small animals from euthanasia or laboratories, she is an avid animal rights activist and is in the process of setting up the bulk of her estate to found, fund, and successfully perpetuate an environmentally friendly small animal non-kill shelter.

Lucinda's wealth, like her life, is the greater extension of who she is, and the world is so much the better for it.

Summary

By now, it should have become evident that money only makes you more of who you are, and we could cite enough personal role models—both positive and negative—to fill a volume of books. We examined what we believe to be very positive role models in this chapter—not to set forth some paeans of praise for who they are, but because they decided early in their lives to stand for something, because their character preceded their wealth, and because one does not find clear water in a swamp.

To be sure there are *antitypes* to the wealth scenario. People who are mean-spirited, greedy, vindictive and ostentatious in the exercise of the wealth and power they have acquired number in legion. There are national leaders from Iraq to Indonesia to give examples of the corruption that wealth for its own sake can create. But hasn't the cosmic magnifying glass shown them for who they are? And aren't they in peril every day of losing their ill-gotten wealth?

Character is the final arbiter of power, and personal power almost always predetermines great wealth. You might acquire wealth by accident, by force, by inheritance, or by pure dumb luck. But unless you have acquired both the character to use it properly and a plan that evolves into a mission, chances are you will lose it in the end.

So, in closing, we offer this delusionist's challenge to you. It comes in two parts. First, list seven wealthy people—from any era—and define what characteristics they possess that cause you to admire them. Then report your awareness of what they have done with their proximate universe. They do not have to be famous people; they may be someone in your own broad circle of involvement. We only ask that you examine who they are and know your subjects accurately. You may find a commonality to your choices that will tell you a great deal about who you are and about your perceptions of wealth.

In part two, we ask you to define your own wealth profile. Write down the ways in which your wealth or abundance has changed your life—that is if you have possession in great measure. If you do not, then you might examine why you do not, and what you would do differently if you did possess wealth. Would you opt for total consumption and self-gratification? Or would you include both service and balance in the mix of what you do? Would you have a plan for intelligent abundance? If not, what would you do to set one in place?

As always, you are at choice in answering these questions, just as you are in setting forth a course of intelligent abundance in your life.

Chapter 11

Quantum Connections

Psychologist Nathaniel Branden once observed that in relationships, one plus one never equals two—that it is either more than two or less than two. And though that sentiment was first advanced in his book *The Psychology of Romantic Love* about love relationships. We think it applies to all relationships, and spawns a kind of quantum math all its own.

It is a universal rule of human intercourse that everything is based upon relationships. We would like to add the word "positive" to that equation. Yet we note, sadly, that millions of people are either utterly lacking in the ability to relate to others or are living the lie that their dysfunctional relationships are actually acceptable. We're here to prompt the delusion that you can have what we call *quantum connections* in every area of your life, provided you are willing to apply some creative rethinking in the way you approach them.

We say that in full recognition of the fact that the vast majority of people are failing in relationships at some level. Many are successful in business and professional associations yet fail to sustain clear, loving bonds within their own families. Others may have dynamic, committed family relationships yet fail to cultivate business associations that will be both beneficial and enduring. Many people are professionally sound, have profoundly loving family relationships, and yet either experience negative interactions within their own communities, or else have no outside social life. Other than clumsy attempts at flirtation, men and women who lack the ability to find rapport with members of the opposite sex number in legion. And oceans of individuals, except for occasional interactive obligations, are isolated from everyone. Some of the latter comes by choice, as a part of the self-possessed super-cocooning desocialization of Generation X. Yet it is also a matter of lifestyle creep that has also come to affect us all to some degree—even the ultra-sociable baby boomers and their media-obsessive GenY offspring.

When you examine the true nature of our lives, everything we undertake, outside the quiet contemplation of our private moments of prayer and meditation, involves some degree of interaction with others. We are either doing it, planning it, or reviewing it at every turn. And each exchange, even one that is seemingly superficial, offers either an opportunity for success or a threat of failure. If this seems onerous, it shouldn't. It is simply the emotional currency of living this life of ours. A successful life is about making connections. And each one may be either more than or less than the sum of its parts.

That sends you back to your matrix thinking as a point of reference. If it is based in Love and comes from the resonance of your attunement with your purpose in life, your interactions at all levels will come from a source of power—true Power. If not, if they crank out of the confusion of your selfish ego desires, they will put you in a position of lack, need, and evident weakness. That weakness will virtually seep into everything you do; it will expose you. And people who are weakened to this degree will have to find their power in pathological ways such as disempowering others and betraying the very images they are initially striving to represent.

Rest assured, just as relationships determine the success of all levels of human intercourse, personal power predetermines the success of any relationship. That is the misconception that sends everyone clamoring to hold onto their own power. This fixation with personal power generates a power struggle which in turn invokes the cycle of attack-and-defend that is such familiar terrain for all of us. Familiar terrain or not, that seeming firmament eventually becomes a quagmire of inner conflict into which most relationships sink.

Make no mistake about it: *For any relationship to be mutually beneficial, power must be shared; it must be freely given and readily received. One must be able to empower others and to grow into the synergy of one's interaction with them without losing command of one's own base of power.*

On the surface, this appears to be another paradox, the ultimate contradiction, an insupportable illusion. It is all of the above and none of the above.

The Power Paradox.

Let us be very emphatic in our advancement of yet another theory: There is no zero-sum game in relationships. Winning at the expense of another will cost you in equal measure. So, unless you focus strongly on zapping the flak—on making every situation better, no matter how challenging it may be—you will invariably find yourself being dragged down to the lowest common denominator.

If you are in a position of dominance in any relationship, and you disempower others, they will start to depart from you the moment that you do. It may not be evident immediately, but inevitably you will lose them. It can come in a number of ways—from open rebellion and retaliation to the little slips of inefficiency, irresponsibility and indiscretion; or it can be the cryptic seeking of other relationships. It can amount to crushing betrayals, or (when one is paired in love) infidelity. But it seldom varies and never fails that mutual empowerment is so much an integral part of every relationship—business, social, and romantic— that it cannot be denied.

When a group admires its leader, it's because he or she is "such a dynamic person." They're powerful; they're charismatic; they have the magic. They convey that power, that sense of invincibility to others. They form a coterie of devotees, a dynamic clique that generates a chemistry all its own. Whether it is a sports team or a business organization, they form a kind of splendid synergy, a quantum leap beyond the measure of the individual self. It happens in a magical season, that rare combination of personal chemistry spontaneously generating a momentum that often seems indomitable.

When two lovers first engage in the euphoria of a passionate relationship, they can feel the power that surges through them, the sense of being greater than they are alone. Their attraction is stronger, their energy levels higher, their capacity for expressions of love seemingly inexhaustible. They can't get enough of one another. Their personal chemistry stretches beyond the bounds of physical limitation; they are driven by a sacred passion.

By the same token, when a love relationship begins to fade, one or both of the partners declares that they "no longer feel important" to the other, an admission that they have somehow lost their power. They feel undervalued, their personal worth diminished; it is a foreshadowing of the end.

When people engage in friendships, in male or female bonding and peer group associations, they do so because they often have shared goals, similar professional aspirations, and congruent political sentiments. There is a power to be found in it, a satisfaction that this is a safe haven for their identity for a while. In youth, these associations are spontaneous and emotional. Later in life, they become more calculated. Belonging to just the right club, the right business association, the proper social atmosphere, all become conducive to one's advancement in the ranks. More than a social comfort zone, it increasingly becomes an issue of power. We are seduced by the warm embrace of pleasure-driven groups and whittle our perceptions to yield to the collective.

Eventually, however, there arrives a crisis of consciousness when a man or a woman feels that he or she has outgrown the group and makes the decision to change affiliations. To do so takes a special courage but requires in equal measure a sense of timing and a touch of social finesse. It also comes with a willingness to take back our ability to individuate.

The prism of power remains the wicked constant in all our interactions, but only if we allow ourselves to be deceived by the mirror images it throws down before us. The issue for us becomes one of understanding that our true power rests with us alone. And if we will merely allow it to come from a higher source, it will enable us to embrace the correctness of everything we do. It overrides the surge for dominance. It transmutes the cluster consciousness. It serves the individual self without glorifying the ego, without engaging in the classic attack-and-defend scenario. It comes as a challenge to each one of us to stand in the truth of who we are, but most of all to know ourselves before we dare to know another.

More easily said than done, for though we want to believe in ourselves, we often lack the conviction to carry it through. Especially in relationships where the opinions of those closest to us can bear such weight upon us, we hold our own identity more fragile than at any other time. In truth, it is not our opponents who most often cause us to fall; it is the friendly fire of those we love. Often in error, they bind us up with the kindness of good intentions, and leave us gravely in doubt and bitter at being misunderstood. It is at this point that we emphasize that loving someone does not require you to abdicate your power to them any more than it requires you to vigorously defend who you are.

It is also at this point that we remind you to look upon those you most admire—those from whom you would draw the model of your life. In almost every case you will find that they stayed the course of their Truth. Even dressed down for their "delusions," they didn't waver from their intentions or who they were meant to be. In doing so, the interweavings of their daily lives with others never frayed. Instead they became more powerful with the passage of time. They came to their success by standing firmly in the light of their convictions without alienating others. And that is what quantum connections is all about.

The First Connection—Your Self.

There is a classic joke among psychotherapists about the egotist and the egoist—that the "egotist" thinks he's the center of the universe; the "egoist" knows he is. Of course, egoism (a Freudian term) is the reference to oneself as the sole arbiter of all moral decision and brings along its own kind of atheistic centering. Philosopher Abraham Maslow extended this self-reference to include the *self-actualized* individual. That is the person who, in modern times, would be most likely to have arête; someone who is complete in their moral centering as well as their accomplishments toward total self-empowerment, toward the renaissance persona. Like so many philosophies from the behavioral sciences, Maslow's profile of *self-actualism* is at least agnostic, and because of its agnosticism draws fire from certain religious sectors as being a God-less philosophy.

In truth, it is impossible for any philosophy to be entirely Godless, because all philosophies are justified only by their reference to the Creative Force of our universe, even when they oppose it. And self-referral, as opposed to "other" referral, is a pivotal point of emphasis of most proponents of self-empowerment. Ultimately as well as initially, we must adhere to our own truths, and not rely on the furtive opinions of others to direct our conduct. We add our support to this belief with the caveat that the ego must serve the higher self—the angelic messenger. Once it is willing to subordinate itself to a Higher Source, to our Creator, there is a peace one experiences that transcends all understanding.

By now, if you've been following at least some of the principles in this delusionist's doctrine, you've been able to determine the core of your destined purpose. You've been able to realize that you inherently possess the gift of flight, that you are capable of great things and (most important), that you are meant to give and receive unconditional love. If you've been able to clear out at least some of your Fear Matrix fixations, you've made room for that loving spirit that dwells with the child inside you to express itself more fully. You're at least in better tune with your

GUT, and your sense of timing has probably improved. Most important, you have learned that it is not only within your power but also a part of your daily bread to become larger than life. You can make every situation in which you find yourself a little better by bringing the light to it, by enlightening others even as you go through your average day. And your power is inexhaustible because, at least in part, you're allowing it to flow through you—down from the fountain of your higher self and not up from the maw of your ego.

If you've been able to grasp all this up to now, just imagine what you can bring to any relationship you share or any connection you make.

You have remarkable gifts to give. You have achieved a level of personal integrity that is unique. You have a power that is all your own. Yet, like any power, it requires a responsibility to wield it with both compassion and wit—with intelligent abundance. Each connection you make also offers you the opportunity to stand in your own truth, to hold to the power of your self without being forced to defend that self to others. That is a delicate balance indeed. And as you soon will see, it is most sorely tested in the most important connection of all—the one you make where your life's mate is concerned.

Love Connections and Euphoria Dynamics.

In truth, love between men and women isn't what it used to be. It's even more so. By all official evidence, permanent love and marriage, "until death do us part" relationships have become socially irrelevant; at least in purely technical terms. As men and women in America at least have achieved a measure of professional and economic parity, marriage is no longer required to build society as we know it. Granted, it's a better idea to marry if one is going to bring children into the world. But even so, the bonds that social convention places upon matrimony grow more tentative with each generation, and prenuptial agreements have become standard at every level of income. Marriage contracts look less like oaths of fidelity than they do preemptive strikes. And almost every futurist's projection seems to include the statistic that the typical adult in the new millennium will be married an average of three times.

What's more, modern romantic relationships have now become more centered around issues of power than they ever were in the past. This of course makes romantic love more of an illusion and more of a contradiction than we might have ever believed possible.

So, why have love pairings and marriages of the heart become more powerful institutions in society than ever before? The divorce rate in the United States since 1997 is actually down. And marriages, by percentage, have held steady—if not, in fact, increased in number.

One can no longer attribute this to the plague-year mentality that pervaded our society in the late '80s and early '90s. The AIDS epidemic spawned that rare period of social fatalism, and brought us to a new paradigm of monogamous paranoia, early marriage, and social cocooning. But HIV is no longer the death sentence it once was. There are currently a number of treatments that are now believed able to put the dread virus into remission. And sexual activity among singles is actually on the rise again. So, in many ways the old rules still apply, because it is in romantic relationships that men and women reveal the best and worst of what they are—when they are their most giving, their most selfish, and their most fatally flawed.

Pheromones kick in to a whorl of mutual attraction that is compelling if not addictive. And there accompanies the frenzy of courtship a special kind of madness, one that turns us into angels and ravening beasts all at once; one in which logic is lost in the sweet savor of passion, at least for a while. This all occurs in the wooing stage, the sweet bliss of *euphoria*. Euphoria stems from a Greek word meaning a state of joy or well-being that has no basis in logic; not a bad place to be, if you can sustain it. The challenge with most of us is that we can't.

It is the belief of some insightful relationships counselors that there are five stages of a love relationship, and only two of them are as sweet as they're meant to be. They are *1) euphoria, 2) the power struggle, 3) reconciliation, 4) rapprochement,* and *5) dynamism.*

We emphasize here that these are not necessarily our determinations. They are actually an amalgam of love connection paradigms by a very astute relationships therapist and best-selling author, Harville Hendrix, spiritual psychotherapist Carl Gustav Jung, and best-selling author and counselor Nathaniel Branden. So, we're being eclectic here, and taking the best of what we think portrays the complex mural of romantic love. But before we get into any observations about relationships between men and women, we believe they are most succinctly predicated upon one paradigm originated by Harville Hendrix—that is the *imago* concept. In brief, the *imago* (the *Latin* for "image"), is the parts of the missing self that we long to find in the opposite sex.*

Especially in seeking longstanding relationships, the imago represents the projected character *images* that exist in the person of the opposite sex that were missing from parent of the opposite sex. In other words, the little child in us seeks to fill the emotional gaps in its love relationship that were never filled by the parent of the opposite sex—the nurturing, the caring, the need for symbiosis. That means if a man had a mother who was introverted, cool, aloof, unemotional, compulsively fastidious, humorless, demanding and obsessively critical, he is going to want (if not desperately seek) a long-term life-mate who is warm, affectionate, emotionally expressive, easygoing, nurturing, supportive and gifted with a terrific sense of humor. He will be drawn to those qualities or the mirage of them—that will be his *imago* fulfillment. If a woman had a father who was an extrovert, warm, garrulous, irresponsible, overbearing, smothering, equivocal, and sloppy, she is going to be secretly in search of

---

* The *imago concept* is defined in its entirety in Harville Hendrix's bestseller *Getting the Love You Want.* Henry Holt. 1988.

a man who is dignified, fastidious, personally and financially solid, retiring (if not shy), very truthful, and willing to give her space. Of course, she is also liable to get a man who is chilly, unfeeling, calculating, demanding, and uncommunicative. And he might possibly end up with someone who is also clinging, hyper-dependent, personally coarse, and downright bawdy.

Please note that this sophisticated imago perception only applies to people who are more self-aware and more actively conscious of what they seek to avoid in their early experience. Less self-directed people—the majority, in fact—will actually superimpose their imago fixations on their choice of mate that very nearly duplicate the parent of the opposite sex, if for no other reason than the fact that these character pathologies put them on familiar ground; they can "deal with them."

Either way, this imago-fixated relationship is doomed to disappointment and eventual failure, because these expressions are needful things. They depict the shadow side of the little child in all of us who is looking for the lost part of itself and who, finding its *imago* expectations unfulfilled, rails and rants at the disappointment it feels.

None of these things will hatch out in the beginning, because there is a sixth sense in the torrid tango of courtship of just what the other party needs. So there is a wish fulfillment expressed that the euphoric lover is more than willing to oblige. Hormones can spawn a strange compliance. And when one is passionately involved, there occurs a sense of completion that seems to pour into the soul.

There exists in this the ultimate contradiction because, in seeking to be fulfilled, we have made the pronouncement that we are incomplete, that we are needful and therefore flawed. This is seldom revealed in the beginning, because the momentum of euphoria denies all contradiction. One becomes virtually drunk on the wine of consummation and the perception of invulnerability that comes from this sudden spontaneous unity of souls. There is a sense of spiritual bonding, a Tantric generator, a sacred sexual synergism that appears to have transformative powers. It is also accompanied by a Pandora's Box tied together with ribbons of expectation. And these expectations, once untied, will soon release a plague of flaws enough to doom these lovers for the rest of their time together.

It is here that we offer one iron law of all romantic relationships: *Lasting romantic relationships are like bank loans. You can only get them when you can prove that you absolutely don't need them.*

The greatest flaws in the expression of oneself seemingly come from the heart when someone says with true belief that "he completes me," or "she is the other half of me that I've been looking for."

There is an undeniable poetry that accompanies such thinking, and in the beginning it certainly seems that way. But in the end, as in the beginning, we only have who we are. And unless we feel entire unto ourselves, we can never feel complete in anyone else. This creates a dilemma for us that goes beyond romantic notion and into the nucleus of our own spiritual striving. There is a sense in us that is cellular, visceral, a GUT awareness that we—powerful on our own—may amplify that power if we couple with our true soul mate. Such loves are the stuff of legend and romance, because they have a basis in truth. That imponderable absolute does exist between two people. It can exist. We've seen it work. We've read about it. We've caught glimpses of it in others. (We probably even know a pair or two who have actually pulled it off!) And so we have to have it for ourselves.

So we stay in Stage One of our mating relationship—*1) euphoria,* for anywhere from two weeks to two years. That is the honeymoon stage of a relationship—the "she (or he) can do no wrong," period when we are convinced that we have found our endless love, ageless and evergreen; the stuff of romantic legends.

Then it happens: It may be a triggering event such as a display of completely opposing behavior or a defining moment of stress when both parties simultaneously revert to the needful child and neither is able to offer either nurturing or consolation. Or you may simply wake up one morning and realize that you are lying beside a stranger, that the mythical hero you once saw through your passionate gaze has somehow been disassembled, and in their place another creature is left, all too fallibly human and somehow devoid of the lofty notions that once set them apart. They sneeze and snore and fart and have morning mouth, and somehow don't look quite as good with their clothes off as you once thought they did.

The masculine aspects (the *animus* qualities) of the woman you first became enamored with—the fact that "she thinks just like a man"—now somehow make her seem pushy and overbearing. The *anima* qualities of your man—the poetic soul in touch with his feminine side—have managed somehow to render him spineless and lacking in resolution. Or, as is the case in even more relationships, your man is all beef, butter and brawn, and has no sense of poetry; or your woman is squeamish and whiny about the least little challenge to her dainty sense of order. His feminine side is non-existent, and her animus is buried, so you can't even begin to relate to one another. (How did you ever in the first place?) Now, everything that used to excite you about your significant other somehow turns you off; they're not fulfilling you in the way you thought they would.

To make matters worse, you realize that you've unwittingly given a large portion of your power away to this other person you've brought into your life. You've entrusted it to them, and now you're shaky about leaving so much of it in their hands. They're not always right. In fact they're often wrong. In fact, you're right more often than they are, and it's time you let them know it. You're going to take your power back, no matter what the cost.

Welcome to Stage Two of your love connection—*2) The Power Struggle.* The rules of any power struggle are both resolute and timeless: The struggle continues until someone surrenders. During that initial changeover in the love connection, however, the power struggle is, more often than not, denied as a factor in the relationship. The couple, still clinging to the lost heroic images of what they once had in the euphoric stage of their courtship, refuse to acknowledge that they are now in open conflict. At least they do at first. And because they do, the hidden friction grows even more intense because it is often expressed through sublimated resentment, periodic withdrawals, and sexual bartering. Later, when the heroic images are a distant memory and the edges of confrontation become more brittle, the power struggle opens up into a public conflict.

In case one has any doubt about how power conflicts between couples manifest, they can be as obvious as arguments over principals and politics or as trivial as what kind of restaurant the family should attend on a given evening. They manifest in dozens of ways—from disapproval of friends to sniping remarks about style of dress and someone's recent girth. At their most civilized, these plays for power work their way into grudging compromises. At their basest and most unseemly, they become pathological, mutually destructive, and even physically abusive.

Without question, most power struggles are ego-driven, usually petty, and diminish both parties, rendering them virtually smaller than life. And intimacy, admiration, reconciliation and trust become the casualties. There is a sense of betrayal that accompanies the power struggle that often reveals itself either through public emasculation or the private sterilization of ridicule. And God help the child who grows up in a family where such power struggles exist, because they are poised on the borders of this domestic civil war. In truth, the unfortunate children of such bondings number in legion and are the rule, not the exception.

There are no truces in a power struggle that offer any lasting value. (A truce, after all, is merely a cessation in hostilities.) Someone simply has to give up so that true reconciliation can follow. The challenge that now comes to the new millennium relationship is that the rules for dominance have changed, irrevocably.

According to the time-honored if outdated tradition of relationships, once the family unit was formed, the man as the acknowledged breadwinner would stand a better chance of maintaining dominance. So the woman, assuming the role of homemaker, would at least offer the appearance of having surrendered. That would possibly set the stage for years of domestic guerrilla warfare. And that in turn reverts to our maxim at the beginning of this chapter: Disempower another, and you will begin to lose them the moment you do. Still, the illusion in the old family paradigm would have persisted. Still, the faux surrender would take place, and the family unit could trudge on under a kind of grudging inertia that would carry them through to completion (or at least until the children were grown). Not any more.

With women forming a major portion of the labor force and often earning incomes comparable to their husband or significant other, the power struggle has assumed a different aspect. And socially impaired is the man who enters into a long-term relationship with a woman who draws a significantly higher annual income than his own.

Despite our protestations to having evolved into a new society that has taken quantum leaps in personal awareness, we are still replete with double standards, and income is one of them. Unless both parties in the relationship are supremely evolved, or unless the man is in a highly prestigious, if lower paying, profession, any pairing in which a man earns measurably less than the woman is in a constant state of peril. Call it visceral, tribal, cellular or simply the instincts of the Alpha pack, it takes a life of its own. And, in the majority of such cases, the underachieving male loses all leverage in the relationship.

Evolvement is the issue here, and couples must be equally yoked if the mutual bonding is truly to endure. They must share a similar sense of life, have a spiritual sense of one another, and be well-matched intellectually, socially and economically. They should also be mutually devoted to one another's level of personal growth. Only then do they have a chance to get to the end game of the love connection—*Stage 5) dynamism.*

The secret of any successful relationship comes with learning how to get through the power struggle and get to dynamism as soon as possible. That mean's getting through *Stage 3) reconciliation,* or the surrender of one and the acceptance of all aspects of one another, and *Stage 4) rapprochement* (the rediscovery of all the good qualities that originally existed one for the other) as soon as possible. That is realizing that *Stage 5) dynamism* is what you always had but would have denied yourself simply through failing to understand that we are all here to lift one another up on our journey to the sky, to be the wind that carries each other aloft.

Dynamism is the stage of enhanced relationship when all the good qualities of each individual are not only valued but also enhanced by the relationship itself. In dynamism, there is a support level that comes to pass between two people that can be absolutely electrifying—a level of admiration for what you have chosen as your life's mate takes on new meaning, one that the world easily reads and readily applauds. There is a celebration of the individual self that is enhanced when the two of you join your indivisible power together. There is a level of what Relationships Counselor David Deida refers to as *intimate communion,* that becomes the most exquisite expression of the private sensual moments of who you are together. All this and more can come to pass far beyond the veil of years and the fever of euphoria, provided we're willing to break a few of the rules that we have been taught.

In order to make a loving relationship last, each of us in our way must love unconditionally, surrender unequivocally, and yet never give up the power of who we are.

Only one who is truly deluded can grasp the truth of such a paradox.

When you are able to love unconditionally, you are not forced into the psychobabble cliché of the longing child looking to the imago for fulfillment of the lost portions of yourself. You are able to love from the totality of the higher self—seeing in your loved one the little child looking to you in trust and faith to share your life's path together. You are able to surrender to that ideal, keeping faith that all the higher aspects of your loved one are the truth of what they are and what they most desire to be. By appealing to that higher nature in them, you bring out the best in yourself. You set yourselves on the dynamic path that strengthens both of you. Whenever your soul-mate begins to waver or descend into his or her fear matrix, you can be the light that brings them up. You can hold your power by doing nothing more than standing in the truth of who you are.

If they express their doubts about your sense of responsibility to them, show them all the ways that you are already larger than life. If they begin to weigh on you with their fears of inadequacy and lack, let them feel the glow of your intelligent abundance. You never have to compromise your principles or defend who you are. You simply have to be loving to others, even when they appear to be critical of you. You never have to tell anyone else they're wrong about you. Solely by standing in your light and keeping the stillness of your conviction, you draw a strength into you that even your severest critic cannot overcome.

All of us can change so much by simply finding ourselves, by locking onto our guiding light and following in the flow of our destined path. By doing this, not only do we remove ourselves from the cycle of attack and defend, we uplift everyone around us, beginning at home, starting first with the sacred self of those we bring into the intimate fold of our selves. And in so doing, we have zapped the flak.

Achieving dynamic love, a love that grows stronger in time, is the fairy tale fulfilled—the one we all long to believe. Then again, making fairy tales come true is the delusionist's directive. We're here to make real the dreams that the rest of the world has abandoned. This is the one you'll enjoy the most, if for no other reason than knowing that there will always be someone there to share it with you.

Having said all this, we must now ask you to understand as well that there is a quality of perfection we desire in our love relationships that is so elusive to us that we tremble even at the thought of seeking it again. We came so close in those early days of contact when our polarity was primed, when we ventured into one another's force fields and were drawn up into that sacred contract of the soul. In that instant, there flashed before us the full kaleidoscope of our potential—all the things we could ever be, everything we could be together, the synergistic Self. The one plus one made more than two.

It is our firm belief that we can all get back to that magical garden in our love relationships as surely as finding the way back home. We can take that quantum leap from euphoria to dynamism, if we're willing to take the extra steps to do so. We stop short of saying you have to work at it, because the term, "work," implies labor, agony, and toil.

Love is not toil. Loving is pure joy. And loving someone unconditionally is prana, ambrosia, and the food of the spirit itself. But like mastering any other aspect of your life, you have to practice it diligently and with a cultivated sense of refinement.

Even though we have been blessed with certain natural talents—in a sport such as skating, in a dance such as ballet, in our ability to play a musical instrument or refine our sense of graphics into painting or sculpting—none of us would expect to play or dance or sculpt at the highest levels of our potential unless we were willing to perfect those skills, to practice them constantly and with the anticipation that we will fall or hit a sour note or wreck a mold somewhere along the way.

How can we expect less of the art of loving? It is a gift to us, to be sure, but we can never take it for granted or possibly hope to believe that its perfection can be sustained unless we give it our best and all that is in us. That is how dynamism is achieved in every aspect of our lives. Perfection is the mistress of persistence.

It also helps to occasionally be practical about how you go about it. If having a plan and designing your patterns of achievement by writing them down and objectifying them works in other areas, then why not your love connection? For that, we offer a seemingly simple procedure: Start by realizing that, in your euphoric state, both you and your significant other brought the best part of yourselves to the experience. You were more imaginative, more captivating, more adventuresome, more considerate, more charming—more powerful—than at any other time in your life.

Write down all the aspects of your significant other that first attracted you to them; include all the eloquent moments, the way they dressed or behaved or talked of their dreams and aspirations. Then make a list of all the wonderful things you became in those early days together. Include all the special moments you shared in those early days and months that brought you to taste your own magic: all that you dreamt of, talked about, shared about yourself; each of the moments when you were all the bold imaginative lover that your significant other believed you to be when you were both willing to be your own fantasy. Now, have your significant other make two similar lists of his or her own. Open a bottle of wine, apple juice, or designer water, and sit down with them in a romantic setting and lovingly compare notes. What we believe you will discover is a treasure that you never really lost. It was only hidden for a while beneath the sheaves of ego.

Personal Friends. And How to Be One.

> A friend may be reckoned the masterpiece of nature.
>
> —Ralph Waldo Emerson
> on "Friendship."
> *Essays and Journals*

Ralph Waldo Emerson, perhaps the most gifted essayist of all time, had a way of distilling from the truth the perfect thought. In his essay "On Friendship," he opens with this poignant observation:

> We have a great deal more kindness than is ever spoken. Maugre *(notwithstanding)* all the selfishness that chills like east winds the world, the whole human family is bathed an element of love like fine ether. How many persons we meet in houses, whom we scarcely speak to, whom yet we honor, and who honor us! How many we see in the street or sit with in church whom, though silently, we warmly rejoice to be with! Read the language of these wandering eye-beams. The heart knoweth.[37]

Nothing expresses our ability to see the light in one another more eloquently than this observation made a century and a half ago. Emerson also noted succinctly that, "The only way to have friends is to be one."[38]

Often quoted, his maxim is rich in meaning, because for many people the measure of friendship is taken in ways that are at best superficial. In the beginning we often form friendships based upon how others may amuse and delight us, but for a friendship to be both durable and deep it requires an understanding of what it means.

In its first definition, a friend is someone with whom we form a bond through "mutual admiration and trust." Trust is a pivotal issue in all enduring relationships, and we might add our additional insistence that true friendships endure through mutual respect, love, and admiration.

In truth, if we are to enjoy the richness of friendships we deserve we should be willing to bring our commitment, our loyalty, and a sense of contribution. It is also important for us to understand that, though we may share our light at all times, we are best served to share our Inner Light with those who would be considerate of our emotional resources.

We couldn't agree more with Emerson that the harmony of human warmth is the currency of who we are. We want to share our best moments with others, to bond with the family of humankind in joyous celebration. These are the easy gifts to give when we join in the circle of friendship. Then again, so often those circles interconnect. And our friendships take as many forms as there are activities in our lives. We have business associations that we define as friendships, club associations from which friendships are formed, and friendships that have seemingly endured since childhood. Close friendships, those soul connections that seem to spin up and away from the hive of social interactions and somehow take their place in our hearts, often seem to come about effortlessly, as if naturally ordained by a higher source.

When we are energetic, loving, attractive and, by force of our spiritual chemistry, only allow positive people to come into our sphere of influence, our chances for making and keeping valuable friendships increase tenfold. These are the fellow travelers in life whom we recognize instantaneously. They live on the enlightened path. They enrich us by their association and by their love of life. And we can do no less than return such goodness in kind.

When we are truly blessed by our friendships, they stand the test of time; they endure the wind and rain of occurrence. On occasion, however, some friends will disappoint us and fall away, often for what seem to be the most inane of reasons. More often than some of us would like to admit, there are also impostors in friendship who connive connections with us that actually become harmful. At best, they waste our time. At worst, we find ourselves the victim in them. We are either exploited for our money or material goods, used for the credibility we can provide to those less stable than we. Or else we're simply drained of energy by those who would use us as a repository for their negativity. In other words, we become a blood bank for what have become commonly known as "energy vampires." And these are to be avoided at all cost.

Although we remain steadfast in our belief that by keeping in our own light and assuming the power of our higher self, we can withstand all potential harm, we also acknowledge that there are many lost souls who carry corruption like a fever into our lives. Our life, after all, is a matter of choice. And that ability to choose is accompanied by a responsibility for discretion. Be discreet. Cut your losses. Move away from energy such as this, and do so as soon as possible.

We are not suggesting that anyone should put barriers up around themselves. What we do recommend, however, is that you determine the degrees of your commitment to others, and apply some of the same standards for a close friendship that you would a long-term mating relationship. For most people, true friendships are earned and won. And shared interests usually predicate the success of them. All we ask that you do is set the same standards for them that you would for your own life. If you would not abide dishonesty, abuse, expedient morality, selfishness and duplicity in yourself, then realize that you are not required to accept it in others—at any level! You may wish them well, and let your best thoughts come to rest on the recovery of their senses. But you are not required to take on their emotional garbage. Neither do you have to let anyone drag you down to his or her level of negativity. To do so places you in the position of enabler in a codependent relationship. And friendships only endure if they are independent, stable and clear—like two trees that stand on their own to share the same sky.

It is also certain that during the course of a friendship, there will be moments that will define them as well as your friend or faux. They will reveal themselves through issues of character in times of stress.

A very wise mutual friend of ours once observed that "Anyone can show good character when times are good. It's when times get bad that we separate the honest man from the scoundrel."

There are moments that define us all for better or worse, and it is then that we can see who holds the standards high with us and who does not.

Recently, a woman we knew had run into some financial difficulty when her husband had suddenly deserted her, leaving her alone to bring up their three children, as well as dropping a mountain of personal debts and credit card defaults on her that would have brought anyone to the edge of their sanity. Rather than file for personal bankruptcy or default on her obligations, she took on two full time jobs, borrowed the money from her father to pay off her credit cards, worked out a payment schedule to each of her ex-husband's friends and associations, and paid them off to the penny within two years. Of course, she filed for divorce (from her vanished spouse). But since she was her family's sole means of support, she had to get innovative and took on a marketing consultancy position for a woman's clothing store. Functioning with astounding competence and flair, she got hired as a vice-president for a prestigious marketing firm and is now making a well deserved six-digit annual salary.

By contrast, two brothers of our acquaintance—charming and likable fellows—sold their chain of hardware stores for more than $10 million to a large international hybrid firm. In the aftermath, they were so elated with the final price that they retired from the business, closed out all their chains, and gave all of their employees two weeks notice (with the advisory that they might be hired back by the new company). Upon receiving notice of their termination, many of the brothers' employees, some of whom had been with the store for more than two decades, expressed shock over the way they were treated. "Well, I should have known better," observed one longtime sales clerk. "They never did have an insurance plan. And I only got one Christmas bonus from this place in the 21 years I worked here."

We use these examples in the business metaphor because they provide us quick revelations of principle, and yet underscore the simple truth that character will tell. We get warnings about people all along the way that we tend to ignore. They may manifest in mean and subtle ways, but they will inevitably make themselves known. And we ask the rhetorical question, here: In whom would you have preferred to invest your friendship? Surely deep, enduring relationships go beneath the paint of charm and into the soul of the seeker and the truth that it reveals.

It at this point that we counsel you to engage in some discerning observations. Use your GUT feel to be sure, but also hold to your truth, and understand your own heart. If someone undertakes to do something that violates your personal code, be ready to zap the flak. And especially if they continue that violation, either speak your mind (with due respect) or set your exit path. In some cases, both may be necessary.

By the same token, once someone has earned your friendship, you should regard that relationship as if it were made of pure gold. Never cease to give it your attention, to reinforce it, to strengthen the bond that forges it. Remember those occasions that make everyone's life special—the birthdays, the anniversaries, the shared occasions, the reunions—and call or write them. E-mail is as quick as a phone call, is something they can keep, and is certainly more cost-effective. Whatever it takes, a friendship is worth the effort. It's not as if anyone's list of true friends had the volume of a Sears Catalog. And even if you expand your list to include casual friends and new acquaintances to whom you would reach out, it only takes a little time to tell them that you care, to tell them that they're special, and that they matter. And for all we ever know our loving contact with these very special people in our lives might be our last.

No life should be measured by the quantity of friendships it sustains. But without the blessings of loyal friends, our lives will have neither measurement nor quantity, and precious little quality.

All Business.

"Love one another as brothers. Do business as strangers."

—an Arab proverb

On the continent of human relations, business forms its own special nation of character and insight. In many ways, the rules of personal relationships simply cannot be permitted without passport. And yet the system of this other world can usually serve us well, if we remember to use our personal integrity as the basis for all our commerce. It also helps to understand that there will be dozens, if not hundreds, of business occasions during our career in which others with whom we interact do not hold to that same level of integrity. In the common vernacular, "There are a lot of sharks out there." In our true sense of the world as we know it, fear still drives the marketplace. And since business setbacks may constitute a genuine potential for harm at least in terms of extreme financial loss, we are well advised to build our alliances with great care and to hold them to the highest standards. That is why the Arab proverb to which we have just alluded holds true.

Even with the best intentions in the beginning, every enterprise is forced by circumstance to trek through the minefield of fear, greed, expedient morality and explosions of ego that come with the business climate. What's more, the broader one's sphere of influence and the greater one's reach as a business entity, the higher become the percentages for encountering corruption. That's why, at the beginning of any business venture, it is essential to qualify your associations. It does not mean you can't love and bless all other people as they go along the pathway to their personal evolution. It does mean you have the choice to place them under closer scrutiny when it comes to placing your professional future in their care.

In the world of business, this is often mistaken for due diligence. Due diligence is usually practiced by means of background checks, financial reviews, résumés and screenings from corporate headhunters in a number of different ways, but it does little to hold people to a higher standard of acceptability. Smart companies conduct thorough due diligence on everyone from suppliers to new clients. Companies initiating an IPO (initial public offering) are subjected to due diligence, as are people in every level of government security. And yet it is often amazing to see how poorly due diligence can be structured and by what superficial means those who undertake it are willing to be satisfied. In the heat of competition and the constant need to gobble up appropriate opportunity, our criteria often fall to a common denominator that is somewhat less than superb.

In our delusionist's view, there is *a process of determination* that takes an even more sophisticated form. And it begins with your inner circle. Initial hirings, corporate officers—founders in fact—form the heart and mind of any company. They should be built by choosing to work with others who bring unique abilities and high character to the mix. And yet, pivotal choices for beginning enterprises are often based upon the flimsiest of reasons.

Starting a business with social friends and relatives (and we recommend against either) can work at times but very often ends in the loss of friendship (if not the business itself). Hiring someone as an officer of your company simply because they claim to have contacts to an industry that you do not is both shortsighted and fraught with admissions of your own powerlessness to advance in your chosen field.

It has become a business cliché for someone to intimate that they have connections, because nothing is more self-empowering than to assume that stance. Of course, if someone tells you outright that they are "well-connected," it is almost certain that they are not.

Business is often done on bravado. But unless it is accompanied by great skill, remarkable experience, and extensive planning, it is troubled in the beginning and ill-fated in the end. More than all this, however, for any business to succeed, it requires the concerted genius of a few good people and the open embrace of millions. In other words, it requires relationships—and very special ones at that.

We had touched on this earlier, but it bears closer examination: And that is that our professional success in a number of areas begins with what Napoleon Hill refers to in *Think and Grow Rich* as the power of "The Master Mind," or what has come to be known as *masterminding.*

By Napoleon Hill's definition, masterminding is "The coordination, of knowledge and effort, in the spirit of harmony, between two or more people for the attainment of a definite purpose."[39]

Masterminding can be applied to any aspect of one's life, from creating a new ecologically centered community to bringing financial strategies to resolve global market challenges. It is a precursor to what came to be known later in marketing parlance as the "think tank," but truly fits any business or creative model we may choose. There are a couple of characteristics of the "mastermind" concept as it has evolved that are both unsettling and reassuring.

The first is that masterminding is viewed as an essential component of achieving your success goals. The second is that, for your mastermind group to truly work effectively for you, it should be populated by people who are smarter, richer and more successful than you are. In other words, in your striving to succeed, you are instantly hit with a classic Catch-22. And it invokes this dilemma: How, if everyone is being presented with the same criterion, do you get anyone to be a part of your mastermind group? If you are best served to find others smarter, richer, more successful, and more skilled than you, then you have to ask yourself the question: "What contribution can I make to this effort?"

"Contribution" is the issue in question. And look to yourself for the answer. Because contribution, by definition, nullifies exploitation. Especially those of higher mind can read it on you like a light, the color of your intention to make a positive difference. If your business or profession is out to make a positive difference—and if it brings the power of innovation with it—your opportunities for success will be greatly enhanced, and you will draw the best people to you. These are the initiators and facilitators of the world; self-actualized individuals, free of dark agenda, and aware that what they undertake can change all things for the better. Through them, and through you all together, there comes to pass a mutualization of power that can literally change the nature of everything you undertake.

We make this appeal to the self-starters of the world—to the visionaries—to those who choose to find their own path in business as they have in life. No employee can give you this; nor can you impart it to them. Besides, if you're not working in your own business, statistics show that you're just a "temp," and have little chance of becoming much more than that.

In sum, all good business relationships are based upon mutual contribution, cooperation, and commitment to a common vision. Goals and objectives may be set out of them. But it is the intention of those involved that makes the ultimate difference. If you surround yourself with people who are results-oriented and who understand the divine synergy that comes with masterminding, you will have found your professional synergism with an added bonus as well—friends who share your sense of life as well as your penchant for success.

Summary. The Final Connection.

There is no time in our lives when we are truly alone. Even in what seem to be our most solitary moments we are surrounded by the life force as it fills us. Our plants breathe in and out with us, exchanging the pure energy of the mutual recreation of our cells. A bird camps on the branch outside our window and peers inside in sweet recognition of the tiny universe we have created. Our creature companions rub against us in show of appreciation at sharing some portion of our lives with them. Our books counsel us. Our media inform us. We are surrounded each day by the cultures of past civilizations and all the limitless futurescapes that technology has set before us. In every movement that we make, we feel the radiance of the world upon us—the traffic of promise, the heat of activity, and the loud hum of potential in everything we do.

Every day that we rise again to face our own horizon is just another brush of the angel's wing.

Our interaction with one another becomes the final bonus—the quantum connection and the consummate door to this life.

Chapter 12

The Eureka! Factor

Every moment of our life is a swing between polar opposites—between the process of constant determination and the spontaneous madness of brilliant pursuit. We work for a while to stabilize ourselves and find safe haven in the wisdom of our quiet thoughts. And when we do, we take the time to contemplate perfection, often as if it were some distant ideal always beyond our grasp. What we have finally come to find is that it is already ours in this moment, now and for all the days to come.

Think with your heart. Feel with your GUT. Calibrate your mystical sense of timing, and you will behold the future: a world not far from this where communication is perpetual, pure, and unimpaired by all the contraption of ego. It is non-verbal and yet entire, because we have all achieved a total sense of one another. In that clarity of self, those declarations of the soul, lies will die the death because we are instantly revealed each soul to its sister. There will be no need for fabrication. The truth of who we are will announce us to our world in every expression of ourselves. Stripped of pretense, we are free to continue with the destiny we have embraced, to make a positive difference in everything we do.

It is our deliverance and yet becomes our covenant as well, if for no other reason than we now accept responsibility for all our thoughts, words, and actions. Knowing that each predicates the other, we will come to understand that we are energy in toto and take responsibility for that fabulous power we've been granted.

In our window to the world, there is no tomorrow, because it surrounds us in the moment. It is our firm conviction that we have already caught up to our hope and merely need to put our personal potential into play. That is our dream fulfillment and our responsibility as well.

Eureka! You have found it: the end game of Delusion, the act of putting into practice all that fills your heart.

By now you have learned the secret of flight. You have come to hold Love in your hands and understand Fear for the brother that it is. Your Great Universal Truth is now a part of your daily discernment, and your sense of timing has become refined, as well as teaching you some patience along the way. You've learned that becoming larger than life is the simple understanding that you can bring the light of your higher self into everything you do. You can always make it better for everyone else around you. You can bring your commitment and love and compassionate understanding; you are the solution to the challenges the world brings into the room.

Knowing all this and putting it into practice imbues you with a power that is yours alone, because you have found your higher self and the parchment of your purpose. You emanate intelligent abundance and know that every day this bounty is flowing through your life in the fullest expression of who you are. And because of who you are, you have made those quantum connections—those friends and loved ones and mastermind associations that you so rightly deserved. You have drawn them into your life because of what you believe, the vision to which you have now committed to your life. You wear your commitment like a plume, and it honors who you are. And simply by standing in your own truth and pursuing it with all that is in you, you will attract a harmony that you might never have thought possible before.

Now, you're ready to lead each day into its fullest potential, to be in the moment and convey its exquisite perfection in everything you do.

It is our delusionist's gift to you that all your days be full, and we offer the following simple framework as a guide and sample of what can be. It is not a structure that you have to follow. We all take our separate paths to reach our chosen place. It is a point from which to start and an expression of being that we can all stop at certain places to share the banquet of life. With that in mind, we invite you to take part in the perfect day, knowing that its perfection starts with you.

The Perfect Day.

To see a World in a Grain of Sand,
And Heaven in a Wildflower,
Hold Infinity in the palm of your hand,
And Eternity in an hour."

—William Blake
"Auguries of Innocence." 1787

Everyone has a different view of what a perfect day should be. And from our delusionist's perspective, it has little to do with doing and all to do with being. It's not about how much you can accomplish or even your body of work, because when all is said and done those moments will occur as a natural consequence of what you have become.

For us, the perfect day is about living in the present and blessing every moment for the gift that it presents. So let's begin together and continue in the awareness that we all will complete it in the way that fills us most.

• Rise from your bed and greet the morning with a "thank you" on your lips, an acknowledgment to our Creator that you recognize the blessing this day presents to you and the treasures that it holds. Somehow we can't emphasize enough the power of gratitude. It is the singular song that is always certain to be heard.

• Breathe deeply of the world around you and realize as you do that you are feeding and being fed the breath of life itself. It is not only a metaphor but also the truth itself. Our breath, our energy, the essence of who we are, affects our immediate environment and brings negative ions (positive energy) into our proximate chain of being. Plants exchange it. Animals feel it. They respond to our light. So our only responsibility is to be enlightened. Bring your joy, and don't forget at what little cost it comes.

Whether we delight or whether we sulk, the sun will shine all day. The birds will fly. The sea will flow. A masterpiece mural of leaves and grass will roll and play about us. It is all a part of life's beautiful ballet, and we may join in the chorus or sit on the side in silent lapses of pity and remorse. (But if you do, you can rest assured that you will confuse your angels. For they've surrounded you with their gifts and wonder at your blindness.)

• Go into the silence, even if it's for a moment, and taste that angelic connection that infuses you with purpose. It is a way of plugging-in to that cosmic conduit, the one that charges us with a renewed clarity that puts everything else we do into perspective. It is among those quiet hymns that find their way to us that we become humbled and risen up at the very same time. It is only then that we can welcome the noise of the world and hear its music clearly, perhaps for the very first time.

• Be the tactile messenger and luxuriate in every sensation that you've been given. If you are with your significant other, embrace them tenderly and feel the exchange of love's energies that come to pass between you. When you bathe or shower, feel the flow of water as it washes over you, and know that it is a kind of christening to cleanse you for the mission ahead. When you eat, bless the food and savor the fruits of the morning. Feel them fill you with a vibrancy that comes from life-filled food.

It's so important to do all these things. That's why you rise a bit early. Each day awaits you like a whole new spring, a brand new season of hope.

• As you go about your day, give the gift of your love. It costs almost nothing and repays you in a thousand different ways. Send it on the wings of laughter and the song of joy in your voice. Give it freely to every living thing and behold the transformation it brings about. Start with your family, with those closest to you, and let the spire of its rapture expand into your day and everyone you encounter. By doing this and nothing more, you have already altered your world, bringing it to a higher level than it otherwise might have known.

• Constantly move in your own vibration. Stay in the light of your truth. Know at times that by virtue of your keeping still, your day will unfold around you. More than you might have once realized, you may be surprised at the flow that it creates when you're simply being yourself. Yet even its moments of madness are teachers, if you will be still and observe. If you will let the storms unfold and settle of their own accord, you will be bathed in their revelation without exposing your self, except to bring in light at the appropriate time.

• You are the light. Remember this above all other things. That is what you bring and what others will come to expect of you.

• But you have been freed of expectation. And your only obligation is to stand in the integrity of that which you have become. That is why you take the time to note your commitments for the day. Whether they are long-term or short-term, once you have made them you are honor-bound to complete them as you promised. Your word is your signature on life. And your promises are statements from your heart. That's why you achieve them willingly and acknowledge the intimate truth that others will honor their oaths to you; denial is not an option.

• And yet negation is not a concern of yours, because you live in every moment without attachment to outcome. You have no concerns from your "mastermind" cortege. They're impeccable in who they are. They have your trust and your confidence in all that you do together. They are your equals in matters of substance and your betters in certain skills, and yet they look to you for solutions because of who you are. And because of who you are, only the best will seek your counsel; for you have little time for fools, and any fool can see it. (It's not that you would be cruel or rude, yet your energy precludes the petty needs of vanity and the assaults of conflict.)

• At midday, you take a moment to listen to your inner voice, to tap into your intuition and the cosmic telephone. It is here, and it happens every day, when you reach out to others. You make the call, write the letter, or send the thoughtful e-mail to give your blessings, to send your love, or just to say "hello." There is no taking measure of the goodness that it carries. It is the constant expression of love that naturally pours forth from you. It cannot be gauged, and you are no longer concerned with keeping score. You simply know that this day will end, and before it does you will drink it fully of every essence that it offers. And you'll fill it in return.

• You take time to feel the rest of your day. You treat it as if what remained would be the last you would ever spend. Knowing this should fill you, not with desperation, but with a masterful urgency to taste the life in each moment. How enriched it is. How each glimmer of light reveals itself as a benediction, touching and transforming every object within view. Suddenly everything around you takes on a life of its own, a psychokinetic celebration that reflects your passion for life. Plants uplift, objects radiate with a glow of affirmation. People bask in the wake of your passage because you have touched them with your heart. Suddenly you're infused with a certain passion to make every moment count—to create, mold, and motivate every instant you are here.

• Your creative urges pour out of you in an endless cascade of thought, and for a span of moments you become your own mastermind. You feel the passion to write them down, to record them on tape, and then it strikes you: time has slowed its hand for you. You are suddenly in a zone, the flow of your own making. And every day can be your end as well as your new beginning. All of us create in our way; everyone has gifts for the world. The art of living comes in finding your secret success.

Eureka! You have found it. And because you have, you have become the freest creature on earth, and you can find the sky. Those with whom you share your thoughts bear witness to your zeal, and they are caught in the fever of enthusiasm you bring. Creativity is a gift to us all, but like any gift it is only a blessing when it is shared.

• There is always a need you feel to savor the new experience, to attempt at least one new thing; in this you find your growth. It comes with beholding that life as what Ernest Hemingway described as "a moveable feast." It is such a gift to us to partake of the banquet we're offered. God is a generous host, and we can do no less than to receive what we're offered in grace and gratitude. Learn a language. Read a book. Applaud another person's art. Develop a skill like Tai Chi Kwan or cooking in cordon bleu. But do it now because, as you know, tomorrow may take you away.

• In a private moment, you review what you have made of your mission statement. You reflect upon it and realize that you are right on course. You have accomplished what you desire. Yet you deliberately leave some things undone—that distant dream, that special goal that gets you up in the morning. You behold it like a far horizon. Yet you realize, it's drawing nearer every day, the answered prayer that awaits your innovation.

• More out of reflex, you continue to practice intelligent abundance, giving of yourself and some of the richness that has become you. Whether it is picking up a piece of litter or tithing to your favorite cause, you are expressing your ability to effect change. There is no gesture that goes unnoticed; our angels are always watching. And you have made it a part of your life to give it the best of yourself. What's best is that it comes with no effort. Goodness becomes a reflex. It grows to be as much a part of you as breathing.

• As your day grows to a close, you listen to your lower egos. Given their proper roles to fill, they become like your children; you recognize them and render them appropriate attention. You feel your body ego cry out to you to send it on a mission, to let it fulfill itself to the limits of its being. Your muscles strain to express themselves; your endorphins plead, telling you they'll keep you young if you let them complete their purpose. You put your body to the test. You feel elation in the challenge, the exercise that you have chosen to let yourself run free. You may run or swim or play your sport, or simply take a walk through the park. But whatever you do, you'll experience your own faultless interaction with the forces of Nature. This is but another blessing, partaking of the serenity that comes after the busy hum of commerce.

• If you have learned anything, it's that life brings us contrast. Challenges come in their disguises, but they are dogs that bark—ferocious until you confront them with both confidence and compassion. Suddenly, they soften and their noise takes another turn away from threat and into the clamor of bluff. No longer the monsters they pretended, they become our companions in growth. Fear is just another way of announcing the arrival of change.

• You are changing. You're constantly growing. But you never forget your source. Not for a moment do you lose sight of what truly matters in life. You return to your home and loved ones and celebrate the time that you can share the laughter and the joy of being alive.

• You feel the flow of media around you, but you make slight note its clamor. It has become the merchant of fear, and you are in love's dominion. You share a comedy or a romance—a film that's silly and old—and realize that those who live longest have learned to laugh the best.

• You know that laughter is the tonic. It's manna. It is joy. It is the cosmic chime that brings us into chorus. In these moments, you share your elation, and always keep in mind to say what is in your heart in every moment. Never forget to say "I love you" to all that you hold dear, but especially to those who by blood have been brought into your life. Let those be the last words that escape from your lips before you say goodnight.

• Into the night, you share your last moments with your significant other. You lock in each other's embrace. You feel your passions flow into a river of your mutual completion. This is the answer to your deepest soul's desire, the other country of the reunited soul. Your love grows more dynamic with each touch of the inner self.

(If you happen to be alone, you also relish the instant that you know you are complete—that this is your best passage for your personal restoration.)

• Again you say thank you to the day and bless the night ahead, knowing that your sleep will be filled with dreams of high intent.

You feel just a little bit spent; there's nothing for which to long. How much more soundly you sleep on those nights when your days have been filled to the rim with the blessings of positive living, of contribution, of sharing, and of unconditional love. And yet the mere experience of it already begins to restore you; the fire for life builds again even as you sleep.

To have cooked in the crucible of life all the precious metal that is in you, to leave nothing for the dregs of doubt and the dross of negativity—that is to have lived.

Eureka! You have found it: the secret that every day can be filled with the richest moments of your life.

Of course, we are the first to acknowledge that everyone's perfect day will be different. We offer only a blueprint here. The building is yours to structure. May it be built with all your dreams, and may all your dreams come true. It's truly why you are here on this glorious campus of our schoolhouse, Earth, partaking of the course of perfect delights.

Dream forever, and live forever in your dreams! That is the delusionist creed.

More to come. School is always in…

Notes

Chapter 2

1. Faulkner, William. In a speech at Washington and Lee University. Lexington, Virginia. 1958.
2. Fowler, H. W. and Sir Ernest Gowers. *A Dictionary of Modern Usage.* Oxford University Press. Oxford. 1965. p. 124 a.
3. *Websters Third International Dictionary.* Springfield, MA. 1961. p. 598 b.
4. Taliaferro, A.A. Ph.D. DD. *The St. Alcuin Tapes.* Dallas, Texas 1982.
5. Ibid. 1991
6. Seldes, George. *The Great Thoughts. Helen Keller.* Ballantine Books. 1985. P. 216.

Chapter 3

7. Seldes, George. *The Great Thoughts.* "Aristotle. Taken from Quotations from *Stobaeus Floritegeum.*" p. 20.
8. Emerson, Ralph Waldo. *Essays and Journals.* "On Self-Reliance" International Collectors Library. Nelson Doubleday, Inc. Garden City, New York. 1968. p. 105

Chapter 4

9. Herbert, Frank. *Dune.* Ace Books (by agreement with Chilton Books). New York. 1965. p. 15.
10. Emerson, Ralph Waldo. *Essays and Journals.* "The Over-Soul." International Collectors Library. Nelson Doubleday, Inc. Garden City, New York. 1968. p. 196

Chapter 7

11. Sheehan, George, M.D. *Running & Being: The Total Experience.* Simon & Schuster. New York. 1978. p. 172.
12. Csikzentmihalyi, Mihaly. *FLOW.* Harper Perennial. HarperCollins. New York. 1990. p.41.
13. MacKay, Charles LL.D. *Extraordinary Popular Delusions and the Madness of Crowds.* "Preface to 1852 Edition." Harmony Books. Crown Publishers. New York. 1980. p. xix.

Chapter 8

14. Camus, Albert. *The Myth of Sisyphus.* "An Absurd Reasoning." (*Le Mythe desisyphie.* "Essai Sur Absurde.") Gallimard. Paris. 1942. p. 46
15. *Encyclopedia Britannica/ 15th Edition.* Vol. 5. Chicago. 1965. p. 860 a.
16. Marcus Aurelius Antonius. *Meditations.* Barnes & Noble Books. NY. 1989. Book. Four. p. 73.
17. Plato. *Apology of Socrates, Crito, and Carta VII.* Tr. Benjamin Jowett. Collier. New York. 1937. p. 38.
18. Fuller, William. *Gnomologia.* (1732). *The International Thesaurus of Quotations.* Linda Thomas Tripp (Editor). Perennial Library. Harper and Row. 1987. p. 51.
19. Chopra, Deepak. *Creating Health.* Houghton Mifflin. New York. 1995.
20. Roth, Paul. *Life Navigation Technologies.* CEX. Los Angeles. 1999.
21. Allen, James. *As A Man Thinketh.* "Effect of Thought On Circumstance." Barnes & Noble Books. New York. 1999. p. 8.

Chapter 9

22. Kissinger, Henry (quoted). *New York Times.* New York. January 19. 1971.
23. Dahlberg, John E.E. (Lord Acton). In a letter to Bishop Mandell Creighton. April 3, 1887. *Life and Letters of Mandell Creighton.* Seldes, George. *The Great Thoughts.* Ballantine Books. 1985. p. 4.

24. Milton, John. "Paradise Lost.(Argument I)."*Paradise Lost, Paradise Regained, and Samson Agonistes.* International Collectors Library. Garden City, New York. 1969. p.25

25. Harrison, Maureen & Steve Gilbert (Editors). *Abraham Lincoln. In His Own Words.* "Letter to A.G. Hodges. 1864." Barnes & Noble Books. 1994. p. 38.

26. Allen, James. *As A Man Thinketh.* "Thought and Purpose." Barnes & Noble Books. New York. 1999. p. 33.

27. Mencken, H.L. *Prejudices.* Alfred A. Knopf. New York. 1927. p. 54.

28. Mandino, Og. *The Greatest Salesman in the World.* Bantam Doubleday Dell. New York. 1974. p. 71.

29. Diderot, Denis. "Penses Philosophique." *French Thought in the 18th Century.* Romian Rollard and Andre Maurois. D. McKay. New York. 1953.

30. Ibsen, Henrik. *An Enemy of the People/ The Wild Duck/ Rommersholm.* Oxford University Press, Oxford, UK. 1999

Chapter 10

31. Kagan, Donald. *Pericles of Athens and the Birth of Democracy.* The Free Press. New York. 1991. p. 211.

32. Marx, Karl. "Critique of the Hegelian Philosophy of Right." *Deutsche-franzöische Yahrbücher.* Dresden. 1844.

33. Chernow, Ron. *Titan.* Random House. New York. 1998. p. 227.

34. Carnegie, Andrew. "Wealth." *North American Review.* June. 1889.

35. Waitley, Denis. "Waitley on Winning." Videotaped speech to Nikken North America National Convention. 1994.

36. Presidential Debates. ABC. NBC. CBS *et al.* Washington University. St. Louis. October 1992.

Chapter 11

37. Emerson, Ralph Waldo. *Essays and Journals.* "On Friendship." International Collectors Library. Nelson Doubleday, Inc. Garden City, New York. 1968. p. 160.
38. Emerson. *Essays and Journals.* "On Frendship." Doubleday. Garden City, N.Y. p. 164.
39. Hill, Napoleon. *Think and Grow Rich.* Fawcett Crest Books. Ballantine. New York. Revised Combined Registry. Edition. 1960. pp.168-169.

Bibliography

Alexander, Franz G. and Sheldon T. Selesnick. *The History of Psychiatry.* Harper and Row. New York. 1966.

Ayto, John. *Arcade Dictionary of Word Origins.* Arcade Publishing. Little Brown. New York. 1990.

Blake, William. "Auguries of Innocence." *Top 500 Poems.* Edited by William Harmon. Columbia University Press. 1992.

Branden, Nathaniel. *The Psychology of Self-Esteem.* Bantam Books. New York. 1980.

Branden, Nathaniel. *The Psychology of Romantic Love.* J.P. Tarcher. Los Angeles. 1980.

Brands, H.W. *TR/ The Last Romantic.* Basic Books. New York. 1997.

Camp, Wesley D. *What a Piece of Work is Man.* Prentice Hall. Englewood Cliffs, New Jersey. 1990.

Camus, Albert. Le *Mythe de Sisyphie.* "Essai Sur Absurde." (*The Myth of Sysiphus.* "An Absurd Reasoning.") Gallimard. Paris. 1942. (1982)

Carroll, Lewis. *The Completed Illustrated Works.* "Through the Looking Glass."Dorset Press. New York. 1995.

Cheney, Margaret. *TESLA. Man Out of Time.* Barnes & Noble Books. New York. 1981.

Chopra, Deepak. *Creating Health.* Houghton Mifflin. New York. 1995.

Chopra, Deepak. *Perfect Health.* Harmony Books. New York. 1991.

Chopra, Deepak. *The Seven Spiritual Laws of Success.* Amber/Allen. New World Library. San Rafael, CA. 1993.

Chopra, Deepak. *The Way of the Wizard.* Harmony Books. New York. 1995.

Csikzentmihalyi, Mihaly. *FLOW.* Harper Perennial. HarperCollins Publishers. New York. 1990.

Day, Laura. *Practical Intuition.* Villard Books. Random House. New York. 1996.

De Becker, Gavin. *The Gift of Fear.* DTP. Random House. New York. 1997.

Deida, David. *Intimate Communion.* Health Communications, Inc. Deerfield Beach. Florida. 1995.

Dent, Harry S. *The Roaring 2000s.* Simon & Schuster New York. 1998.

Durant, Will. *The Renaissance. The Story of Civilization V.* Simon and Schuster. New York. 1953.

Eliot, T.S. *"The Cocktail Party." The Complete Poems and Plays. 1909-1950.* Harcourt Brace. Orlando, FL. 1980.

Emerson, Ralph Waldo. *Essays and Journals.* Inernational Collectors Library. Nelson Doubleday, Inc. Garden City, New York. 1968.

ENCARTA World English Dictionary. St. Martin's Press. New York. 1999

Encyclopedia Britannica/ 15th Edition. Vol. 5. Chicago. 1965. p. 860

Fehrenbach, T.R. *Fire and Blood.* MacMillan. New York. 1973.

Fisher, Mark. *The Millionaire's Secrets.* Simon and Schuster. New York. 1996.

Friedman, Thomas L. *The Lexus and the Olive Tree.* Farrar Straus & Giroux. New York. 1999.

Fowler, H. W. and Sir Ernest Gowers. *A Dictionary of Modern Usage.* Oxford University Press. Oxford, United Kingdom. 1965.

Fuller, R. Buckminster. *The Critical Path.* St. Martin's Press. New York. 1981.

Gard, Richard A. (Editor). *Buddhism.* George Braziller, Inc. New York. 1962.

Gelb, Michael J. *How to Think Like Leonardo da Vinci.* Delacorte Press. Bantam Doubleday Dell Publishing Group. New York. 1999.

Glassner, Barry. *The Culture of Fear.* Basic Books. New York. 1999.

Glut, Donald R. and George Lucas. *The Empire Strikes Back.* Ballantine Books. New York. 1995.

Gray, John. *MEN ARE FROM MARS/ Women are from Venus.* HarperCollins. New York. 1992.

Gunther, John. *PROCESSION.* Harper & Row. New York. 1965.

Halberstrom, David. *The Fifties.* Villard Books. Random House. New York. 1993.

Hanh, Thich Nhat. *Living Buddha, Living Christ.* Riverhead Books. G.P. Putnam & Sons. New York. 1995.

Harrison, Maureen & Steve Gilbert (Editors). *Abraham Lincoln in His Own Words.* Barnes & Noble Books. 1994.

Hendrix, Harville. *Getting the Love You Want.* HarperCollins. New York. 1989.

Herbert, Frank. *Dune. Ace Books* (by agreement with the Chilton Company) New York. 1965.

Hertzberg, Arthur. (Editor). *Judaism.* George Braziller, Inc. New York. 1962.

Hill, Napoleon. *Think and Grow Rich.* Fawcett Crest Books. Ballantine. New York. Revised Combined Registry. Edition. 1960.

Hitler, Adolph. *Mein Kampf.* Mariner Books. New York. 1999.

Hoffer, Eric. *The Ordeal of Change.* Buccaneer Books. New York. 1996.

Hollbrook, Stewart. *The Age of the Moguls.* Ayer Company. New York. 1981.

Holy Bible. King James Version. The World Publishing Company. Cleveland, Ohio. 1971.

Ibsen, Henrik. (James MacFarlane Editor). *Enemy of the People/ The Wild Duck/ Rommersholm. Oxford University Press. Oxford, UK. 1999.*

Jaynes, Julian. *The Origin of Consciousness in the Breakdown of the Bicameral Mind.* Houghton Mifflin. Boston. 1976.

Jung, Carl Gustav. *DREAMS.* Princeton University Press. Princeton, New Jersey. 1978.

Jung. Carl Gustav. *Man and His Symbols.* Doubleday. Garden City, New York. 1964.

Jung. Carl Gustav. *The Secret of the Golden Flower.* "Commentaries." Harvest Books. Harcourt Brace Jovanovich. New York. 1962.

Jung, Carl Gustav. *Word and Image.* Princeton University Press. Princeton, New Jersey. 1979.

Jung, Carl Gustav. *The Undiscovered Self.* Amereon, Ltd. London 1976.

Kagan, Donald. *Pericles of Athens and the Birth of Democracy.* The Free Press. New York. 1991.

Kazantzakis, Nikos. *The Saviors of God.* A Touchstone Book. Simon and Schuster. New York. 1960.

Knightly, Philip. *The First Casualty.* Harcourt Brace Jovanovich. New York. 1975.

Knowles, Elizabeth (editor). *The Oxford Dictionary of Phrase, Saying & Quotation.* Oxford University Press. New York. 1997.

Korda, Michael. *POWER! How to Get It, How to Use It.* Random House. New York. 1975.

Kordich, Jay. *The Juiceman's Power of Juicing.* William Morrow. New York. 1992.

Kurzweil, Ray. *The Age of Spiritual Machines.* The Penguin Group, New York, 1999.

Lewis, C.S., *The Abolition of Man.* Macmillan. New York. 1973.

MacKay, Charles LL.D. *Extraordinary Popular Delusions and the Madness of Crowds.* Harmony Books. 1980.

Manchester, William. *The Glory and the Dream. Volume II.* Little Brown. Boston. 1973.

Marx, Karl. "Critique of the Hegelian Philosophy of Right." *Deutsche-französische Yahrbücher.* Dresden. 1844.

Maslow, Abraham H. *The Farther Reaches of Human Nature.* Viking Compass. Viking Press. 1972.

May, Rollo. *The Courage to Create.* W.W. Norton. New York. 1975.

Mencken, H.L. *Prejudices.* Alfred A. Knopf. New York.1927.

Milton, John. *Paradise Lost, Paradise Regained, and Samson Agonistes.* International Collectors Library. Garden City, New York. 1969.

New Larousse Encyclopedia of Mythology. Prometheus Press. Hamlyn Publishing Group, Ltd. 1968.

Perot, Ross. *United We Stand.* Hyperion. New York. 1992.

Prescott, William H. *History of the Conquest of Mexico.* The Modern Library. Random House. 1967.

Ponder, Catherine. *The Dynamic Laws of Prosperity.* Prentice-Hall. Englewood Cliffs, NJ. 1962.

Popcorn, Faith, and Lys Marigold. *Clicking.* HarperCollins. New York. 1997.

Posner, Gerald. *Citizen Perot.* Random House. New York. 1996.

Random House Dictionary of the English Language. Random House. New York. 1967.

Ray, Paul H. and Sherry Ruth Anderson. *The Cultural Creatives.* Harmony/Crown. New York. 1999.

Renou, Louis (Editor). *Hinduism.* George Braziller, Inc. New York. 1962.

Robbins, Anthony. *Personal Power 2: The Driving Force.* Volume 13. Robbins Research International. San Diego. 1996.

Schucman, Helen and William Thetford. *A Course in Miracles.* Foundation for Inner Peace. Viking. 1975.

Seldes, George. *The Great Thoughts.* Ballantine Books. New York. 1985.

Saxon, A.H. *P.T. Barnum.* Columbia University Press. New York. 1989.

Sheehan, George, M.D. *Running & Being: The Total Experience.* Simon & Schuster. New York. 1978.

Silverman, Keneth. *Houdini!!!* Harper Trade. New York. 1977.

Solzhenitzin, Aleksandr. I. *The Gulag Archipelago.* Harper and Row. New York. 1974.

Stanley, Thomas J. and William D. Danko. *The Millionaire Next Door.* Longstreet Press. Atlanta. 1998.

Staunton, Howard (Editor). *The Complete Illustrated Shakespeare.* Park Lane Books (Crown). New York. 1969.

Taliaferro, A.A, PhD. DD. *The St. Alcuin Tapes.* Dallas., Texas 1982.

Thomas, Lewis. *The Lives of a Cell.* Viking. New York. 1974.

Thurow, Lester C. *The Zero Sum Society.* Basic Books, Inc. New York. 1980.

Toffler, Alvin. *POWER SHIFT.* Bantam Books. New York. 1990.

Too, Lillian. *The Complete Illustrated Guide to FENG SHUI.* Barnes & Noble Books. New York. 1996.

Tripp. Rhoda Thomas. *The International Thesaurus of Quotations.* Perennial Library. HarperCollins. New York. 1970.

Waitley, Denis. "Waitley on Winning." Videotaped speech to Nikken North America National Convention. 1994.

Wallace, Irving. *The Fabulous Showman/The Life and Times of P.T. Barnum.* Alfred A. Knopf. 1959.

Webster's Third International Dictionary. Springfield, MA. 1961.

Wik, Reynold M. *Henry Ford and Grass Roots America.* University of Michigan Press. Lansing, MI. 1972.

Wilhelm, Richard and Carey F. Baynes (translators). *The I Ching (or Book of Changes).* Princeton University Press. Princeton, New Jersey. 1967.

Williams, John Alden (Editor). *Hinduism.* George Braziller, Inc. New York. 1962.

Williamson, Marianne. *A Return to Love.* HarperCollins. New York. 1992.

Zukav. Gary. *The Seat of the Soul.* Simon and Schuster (Fireside Books.). New York. 1997.

About the Authors

Robert Joseph Ahola is the author and co-author of six previously published works, including *101 Ways to Make a Difference, Personal Identity, The Silent Healer, and Creatures in our Care*. A producer of over 300 films and documentaries, Robert is also an accomplished playwright and filmmaker. *Delusion is Good* is his first collaboration with Paul Peccianti.

Paul John Peccianti is a leading motivational speaker, lecturer and personal counselor. A top executive with a multinational corporation, Paul has a master's degree in clinical psychology. He has used that unique combination of skills to design and formulate a number of success technologies. *Delusion is Good*, designed and written with Robert Ahola, is his first book based on many of those success skills.